THE ECONOMIC HISTORY OF ORISSA IN THE 19TH CENTURY

The Economic History of Orissa in the 19th Century

PURNA CHANDRA DAS

Commonwealth

The Economic History of Orissa in the 19th Century

Edition 2022

ISBN 81-7169-002-2

Published by :
COMMONWEALTH PUBLISHERS (P) LTD.
4831/24, Govind Lane,
Ansari Road, Darya Ganj,
New Delhi - 110002
Ph. : 23272541, 23242541
e-mail : commonwealthpublishers2016@gmail.com

Distributed by :
ARJUN PUBLISHING HOUSE
4831/24, Govind Lane,
Ansari Road, Darya Ganj,
New Delhi - 110002
Ph. : 23272541, 23242541
e-mail : arjunbooks2001@gmail.com

Laser Typesetting by :
Dimple Computers
Delhi

Printed at :
Milan Enterprises
Delhi

Contents

Abbreviations

Aitchison Treaties:	Collection of Treaties, Engagements and Sunands relating to India and neighbouring countries.
ALC	Acts of Legislative Council.
ARG	Abstract of Regulations of Government.
BCHR	Balasore Custom House Records.
BSCO	Board of Customs, Salt and Opium.
BJP	Bengal Judicial Proceedings.
BJP(C)	Bengal Judicial (Civil) Proceedings.
BJP(Cr.)	Bengal Judicial (Criminial) Proceedings.
BLCP	Bengal Legislative Council Proceedings.
BPP	Bengal Public Works Proceedings.
BdRP	Board of Revenue Proceedings.
BdRC	Board of Revenue Collections.
BRC	Bengal Revenue Consultations.
BRP	Bengal Revenue Proceedings.
BSR	Balasore Salt Records.
CPC	Calendar of Persian Correspondence.
CRR	Cuttack Revenue Records.
CSR	Cuttack Salt Records.
DSM	Diary of Streynsham Master.
DWH	Diary of William Hedges.

EIRF	East India Report of Famine Commission, presented to both houses of Parliament.
GAROD	General Administration Report of Orissa Division (Annual).
JASB	Journal of Asiatic Society of Bengal.
Maddox Report	Final Report on the Survey and Settlement of the Province of Orissa, 1890-1900 by S.L. Maddox.
NAI	National Archives of India, New Delhi.
OHRAJ	Orissa Historical Research Journal.
Orissa Records	Guide to Orissan Records.
OSA	Orissa State Archives, Bhubaneswar.
PBCSO	Proceedings of Board of Customs, Salt and Opium.
PBR(M)	Proceedings of Board of Revenue, Miscellaneous.
PBT	Proceedings of Board of Trade.
QAR	Quinquennial Administration Report, 1900-1901 to 1904-1905.
RAB	Report on the Administration of Bengal.
RAC	Report of the Administration of Customs Department, Bengal Presidency.
RADSMO	Report on the Administration of the Department of Salt, Madras Presidency & Orissa.
RAR	Report on the Abkari Revenue.
RASD	Report on the Administration of Salt Department.
RBR	Records of the Board of Revenue.
RCF	Report of the Commissioners appointed to enquire into famine in Bengal and Orissa, 1866.
RCC	Report of the Commissioners appointed to enquire into certain matters, 1884.

Revision Settlement	Final Report on the Revision Settlement.
RIC	Report on the Indian Irrigation Commission.
RIF	Report on the Indian Famine Commission.
RIHC	Report of the Indian Hemp and Drug Commission, 1893-94.
ROC	Records of Orissa Canal Project.
RSB	Final Report on the Settlement of Balasore.
RSC	Report of the Select Committee of House of Commons on the affairs of the East India Company.
Rundell's Report	Report on the manufacture of Salt and the system of Administration of Salt Revenue of Balasore, Cuttack and Puri Districts forming Orissa Division of Bengal Presidency.
Settlement of Aul	Final Report on the Survey and Settlement of Killa Aul.
Settlement of Darpan	Final Report on the Survey and Settlement of Killa Darpan.
Settlement of Khurda	Final Report on the Survey and Settlement of Killa Kanika.
Settlement of Keonjhar	Final Report on the Survey and Settlement of Keonjhar State.
Settlement of Kujang	Final Report on the Survey and Settlement of Killa Kujang.
Settlement of Khurda	Final Report on the Survey and Settlement of Khurda Government Estate.
Selection of Papers (Famine)	Selection of Papers relating to Famine of Bengal, 1896-97.
Selection Records (Districts)	Selection from Records of the Bengal Government, XXXV (Reports of the Districts of Puri and Balasore).

Selection Records (Feudatory States)	Selection of Records on Feudatory States of Orissa Division and rules applicable to them, Part I, Calcutta, 1907 (Confidential).
Selection Records (Settlement)	Selection from the Records of Bengal Government, XXIV, No. 3 (Paper on the Settlement of Cuttack and on the State of Tributary Mahals).

Introduction

Raja Mansingh annexed Orissa to the empire of Akbar in 1592. This territory was apportioned into five Sarkars and included into the Bengal Suba.[1] The Tarkars were Jaleswar, Bhadrakh, Cuttack, Kalinga Dandapat and Rajmahendri. Rajmahendri and a part of Kalinga Dandapat were transferred to the administrative control of Qutbsahi dynasty of Golconda after the settlement of Akbar was brought into force. Again after the death of Aurangzeb, Orissa was parcelled out to the 'Nawabs' of Bengal who were virtually independent kings. Frequent attacks of Marathas changed the political history of Orissa and finally Orissa was owned by Raghuji Bhonsle of Nagpur in 1751 and continued to remain under Maratha control till the British conquest of Orissa in 1803. Orissa during the Maratha rule was constituted of two distinct political divisions : Mughalbandi and Garhjats. The Mughalbandi formed a unit managed directly by the Maratha Governors whereas the Garhjats were held by ruling Chieftains.

The British merchants long before their appearance as rulers in the political horizon of Orissa established their commercial establishments at Hariharpur or Harispur, the modern Jagatsinghpur in Cuttack district in the year 1633.[2] Subsequently the English factories sprang up at Pipili in Balasore district and Balasore proper.[3] The British factory of Balasore

1. Abul Fazl, *Ain-i-Akbar i*, translated by H.S. Jarrett, Vol. II, p. 138.
2. *Bengal District Gazetteer, Balasore*, p. 37.
3. *Ibid*, p. 33; W.W. Hunter, *History of Orissa*, Vol. II, p. 39.

developed into an important centre of their maritime trade. After the battle of Buxar, Clive received the Diwani of Bengal, Bihar and Orissa on August 12, 1765. Following the event Clive became eagerly interested to get the possession of Orissa proper from Maratha control through negotiations. He deputed Thomas Motte to Sambalpur to obtain the permission for diamond trade. He was told by Clive to meet the Maratha Subadar at Cuttack on his way to Sambalpur, for a political negotiation. Motte handed over the letter of Clive to Bhawani Pandit and influenced him to pursue the Maratha ruler Janoji Bhonsla to cede Orissa to the Company on payment of a fixed amount per year. But nothing positive came out of the discussion at Cuttack. Negotiations in this manner continued for a long time from Clive to Cornwallis but nothing substantial was achieved. Finally, this affair was left to Lord Wellesley to triumph over it. The British occupation was declared on August 3, 1803. Madras army under Col. Campbel and Col. Harcourt entered into Orissa. The second British army marched from Bengal consisting of 500 sepoys, 21 gunners and 6 pounders. The third battalion led by Col. Furguson was directed towards Balasore from Medinapur. Col. Harcourt, Melville and Furguson, defeated the soldiers of Orissa and finally Orissa was ceded to East India Company by Raghuji Bhonsla II.[4] By the conclusion of the treaty of Deogaon on December 17, 1803 Sansaheb Raghuji Bhonsla II ceded to the honourable Company and their allies in "perpetual sovereignty" the province of Cuttack including the ports and district of Balasore.[5] Treaties with the Garhjat Chiefs were also confirmed by the Maratha ruler during the course of the war. The Feudatory Chiefs who were thus brought to the orbit of East India Company numbered 16. Two more Garhjats were added to it in 1837. Thus during the time of British conquest, three districts of Balasore, Cuttack and Puri known as Mughalbandi and 16 Tributary Mahals constituted the Province of Orissa in 1803 which was identified as the province of Cuttack or the

4. Harcourt to Shawe, Private Secretary to Wellesley, December 1, 1803 (O.S.A.).

5. *Bengal District Gazetteer, Calcutta*, 1906, p. 34.

Zilla of Cuttack. Orissa which came under the British control stretched between Medinapur to Ganjam and Sambalpur to Bay of Bengal. It covered an area of 24,307 square miles.[6] The geographical tract stretching along the sea-board over a surface of 8,000 square miles was called as Mughalbandi.[7] It contained a population of about 11,25,000 as estimated by Richardson.[8] The hilly regions stretching towards central India formed the Tributary Mahals having a population of about 3,37,500 covering an area of 16,307 miles.[9]

The 16th century marked a period of transition in the economic life of the people of Orissa. This period experienced a feudal economic system. The Hindu landed proprietors like the Bhanja Rajas acknowledged the Afgan suzerainty and agreed to pay the fixed revenue to Sulaiman. Sulaiman Karani till his death agreed to pay the tribute to Akbar and virtually accepted the suzerainty of the Mughal emperor. After the defeat of Daud, the son of Sulaiman at Tokaroi in 1575 by Munimkhan and Raja Todar Mall, a truce was signed.[10] But the refusal of payment of tribute by Daud led to his complete defeat. Orissa then became a part of Mughal empire in July, 1576. Todar Mall was sent by Akbar to Orissa for the finalisation of a standard regulation system of Revenue collection. The main features of this regulation were (i) Survey and measurement of land, (ii) classification of land and (iii) fixation of rates.[11] He introduced a system called *Taksim Jama* and *Tankha Raqmi* in 3 Sarkars of Jaleswar, Bhadrakh and Cuttack in the initial stage. Measurement by *Barah Dasti Padika* or rod of twelve span was made by him.[12] The Mughal rulers

6. Maddox Report, Vol. I, p. 1.
7. *Ibid.*
8. BRP, March 18, 1815, No. 29, J. Richardson to Government, December 20, 1814.
9. *Ibid.*
10. Smith, V.A., *Akbar the Great Mughal*, pp. 129-30.
11. *Ain-i-Akbari* (Transd.) Blochman, H., Vol. I, Calcutta, 1873, pp. 13 31.
12. Stirling, A., Orissa Chronology and History, Asiatic Researches, Vol. I, 1822.

confirmed the collection of land revenue by claiming the bulk of the surplus produce from the peasants. Zabt system was introduced. The rulers became interested to increase the state revenue and thus encouraged the Zamindars to reclaim uncultivable lands and develop cash-crop cultivation. Consequent upon this a new class of agricultural entrepreneurs emerged in the rural economy throughout the Mughal period.[13] The Mughal regime in Orissa attended a degree of centralised authority which was unprecedented during the whole of Gajapati kings. It is the most important factor of medieval Orissa that the seeds of capitalism were sown.

The period from 1740-1751 was a period of unsettled economy in Orissa. After the treaty between Ali Vardi Khan and the Raghuji I in 1752 Orissa was parcelled out to the control of Nagpur, and revenue collection for about 50 years continued to remain in the hands of Maratha rulers. The Bhonsla ruler within these 50 years mainly aimed at increasing revenue income from this province to meet the pressing demands of home charges in the shape of mounting expenditures of the vast and almost idle army of Nagpur. Both the Bhonsla and the Company put conflicting claims over the revenue collecting authority of Orissa. Enhancement of revenue was demanded from the Subadars of Orisaa To keep up the semblance of a well organised administration the Maratha rulers followed the Mughal administrative system. The province was divided into 5 *Chaklas* with 150 *Parganas* and the revenue collection was entrusted to 32 *Amils* or Revenue Commissioners, in the Mughalbandi region. In the Garhjat regions a variable amount of quit-rents or *Peskhas* was fixed over the hereditary landed proprietors.[14] Towards the close of 18th century the size of the revenue collection agencies increased while the revenue paying capacity of the cultivators decreased. Agricultural development was never thought of properly by

13. Habibulla, A.B.M., *The Foundation of Muslim Rulein India*, 1971, p. 257.

14. BRP, August 1, 1822, Stirling to Government, No. 5, October 15, 1821.

the rulers during the Maratha period, but the only thing over which they were very much careful was the increase of the incidence of taxation on raiyats. To help this economic degeneration in every level frequent famines caused by drought and floods told upon the saving capacity of the people pressing them into a state of pauperisation. In this declining agrarian economy by the close of 18th century the European merchants in general and the East India Company in particular had a remarkable role to play for regenerating the bankrupt agrarian economy.

The British East India Company participated in the commercial activities of Orissa in the early part of 17th century. British interest on the Orissan trade was confined to the textile goods. With the interest to invest more capital the British East India Company established factories at Hariharpur on May, 1633,[15] and at Balasore on June 1633 and subsequently at Pipili in 1634.[16] This Pipili port was inhabited by the Dutch, much earlier than the coming of English to this spot of commercial activities. Britishers were deeply attracted towards Balasore as the town was an emporium of cotton yarn and tasar. Throughout the 17th century the English merchants conducted the import and export business between Balasore and Huli via Pipili. Gradually the factory at Balasore had to face the problem of shortage of funds due to the decline of the demands on the British goods. They resorted to the barter system to sell the British broad cloths and lead in exchange of rice, tasar and cotton, but that system could not continue for a longer period due to the rapid growth of private trade and the demand of bribes by the local rajas. In the first half of 18th century the British East India Company had to confront the challenges of the foreign companies and Muslim authorities in Orissa. They had also to fight against the *Dadani* merchants to safeguard their investments in Textile Industries in Orissa. Balasore factory was put under the armed guards for the rest of the 2nd half of 18th century. In 1766 when Thomas Motte

4

15. English Factories in India, 1637-41, Vol. XXIX-XXX.
16. DSM, II, 76, Nos. 1, 52 & 290.

was deputed to Sambalpur darbar by Clive he observed that the glory of Balasore factory for textile industry was completely lost. Thus Balasore lost the importance as a commercial base by the 2nd half of 18th century. Besides all the ports of Orissa were closed down for big vessels due to the silting of rivers and these business centres became barren towards the beginning of 19th century.

In 1803 when the Company Government added Orissa to the Bengal administration, only rice and salt were exported to a considerable amount through the ports of Balasore, Dhamara, Chudamani mainly as other ports like Lychanpore, Saratha and Subarnarekha were found to have been unused by the business community due to silting of rivers. After the discovery of False point in Cuttack district following the years of famine all attentions of the Government were diverted towards the port and it grew as an important port both from business and defence point of view. Construction of Ravensport or Chandabali in 1872 helped the Company Government to accelerate the seaborn trade in rice, salt and other commodities of importance.[17] Government intended to improve the conditions of the ports of Orissa during the 2nd part of 19th century to yield better revenue from portal communication, but failed miserably due to inclemency of nature.

Maratha misrule led to the decentralisation of the Governmental responsibility over the growth of a non-producttive parasite class on the medieval agrarian economy of Orissa. On the other hand this Maratha misrule brought an end to the flourishing internal and external trade. When the trade became standstill, the agrarian Orissa faced a challenge from the middle class *Baboo* society which was based on money speculation in the land tenure system of the people of Orissa. The establishment of the Company rule brought unity among the

17. BRP, November, 1868, H.L. Dampier, Secretary, Government of Bengal to Secretary, Government of India, No. 3345, October, 22, 1866.

Oriya and Maratha bureaucrats, money lenders and revenue collectiors. These changes brought about economic dislocation in the social life followed by the creation of large-scale landed estates and the replacement of the Oriya revenue officers by the Bengali speculators. Towards the end of 18th century resistance movement by the Zamindars and their paikas against the bureaucratic oppression of the Maratha Fauzadars or Bargis began. In this declining agrarian economy, the East India Company had an important role to play in giving a new shape to the economy of Orissa. From the medieval time the rulers were interested in paddy cultivation for exportation to earn better profit for the growth of economy of Orissa. In this deplorable economic condition, the rate of wage was kept low to minimise the cost of production of a variety of goods and to earn good profit for the money lenders only. In this state of economic condition the gradual elimination of the Maratha and Oriya revenue officers from the administration, and ignorance of the foreigners in regard to the prevailing revenue system compelled the Company Government to have settlements to get more *Jama* out of the revenue settlements. To add injury to this, phenomenal, natural calamities, paucity of capital investment on agriculture to provide better irrigational facilities and to construct embankments to save agricultural fields from inundation forced the Orissan economy to decline. Realising the fact that rice was the staple food of the people, the Government decided to extend the British revenue policy to Orissa. This new revenue policy proved fatal to the agrarian economy and in the long run crippled the economic life of the province which was subject to the vagaries of nature throughout 19th century.

The economic condition of the people of Orissa was never good as they were mainly depending on the agriculture when they were not very sure to earn their subsistence out of it. On the other hand there existed no industries as the alternative source of subsistence of the people. Before the coming of the Britishers, many small scale industries flourished in Orissa like Salt Industry and Weaving Industry. After the monopolisation of Salt Industry by the Company's Government and the importation of English-made cloths these two main industries that had been affording subsistence to many could come to a close. Besides these two there existed other small scale industries which were in a state of decline due to lack of patronisation and due to stiff economic competition with the finished goods in the markets of Orissa. Thus the economic prosperity of this country on the eve of the British conquest was in a state of deplorable condition.

Many a work has been done on the administration of Orissa both under the East India Company and under the Crown on different aspects by different researchers. Such less has been done on the economic history of Orissa during the whole of 19th century. This is my humble attempt to bring out a detailed economic history of Orissa in the 19th century. I have given attention also to the enonomic policies introduced by the Britishers giving nothing in return towards development. The present work touches the most important aspects of economic life of the people and the calousness of the British authorities to ignore them. The new land revenue policy, salt policy, excise policy, trade policy and industrial policy and their consequenees are thoroughly examined and highlighted in this work. This may be treated as an humble contribution to the economic history of Orissa during 19th century.

This work is primarily based on official records preserved by the Governments in the Board of Revenue Record Room and Library, Orissa, Cuttack; Orissa State Archives, Bhubaneswar; West Bengal State Archives, Calcutta and National Archives, New Delhi. I have also made extensive use of local dailies and weeklies. I have also studied some of the original published books of different research scholars. To my mind, it appears that these relevant records were not widely studied by scholars to throw light on the economic history of Orissa for the whole of 19th century.

It is my pleasant duty to express my deep sense of reverence to my learned teacher Dr. M.N. Das, Ex-Vice-Chancellor, Utkal University who infused inspiration in me for my research work. I acknowledge my deep sense of gratitude and indebtedness particularly to Dr. K.M. Patra, Professor of History, Utakal University who has been rendering valuable advice always and who was never hesitant to spare his valuable time in spite of all his pre-occupations. He has never felt tired at the time of discussions on matters relating to this work throughout the period of the preparation of this work.

I also wish to acknowledge the valuable advice given by Dr. Jagdish Raj, Professor Queen's Land University, Australia and Dr. H.S. Srivastav, Retd. Professor of History, Gorakhpur University.

I must be thankful to the Archivist of the Orissa State Archives, Bhubaneswar, the Archivists of West Bengal State Archives, Calcutta, the Archivists of the National Archives. New Delhi for their help in providing relevant documents without any hesitation.

Salipur College, Salipur. PURNA CHANDRA DAS

1

Land Revenue Policy and Settlements

Land System on the Eve of British Occupation

The Marathas ruled Orissa for a period of about 52 years from 1751-1803. For administrative convenience they divided Orissa into two distinct revenue divisions, *Mughalbandi* and *Garhjat*. *Mughalbandi* stretched along the sea coast of nearly 8,000 square miles[1] and was kept under the direct management of the Marathas. The hilly region held by the feudal chieftains, who were allowed to rule on a fixed quit rent or tribute to the Maratha Government hereditarily, were called *Garhjats*. These chieftains were possessors of *Killas* or *Garhs*, but the *Garhjats* were not subject to any ordinary British law.

The Mughalbandi was further divided into four divisions such as Cuttack, Bhadrakh, Soro and Balasore. Each division was called a *Chakla*. The *Chaklas* were divided into *Parganas* and *Parganas* were again subdivided into *Mahals* which consisted of a number of *Mauzas* or villages. Broadly the *Mughalbandi* was divided into 150 *Parganas*. Each *Pargana* was generally subdivided into two, three, four or more *Mahals*.[2]

1. Maddox Report, Vol. I, p. 1.
2. BRC, August 1, 1822.

An officer, with the designation of *Amil* was appointed to take care of the administration of a group of *Parganas*. Thirty two such *Amils* were engaged for the purpose of revenue collection.[3] These *Amils* were responsible to the Government for the revenue assessed in their respective divisions to which they were attached.

In course of time, the Maratha Revenue Officer left the management of the land revenue administration to persons who agreed to pay the highest amount for any particular area. The Headmen of the villages were taken commonly into confidence by the *Amils* who were identified as *Mukaddams*. The *Mukaddams* were kept under the supervision of *Talukdars* or *Chaudhurys* or *Kanungos*. The *Mukaddams* were allowed to enjoy some hereditary rights of office and received a portion of land as *nankar* known as *pitrali* or patrimonial property.[4]

Under the Marathas the conditions of the cultivators remained far from being satisfactory due to illegal exaction of the revenue officers. The Marathas never paid any attention to the material prosperity of the cultivators of Orissa as they remained far from the province at Nagpur. They always, ignoring the economic conditions of the people, instructed their officers to be careful about the collection of revenue regularly. In the beginning the officers were sympathetic towards the cultivators but gradually the cultivating class remained unnoticed by the revenue officers. They became interested only in the exaction of more revenue to satisfy their masters for their comfort and lavish expenditure.

Andrew Stirling in his account of Geographical, Statistical and Historical of Orissa Proper or Cuttack stated that the *Jama* of Cuttack under Maratha or the whole *Mughalbandi* area was Rs. 1,35,00,000. This income included land revenue, duties from import and export through small ports like Golrah

3. Patra, K.M., *Orissa under the East India Company*, p. 1.
4. BdRC, Vol. 586, No. 14189, p. 300.

Harishpur, Bishenpur and Manikpatna; duties from cotton and metal trade and duties from Salt Industries.

A. EARLY BRITISH POLICY

Soon after the British conquest in 1803, the British administrators paid immediate attention to the problem of land system and revenue collection as the prosperity of the British rule depended on it because land revenue was the mainstay of their financial system. They retained Maratha divisions of *Mughalbandi* and *Garhjat*.

Kanungos, *Patwaries* and *Sarbarakars* were the main officers for revenue collection in the pre-British days. The British Government before the introduction of the new regulation for Settlement retained these officers and with no change instructed them to collect the *Jamas* effectively. They were called to work under the Commissioners, appointed to look after the administration of Orissa.

Temporary Settlements (1805-1837)

By the regulation 12 of 1805 the British imposed the first land Revenue Settlement in Orissa on an elaborate scale. A yearly *Jama* of Rs. 13,14 825 was fixed on the province. The financial burden on the land holders became heavier in comparison to the collection of *Jama* by the Marathas. As a result of this more than one-third of the province came under the direct management of the British Administration, when land owners refused to pay land revenue. These lands came to be known as *Khasmahals*.[5] These *Khasmahals* were kept under the management of Tahasildars, to be supervised by Collectors.

The next triennial settlement of 1805-06 to 1807-08 was made by George Webb, the Collector of the whole of Orissa under the regulation 12 of 1805. This settlement yielded a

5. Toynbee, G. *A Sketch of the History of Orissa*, p. 40.

Jama of Rs. 14,35,354 giving a net increase of Rs. 1,20,529. The capacity of payment by the proprietors, the conditions of agriculture and agriculturists were never taken into consideration at the time of this new settlement.[6] The British administration abolished the practice of remission of rent, what had been done by the Marathas during the time of natural calamities. This resulted in the accumulation of arrears of revenue due to the Government by the proprietors. In the subsequent year the process of sale of estates started. Many Oriya landlords were replaced by Bengali speculators who could visualise the realisation of huge profit by small investment on lands.

On petition made by the Zamindars the Government modified the original scheme of settlement and to that effect the Governor General in Council passed a new regulation, that provided for a 4 year settlement after 1808.[7] The question of affecting a permanent settlement was then thought of but it was opposed by the Collector of Cuttack on the ground of non-availability of reliable information about the land system and the institution of cases to hold land rent free under the regulation 12 of 1805 by the proprietors. The regulation 6 of 1808 provided for one year settlement that would be followed by a triennial settlement from 1809-10 to 1811-12. This regulation further declared that the assessment of 1811-12 would remain fixed for ever in case the arrangement would receive sanction of the Court of Directors. Charles Buller was appointed as a special Commissioner in Orissa. His settlement increased the annual *Jama* with an addition of Rs. 64,042 making the total *Jama* of Rs. 15,02,954.[8]

At the end of the year 1812-13 the regulation 1 of 1813 was pushed for enactment that directed for one year's settlement to be followed by a 2 years' settlement.[9] The Board of Revenue was directed by the regulation to prepare a report

6. Patra, K.M., *Orissa under the East India Company*, p. 11.
7. Toynbee, G., *A Sketch of the History of Orissa*, p. 45.
8. Patra, K.M., *Orissa under the East India Company*, p. 13.
9. Toynbee, G., *A Sketch of the History of Orissa*, p. 47.

for enforcing a permanent settlement in Orissa taking the state of cultivation and the condition of the estates into consideration. The settlement of 1812-13 ended in a great failure which only increased the Government demands. A new settlement followed in quick succession in 1813-14 for 2 years.[10] John Richardson, a member of the Board of Revenue was appointed to supervise the work of this settlement and he arrived at Cuttack in 1813 He took much pain to influence the landlords to agree for a higher *Jama* for their estates. On the hope of getting a permanent settlement they agreed to Richardson's proposal. As a result of the agreement the 2 years' settlement was completed by the end of October, 1814 by Richardson.[11] In 1815 a resolution was passed that extended the validity of the settlement of 1814 for one year more. It extended the option to relinquish the management of the estates when the Zamindars would feel dissatisfied. That option resulted in the sale of estates of 53 Zamindars. At the end of this settlement, the regulation 6 of 1816 embodied another triennial settlement in 1816-17.[12]

Against the settlement of 1816-17 a rebellion was lodged by the *Paikas*, popularly known as Paika Rebellion. To study the subsequent result on the revenue settlement a brief sketch of the Paika Rebellion of 1817 is of much importance.

The territories of Khurda (a seat of ruling dynasty) situated in Puri district, the storm centre of the rebellion was almost ruined by the British maladministration. The *Paikas*, a kind of local militia rose in a body against the British as they suffered heavily due to the short-sighted policy of the Government. Major Fletcher, who managed Khurda after the British conquest had resumed the service lands of the *Paikas* which they had been enjoying from time immemorial. They were deprived of their rights over their lands. In such a state of discontentment the leadership appeared in Jagabandhu Bidyadhar Mahapatra Bhramarbar Ray popularly

10. Malley, S.S.O., *Bihar and Orissa Gazetteer, Cuttack*, p. 179.
11. BdRP, May 13, 1819.
12. Malley, S.S.O., *Bihar and Orissa Gazetteer, Cuttack*, p. 179.

known as Jagabandhu who was the *Bakshi* or the military commander of the Raja of Khurda before the British conquest. He was second to the Raja in rank. His family held the valuable estate of Roranga at a low rent for several generations. The estate was in possession of Jagabandhu in 1803. Subsequently he became the victim to the plot engineered by the *amalas* of Revenue Department and a Bengali speculator, Krishna Chandra Singh. He was deprived of his estate in 1813. Consequent upon this Jagabandhu became pauper. He was not prepared to go to the Court of Law for justice as he had lost faith in the integrity of the British officers. He carved for vengeance at the first opportunity.[13]

In March, 1817 a body of *Khonds* from Ghumusar, a border estate in the Ganjam district entered into Khurda. British Government was not able to know the intention of *Khonds* and for which, it could not take any steps against this march. *Paikas* under the leadership of Jagabandhu joined with the *Khonds* and broke out in open rebellion. They attacked the police station and other Government buildings at Banpur and looted the treasury. After their victory at Banpur they marched to Khurda and set fire to all Government buildings and looted the treasury at Khurda. Soon after the whole of Khurda and the neighbouring area fell into the hands of the rebels.[14] The Government took immediate steps to suppress the rebellion. But the rebels captured many British officers and killed them. Troops despatched to quell the trouble, retreated to Cuttack. Subsequently martial law was proclaimed at Khurda and was extended upto Puri on April 14, 1817.[15] The rebellion was spread to all over the Eastern and Southern parts of Orissa. But by the end of October, 1817 the rebellion is said to have been stamped out. Order was restored in the territories under military operation. Martial law was withdrawn. Jagabandhu remained absconded for a long time and

13. BRP, No. 15, July 17, 1818, Ewer to Government, May 13, 1818.
14. Toynbee, G., *A Sketch of the History of Orissa*, p. 16.
15. Orissa Records, Vol. II, Bayley's Report on Paika Rebellion, August 10, 1817, pp. 10-18.

ultimately he surrendered in 1825 and remained as a prisoner of the Government at Cuttack where he died in 1829.[16]

The rebellion was suppressed but the Government called for reports to ascertain the real cause of this historic event. Enquiries were conducted. The enquiries revealed about the grave errors in the land revenue policy, system adopted by the Government in the earlier settlement. Finally Watson pointed out that the postponement of the permanent settlement of land revenue had caused the real disappointment in the minds of the Zamindars. He was of opinion that "it is a permanent settlement alone which can correct the prevailing abuses in the internal detail of the collections, repress disorders by personal influence of the land holders...". Watson wanted that atleast a settlement for a long term such as 15 or 20 years should be made.[17] Trower contradicting the opinion of Watson said that it was the "system of anticipation" which was the root of all evils in the land revenue system of Orissa.[18]

Government was not satisfied with the report of the officers and appointed a commission to make further enquiries on the matters. Beside an officer with the title of Commissioner of Cuttack was appointed to set the administration into order. Robert Ker was appointed and he arrived at Cuttack on June 10, 1818.

Ker strongly recommended for enacting a new regulation to preserve the native land holders from further ruin. His recommendation was accepted by the Government and a new regulation (Regulation 10 of 1818) was promulgated in November, 1818.[19] The principal objects of the said regulation were to enable the Collectors to arrest and put in confinement the defaulter and to substitute the mode of enforcing payment

16. Orissa Records, Vol. II, Report of W. Blunt to Chief Secretary to Government, No. 44, June, 4, 1825.
17. *Ibid*, Watson to Government, May 3, 1817, pp. 6-7.
18. BRP, No. 22, May 13, 1819, Tower to Stirling, November 26, 1818.
19. BRP, May, 1820, Stirling to Blunt, Commissioner of Cuttack, February 29, 1820.

as he might deem it preferable to the sale of his lands. The Government also adopted a new measure for improving the situation in Orissa. The triennial settlement of the regulation 6 of 1816 was extended for 3 years more upto the end of 1821-22 by virtue of the new regulation 13 of 1818. The *Jama* was reduced by more than Rs. 1,00,000 and was fixed at Rs. 15,27,834 as against the previous *Jama* of Rs. 16,37,924. By this the over-assessed estate got relief and Government anticipated regular payment of revenues from those estates. Thus within a few years of the rebellion, the Government took decisive steps to end the chaotic condition and to reform the administration. By 1823, normalcy was restored and Government took the next step in the land revenue policy. Finally the *Mahalwari system* of settlement in the ceded and conquered provinces including Orissa was introduced duly approved by the Governor General in Council. This system was recommended by Mackenzie.[20] The regulation 7 of 1822 marked a beginning of a new phase in the history of land revenue administration in Orissa by clearly enunciating the change of policy of Government.[21] The existing settlement of Orissa was extended for 5 years until 1826-27 by the new regulation.

In these circumstances, Lord Bentinck decided to revolutionise the whole system in 1833. He formulated certain principles and soon embodied in the regulation 9 of 1833 and the circular letter was issued to the Commissioner to expedite survey and settlement proceedings.[22] The regulation once more extended the existing Cuttack settlement for 5 years, and Act VI of 1837 declared that the settlement should continue until a new one was made. The first regular settlement with a survey and record of rights was made in 1838[23] giving effect to a long term settlement for 30 years in Orissa.

20. BRP, August, 1822, Resolution of Governor General in Council, August 1, 1822.
21. B. Powel, *Land System of British India*, Vol. I, p. 475.
22. BRP, No, 37, September 9, 1833, Regulation 9, 1833.
23. B. Powel, *Land System of British India*, Vol. I, p. 475.

B. SETTLEMENT OF 1837-38

Henry Ricketts, the Commissioner, Cuttack, took interest in the operation of the settlement work. He reported that the whole establishment was complete both in Settlement and and Resumption Department in 1838[24] On the work of investigation of rent free tenures, 19 Deputy Collectors were engaged. They also tried arrear resumption suits under the control of the special Deputy Collector. From among 19 Deputy Collectors 15 Deputy Collectors were engaged in both Settlement and Resumption Departments under the supervision of 4 covenanted Deputy Collectors. They were further kept under the supervision of 3 Collectors. Henry Ricketts was succeeded by A.J.M. Mill who had lot of experience as a Collector of Cuttack. He expedited the settlement work smoothly. Finally the decision to appoint a special commissioner for settlement work was affected.

Under the jurisdication of the special commissioner there were 14 Deputy Collectors in the district of Balasore. They were entrusted with the settlement work and were also trying resumption cases. There were 12 Deputy Collectors employed under the Collector, Cuttack, out of which 9 officers were required to work in general settlement operation. One was engaged in the demarcation of boundaries and the remaining 2 were engaged in the settlement of resumed lands. In the district of Puri there were 8 Deputy Collectors who were asked to work in the settlement matter.[25]

Besides these set of officers, there were some Deputy Collectors kept under the control of the special Deputy Collector for settling arrear resumption cases. When the settlement and the resumption operation was going on by the Indian Deputy Collectors, the Government declared it as slow and consequently expensive. The Commissioner hoped

24. BRP, October, 1838, Commissioner, Cuttack to Secretary, Sadar Board of Revenue, No. 69, October 9, 1838.
25. BdRP, 1840, Secretary, Sadar Board to Secretary, Government of Bengal, No. 20, 1839.

that the survey and measurement of the 3 districts would be completed by the end of April, 1844.[26]

As per the minutes of A.J.M. Mill, the Commissioner, Cuttack, the expenditure for the settlement operation was Rs. 20,36,348.[27] The settlement of 1838 resulted in a *Jama* of Rs. 13,84,190 against 25,87,993 acres as detailed on page 11.[28]

Mill was of opinion that a fair and moderate assessment had been made on the estates and the estate holders were satisfied with the terms on which they had been allowed to engage for their estates during the settlement of 1838. The estates were assessed village by village known as *Mauzuwar.*[29] The settlement also fixed the percentage of allowance for the under-tenures such as *Mukaddams, Sarbarakars* and others like the village barber, watchman, blacksmith, washerman etc. They were allowed to be in possession of their petty *jagirs.* In large estates *Patwaris*, village Accountants were remunerated by a grant of land whereas in small estates the Zamindars were allowed to make their own arrangements. The settlement thus had tremendous impact on the Zamindars and the raiyats from the social aspects. The Government revenue was increased and consequent upon this the Government was benefited in every respect.

In 1856 the revision was undertaken. In 1867 Bengal Act X extended the settlement of 1837 for a term of 30 years as the great Orissa Famine forced the Government, rendering an immense loss of life and property. This extension of the term of settlement of 1837-38 for another period of 30 years allowed the people to regain the loss. The 30 years settlement was based on a careful survey in the field and the importance of individual's rights of land holders of each and every category and under tenants.

26. BdRP, No. 96, December 14, 1841.
27. *Ibid,* January 23, 1847.
28. BRP, August, 1900, P.C. Lyon, Director, Land Records to Board of Revenue, LP. No. 1549S, July 24, 1900.
29. Baden Powel, *Land System of British India*, Vol. I, p. 475.

District	Total Area (Acres)	Unculti-vated Area (Acres)	Assessed Area (Acres)	Mufasil Jama or Assets (Rs.)	Sadar Jama	
					Percent-age	Amount (Rs.)
Cuttack	11,74,900	6,97,000	6,21,000	11,21,000	64	7,14,1000
Balasore	9,13,993	5,54,000	5,93,200	5,75,600	65	3,77,290
Puri	4,99,100	3,77,000	2,02,400	4,41,600	66	2,92,800
Total:	25,87,993	16,28,000	14,16,000	21,38,200	65	13,84,190

The settlement was made with the Zamindars, the majority of whom held propriety rights under the Mughals and Marathas. They were recognised as Rajas of Killas. They had received permanent settlement of their lands during the early settlements. There were a few estates which were originally parts of *Rajwara*, since the time of Marathas, and were treated as appertaining to the Mughalbandi or Crown domain. These estates like Killa of Dampara, Balrampur, Chousathipara etc. were known as *Killazat estates*, and occupied an anomalous position.[30] Mansingh left these estates as part of the *Rajwara* but during the time of the Marathas they were required to pay regular *jagirs*. These Rajas belonged to the Ancient Hindu stock allied to the Chiefs of Garhjat States. On the eve of the British conquest states of this category were in the roll of the temporarily settled estates. These estates were absorbed into the class of ordinary temporarily settled estates.

Besides, this settlement recognised the *Talukdars*, rent collectors, village Headmen and holders of village *jagirs*, as the holders of larger revenue free properties and soon they were allowed to be recognised as Zamindars. The origin of Orissan Zamindars thus had its relation with this settlement. Minor revenue officials like *Padhans*, *Mukaddams*, *Sarbarakars*, and the purchaser of the recipients of propriety rights in small plots of lands either from the Zamindars or *Mukaddams* were identified as *Khariddars* or *Sikim Zamindars*.

The Hindu rulers were in practice of assigning lands to brahmins for their maintenance who were in return required to perform the duties of priests in Monasteries. The monasteries were also assigned with lands for their day to day management. These grants to the brahmins and monasteries as well were subject to the revenue exemption. During the time of Muslim rule attempts were made to settle these lands in order to exact revenue for royal treasuries. Marathas also worked hard to set this practice right but miserably failed due to its

30. Malley, S.S.O., *Bihar and Orissa Gazetteer, Cuttack*, p. 181.

strong root in the social tradition of this country. After the British conquest enquiries were made according to the resolution 12 of 1805 which resulted in the recognition of these types of land tenure as *Lakhraj Bahal. Lakhraj Bahals* were confirmed as revenue free lands. The proprietors of these lands were known as *Lakhraj Bahaldars.*

The *Lakhraj Bahals* were of 2 categories, (a) Brahmottar, those with full propriety rights and powers to alienate, (b) *Debottar* or *Pirottar* those who held lands in trust for endowment without power to alienate.[31] The usual abuses were prevalent in almost all cases in relation to the second category of lands. This became complicated in the case of Khurda. The resumption proceedings which were really part of decennial settlement, completed in 1834, in section 8 of the ruidad or final proceedings confirmed by the Government the position of the *Marfatdars* and *Sevakas* as clearly defined had no right in Khurda to transfer their trusts or services or to alienate the lands attached to several endowments.[32] All such persons were classed at the settlement under which they held the lands as mere servants of the idols and liable for dismissal by the Collector for misconduct. However the type of restriction was not applicable in other parts of this country as applicable in Khurda in case of endowments.

1. Class of Raiyats

At the time of British conquest the cultivators of Orissa were found to be divided into 2 classes such as *Thani* or resident and *Pahi* or non-resident raiyats. The term *Thani* is the corrupt acceptance of the term *Sthaniya* i.e. local. The *Thani* raiyats had the hereditary rights of occupancy in their lands whereas the *Pahi* raiyats were mere tenants at will. The advantages enjoyed by the *Thani* raiyats were enormous. He held his homestead and garden lands rent free. His lands were

31. Settlement of Khurda, 1897-98, p. 195.
32. *Ibid.*

the best in the village and he had the preference in the reclamation of new lands. He had the rights to pasture, firewood and thatching grass. He had thus a hereditary right of occupancy and cound not be ousted so long as he paid his rent. The enjoyment of these advantages virtually increased his importance as well as image in the eyes of his neighbours, that could strengthen his credit with money lenders. His rent was much higher than that of *Pahi* raiyats or non-resident raiyats.[33] He groaned under the extra contribution and impositions exacted from him by his landlords and these demands were often so excessive that his profit of cultivation was subject to be swallowed up by the landlords pressing him into despair ultimately to abandon his home, prestige and image in the society. On the other hand the *Pahi* raiyats paid much lower rent to the landlords, but were liable to be turned out of his holding at any moment.[34] After the settlement of 1837-38 the *Thani* rents remained almost unaltered while the rents of the *Pahi* raiyats which were not regulated for years together by law rose higher due to stiff competition among them.

Besides the above 2 categories of raiyats, there existed in this land *Tankidars*, *Baziaftidars*, *Chandinadars*, *Jagirdars* and *Sikim Raiyats* or under raiyats.

(i) *Tankidars*

They held small areas assessed permanently at a quit rent. A group of *Tankidars* who agreed at the decennial settlement to periodical enhancement in proportion to the enhancement of ordinary raiyati rents over the whole estates on condition that no enquiries should be made into their titles. Government orders confirmed this type of *Tankidars*. They are identified as *Rafatankidars*.[35]

33. Malley, S.S.O., *Bihar and Orissa Gazetteer, Cuttack*, p. 195.
34. *Ibid.*
35. BRP, October, 1839, Government of Bengal's Letter No. 1518, October 22, 1839.

(ii) *Baziaftidars*

They held resumed rent free lands at somewhat liberal rates. From most of these tenants the proprietors never realised any rent.[36] Some of these were objected to under section 103 and a few were also tried judicially under section 106. The majority were retained.

(iii) *Chandinadars*

In the case of cultivating classes their homesteads were generally used from their agricultural holdings but the shopkeepers, artisans and the labouring classes who had no arable lands in the village paid rent for their homestead only and were called *Chandinadars*. The term originally implied inferiority as on this class fell the obligation of supplying forced labour but this obligation having fallen into disuse the word *Chandina* came to be used for all homestead lands.

(iv) *Jagirdars*

The Jagirdars held lands rent free or on low rent in return for the services rendered to the landlords and were liable to ejectment on failure to perform duties and those commonly known as *Desheta Jagirdars*,[37] who performed services to the village community. The system of giving *jagirs* to the village servants like barber, washerman, carpenter, potter and astrologer prevailed in Orissa from ancient time and their lands were always exempted from land revenue. The general custom was, for these village servants, to get small payments of paddy or cash annually from the raiyats.

Paikas (militia), village watch or *Chaukidar*, jungli *Paika* (forest watchman), *Dalai*, *Tandakar* and other communal *Jagirdars* were also treated in the same manner and were known as *Jagirholders*.[38] *Gariba prajas* like (Bauri, Kandara,

36. Settlement of Darpan, 1901, p. 11.
37. Malley, S.S.O., *Bihar and Orissa Gazetteer, Cuttack*, p. 197.
38. Settlement of Khurda, 1897-98, pp. 67-68.

Sabar, Damos, Panas, Kelas, Khonds, Matias, Kalinji, Sodhas and poor widows and orphans) belonged to exempted class in the revenue roll.[39] This was applicable in some parts of Orissa in the Settlement of 1838. Mill had remarked that the rent free claims had been judiciously investigated which numbered 2,77,925 (Cuttack 1,49,449, Puri 46,803, Balasore 81,673).

2. Results

A.J.M. Mill remarked, "this great work was undertaken with a far higher view than to improve the exchequer."[40] It was aimed at fixing the area of each estate and the valuation of the lands. Due to lack of careful consideration about the capabilities of the estates it had pushed many poor Zamindars into poverty. The purpose was also to finalise the boundaries of estates and to decide the disputes relating to the rights and interest between the landlords and the tenants on the spot. The rights of *Mukaddams* and *Sarbarakars*, *Padhans*, *Khariddars* and such other tenure holders had been separately ascertained and recorded. Mill concluded that the settlement operation had permanent blessingss for the people. He believed that a fair assessment had been made on the estates and the proprietors were well satisfied with the terms and conditions with which they were allowed to make arrangements within their estates. The *Malikana* allowance to cover the risk of collection was limited to 30 per cent but later on it was reconsidered with liberal terms in 1840 by Auckland that had increased the allowance to 35 per cent and in some particular cases to 40 per cent where it was justified. This settlement further had fixed the *jagirs* of village staff. In big estates the *Patwaris* were remunerated by grant of land.

3. Problem of Sale Law

At the very outset the sale law created a lot of commotion in the Revenue Administration following 1838. It had already

39. *Ibid*, p. 69.
40. BRP, January, 1847, Minutes of A.J.M. Mill, January 23, 1847.

been noticed by the first commissioner of the province regarding the irregularity in payment of revenue. Mill in his minute observed that this system was "far more suited to the existing state of things than periodical sales at fixed times of the year."[41] The successor of Mill however had proposed the introduction of resolution 10 of 1818. The Board agreed to this proposal and viewed to have a fixed date of payment like the practice in Bengal. The Board decided to fix April 8 and November 8 as the last dates of payment of revenue failing which their estates would be sold on the 1st of May and 1st of December. After a prolonged correspondence it was decided by the Board that the old system of "dustuk system" should be replaced by the system of periodical sale of estates liable for, due to non-payment of dues in fixed time. The "dustuk system" was however abolished from January 1, 1854,[42] and in lieu of that April 28 and November 8 were fixed as dates for 8 annas demands and 16 annas demands respectively. According to this new policy only in Cuttack district as many as 32 estates were sold between 1831-32 to 1841-42 amounting a sadar *Jama* of Rs. 16,279 against the sale proceed of Rs. 34,232.[43] Henry Rickets emphasised that the settlement had doubled the value of the estates but during the time of natural calamities, as no remission of revenue was granted to any single proprietor, the number of sale naturally increased.

4. Changes during 1837 and 1897 Settlements

There took place a lot of social, economic and natural changes during the long period of 60 years from 1837 to 1897. The population increased by over 80 per cent. Cultivable lands were added by 30 per cent. Roads were constructed and communication facilities were mostly improved consequent upon the growth of trade and commerce. Agricultural products increased to a considerable degree due to irrigation facilities, afforded to the agriculturists following the

41. BRP, January, 1847, Minutes of A.J.M. Mill, January 23, 1847.
42. Maddox Report, Vol. II. p. 393.
43. Henry Rickets' Reports on the District of Cuttack, pp. 68-69.

years of Famine. The prices of staple foods and crops were increased to a considerable rate that yielded heavy profit to the cultivators. This material development was accompanied by an increase in the rent of *Pahi* raiyats, the only class who were not fixed with a rent in the settlement. The advancement of their rents took place in the meanwhile. The increase in rent for them ranged from Rs. 1-14-6 to Rs. 2-11-6 in Cuttack, Rs. 1-2-11 to Rs. 1-11-1 in Balasore and Rs. 1-7-8 to Rs. 1-13-8 in Puri.[44]

On the other hand there took place a sizeable decrease in the area of *Thani* raiyats. These tenancies as the resident tenants occupied the best possible lands in the villages. They were assessed at much higher rates than the *Pahi* tenants. The decrease was only due to Famine as confirmed by Maddox, the Settlement Officer.[45]

Multiplication of estates as well as landlords became the striking features during this time. The estates rose from 3,571 to 6,377 and the landlords increased from 8,000 to 42,400 with the corresponding increase of lands in the direct possession of landlords.[46] The following table gives a clear picture of the increase.[47]

District	*Settlement of 1837*		*Settlement of 1897*	
	Area	*Valuation*	*Area*	*Valuation*
Cuttack	42,300	Rs. 75,400	85,800	Rs. 2,23,200
Balasore	20,400	Rs. 25,100	46,600	Rs. 81,100
Puri	26,00	Rs. 46,800	40,100	Rs. 80,200
Total	88,700	Rs. 1,47,300	1,72,500	Rs. 3,84,500

44. BRP, July, 1900, P.C. Leyon to Board of Revenue, No. 1549S, July 14, 1900.
45. RAB, 1901-1902, p. 120.
46. *Ibid.*
47. Maddox Report, Vol. I, p. 120, P.C. Leyon to Board of Revenue.

This interim period thus brought tremendous changes on the condition of the landlords, tenants and the Government too.

C. THE SETTLEMENT OF 1897

1. Principles of Settlement

The hopes of Orissan Zamindars were pushed into oblivion as the permanent settlement could not be materialised by the Government. Temporary settlements were affected one after the other only to get a fixed *Jama* for the Government in temporarily settled estates. The question was reopened by the Orissa Landlords' Association through petitions. Prior to that petition the editor of the Utkal Sabha held a meeting at Cuttack town to discuss matters relating to the coming settlement which was not only attended by the membersof the Landlords' Association but by all the Zamindars of the town. Utkal Gauraba Madhusudan Das in his presidential address supported the cause of the Zamindars and urged upon the Government to resolve on the matter of a permanent settlement taking all the assessed and unassessed lands into account through intelligent officers.[48] The petitioners were informed by the Commissioner that they should wait till the Government had ascertained about the material benefit of the people. Charles Elliot, the Lt. Governor during his visit to Cuttack had informed the petitioners in the meeting held at Lalbag that there was not the slightest chance of permanent settlement being made.[49] Again in 1897 the Association appealed the Government for a long term settlement. Consequent upon the prayer of the landlords the uncertainty was removed.

The settlement work extended for a period of 10 years commencing from 1889. It covered the districts of Cuttack, Puri and Balasore with the exception of certain permanently settled estates known as Killas. The areas covered by the operation

48. *Utkal Dipika*, Vol. No. 44, November 16, 1889.
49. BRP, Nos. 19-21, May, 1897.

amounted to 5,053 sq. miles as detailed below with 11,056 villages.[50]

Cuttack	2,194 sq. miles	4,876 villages
Puri (excluding Khurda)	1,147 sq. miles	2,287 villages
Balasore	1,712 sq. miles	3,893 villages
Total	5,053 sq. miles	11,056 villages

Khurda Government estates made an addition of 967 sq. miles to this that was brought under the operation in 1,377 villages. The settlement operation was decided to have started on certain problems, survey of the areas, the preparation of the record of rights, the settlement of rents and the settlement of revenue.

2. Survey Operation

The survey operation began in 1889 under the guidance of Paterson. There took place number of obstructions in the process of survey work regarding the fixation of units but ultimately the existing village was adopted. The average cost of survey work became Rs. 39 per sq. mile.[51] This work was conducted by the village *Patwari* and other local people at first but the attempt was abandoned on the pretext of slow progress. The trained *amins* were employed from the North-West province for this purpose soon. For the expedience the cadastral survey work was placed under the control of Colonel Sundeman as the Director of Survey and Lt. Crichton as the Superintendent. The survey work was completed in September, 1894. The Survey Department further extended the operation

50. GAROD, 1899-1900, Pr. 88, pp 21-22.
51. BRP, July, 1900, P.C. Leyon to Board of Revenue, No. 1549S, July 24, 1900.

work to the lands belonging to the temper of Lord Jagannath totalling 105 sq. miles at the expenses of the temple authorities.

Making an exception of the lands of Lord Jagannath the survey operation was mainly confined to the temporarily settled estates. But some permanently settled estates were also surveyed due to their territorial links with the temporarily settled estates.

Along with the survey work the *amins* of the Survey Department of India were entrusted with the task of preparing the record of rights. The *amins* were asked to complete the work cautiously basing on the facts on the spot. The records so prepared were 4 in number—*Khewat* in which were entered the names, *tauzi* number, areas and proprietors of each estate of which any lands were situated in the village; *Khasara* or field index to the map containing one entry for each field or separate plots belonging to one cultivator specifying the names of the owner and occupier, its area, the crop borne in it and the description of the nature of the soil; *Khatian* or abstract record containing a list of tenants of the village with details of land held by each, the rent payable by them and the class of tenancy to which the holding belonged and *Parcha* which was prepared simultaneously with *Khatian* and handed over to the tenants to enable them to understand what was being entered in the record and to check its occupancy.[52]

After the preparation of these records by the field officers of the Survey Department they were compared and checked finally in the office of each camp and then were handed over to the Settlement Department for the fixation of rent and status. This rent fixation work was to be executed by a responsible revenue officer. This work was kept in charge of one settlement officer but due to pressure of work 2 settlement officers were appointed, one for Cuttack and Puri and the other for Balasore

52. BRP, July, 1900, P.C. Leyon to Board of Revenue, No. 1549S, July 24, 1900.

alone. The most difficult task of assessment of rent of these estates then came which became extremely a difficult job because of the long gap between the present and the last settlement.

Sir Alexander Mackenzie, the Lt. Governor of Bengal was not satisfied with the progress of rent fixation and thus became more interested to appoint more revenue officers for the work. He had suggested the Government of India to delay the settlement operation work in North Bihar and to allow the officers engaged there to work in Orissa for the completion of the work in time. The proposals were approved and accordingly the Bihar officers were engaged in this work.[53]

3. Scheme of Settlement

Mackenzie prepared a scheme for the settlement of rents in Orissa that recommended the enhanced rate of rents due to the facts that there were large number of tenants who were enjoying a fixed rate of rents since a long term of 60 years and that many of them were assessed at a privileged rate of rents below the ordinary rates and that the culturable lands were increased and were in possession of both the Zamindars and tenants for the cultivation was largely extended to these lands. The scheme was substantiated in the following manner:

(i) In the case of *Pahi* raiyats of Orissa (whose rents the Zamindars were empowered to enhance and did enhance during past 60 years), the existing rents should be taken to be fair rents unless application was made by the Zamindars for enhancement or by the raiyats for reduction.

(ii) In case of *Thani* raiyats whose rents had not been altered during the term of the last settlement rents should be proposed to them which would be somewhat lower than the rents paid by the *Pahi* raiyats.

53. RAB, 1895-96, Pr. 127.

The rents as proposed if accepted by the raiyats should be recorded with their consent as the fair rents. If the rents proposed were not accepted then fair rents should be settled in accordance with the provisions of Chapter 10 of the Tenancy Act following the Civil Procedure Code and Tenancy Act rules. The enhancement would be mainly based on the rise of prices that had taken place.

(iii) In case of *Baziaftidars* and other privileged tenants rents should be proposed in a similar manner. But it would be somewhat lower than those fixed for non-privileged tenants and should, if accepted, be recorded as fair rents. If not accepted, rents were to be settled strictly in accordance with the procedure laid down in Chapter 10 of the Tenancy Act and the Government rules made under it.[54]

Under the above consideration the excess lands in possessions of the tenure holders were ordered to have been assessed to rent and settled with them as *raiyati* holdings. An acceptable rent settlement was made and recorded for all the tenants including those having holdings at privileged rents for the term of the settlement due to expire in 1897. The existing rate of the rent of the *Pahi* raiyats remained unchanged and the rate of the rent of *Thani* raiyats was not ordinarily enhanced more than half the difference between the *Thani* rate and the village rate which was calculated on the basis of *Pahi* raiyats.

In the case of other raiyats like *Tankidars, Baziaftidars, Chandinadars* and *Jagirdars* rent settlement was also made accordingly.

The rents of *Tankidars* or holders of small area, permanently assessed at a quit rent were not disturbed but excess areas in their possessions after 1838 were assessed in the like manner of the revenue and rent free holders.

54. Maddox Report, Vol. II, Appendix No. 11, Government of Bengal to Government of India, No. 238TR, May 12, 1897.

Nisi Baziaftidars and *Kamil Baziaftidars* who were holding resumed rent free lands were liberally assessed much below the rate of *Thani* and *Pahi* raiyats as they were found in hardship caused by the sudden enhancement of rents. The *Jamabandi Khariddars* or purchaser or recipients of rights as a proprietor of lands from the Zamindars were treated as tenure holder and thus were assessed at an enhanced rate. The rents were settled for them by deducting from the gross assets of each tenure a percentage equal to the percentage granted to them at the last settlement.[55]

The *Chandina* holders who were paying rent for their homestead at the full rate during the last settlement either in towns or villages were not required to pay rents at an enhanced rate. The *Chandina* tenancy constituted of inferior class such as Gaurs, Sarakitanti, Golatanti, Bengalitanti, Patra, Rangani, Bauritanti, Kolhu, Tamuli, Tulavina, Gurias, Keutas, Khatians, Gokhas, Kartias, Nulias, Golas, Mastanas, Sundhis, Chamars, Mochis, Baiso Bania, Sonari, Thatari,. Kansari, Kachera, Thoria, Chitrakar, Kumutis and Telengas.[56] However, excess areas in possession of *Chandina* holders were assessed to rents. As a result of which a nominal enhancement could be added to the revenue. The status of the *Chandina* holders has been recognised and defined and they were protected from eviction except in execution of a decree for arrears of rent.[57] The *Jagirs* of the village servants were considered carefully and regranted to them in this settlement. But the Jagirs to *Chaukidars, Chandinadars, Patwaris* and *Khandayiats* were resumed and rent was fixed. The holders of confirmed revenue free lands who possessed the permanent rights to hold their lands free of land revenue or *Lakhraj Bahaldars* were not at all disturbed in this settlement and were allowed to enjoy revenue free lands. But excess lands in their possessions after 1837 settlement were taken into consideration for revenue payment.

55. BRP, July, 1900, P.C. Leyon to Board of Revenue, No. 1549S, July 24, 1900.
56. Settlement of Khurda, 1897-98, p. 57.
57. Malley, S.S.O., *Bihar and Orissa Gazetteer, Cuttack*, p. 196.

Thus the rent assessed in this settlement became Rs. 38,67,600 against the previous assessment of Rs. 21,38,200 which was raised to Rs. 34,09,900 by the Zamindars in the interim period giving an increase of 13 per cent over the existing assets of Rs. 34,09,900. The increase was caused due to excess rents obtained from the tenants known as *Nisi Baziaftidars.*[58] The new assessment of Rs. 38,67,600 was made from 3 districts (Cuttack—Rs. 20,72,900; Puri excluding Khurda—Rs. 6,43,300 and Balasore—Rs. 11,51,400) in 1897.

As regards to the fixation of percentage of revenue on the assessed amount or assets became the question of controversy. Sir Alexander Mackenzie consulted the Collectors of 3 districts, Macpherson, the Director of Land Records and Agriculture and S.L. Maddox, the settlement officer in a conference at Lalbag, Cuttack on January 9, 1897 on the question of fixation of percentage of Government revenue. Three considerations were taken into account in the meeting. Thirty-five per cent was allowed to the Zamindars in the last settlement. The normal 50 per cent of assets as the revenue was applicable all over India, duly approved by the Government of India. In other exceptional cases the Government had approved the percentage between 50 to 65. The decision was arrived at 55 per cent to be taken as revenue from the assets.[59]

The above proposal was carefully considered by the Government of India and the basis of assessment was suggested in the following manner to the Secretary of State for India for his approval.

In the place of 60 to 70 per cent of revenue of the last settlement, the Government share of assessment should be fixed at from 55 to 60 per cent as land revenue. But the cost of the land record establishment should be met by a separate cess as in other provinces. In view of some special circumstances the Government of India would ordinarily be contented with from

58. BRP, July, 1900, P.C. Leyon to Board of Revenue, No. 1549S, July 24, 1900.

59. Maddox Report, Vol. II, Appendix No. 10.

50 to 55 per cent. Whenever it would be proposed to take below 50 per cent or above 55 per cent, the sanction of the Board of Revenue should be obtained. Within these limits the settlement officer would use his discretion with reference to the circumstances of each case.[60]

George Fransis Hamilton, the Secretary of State approved the above suggestions in his correspondence to the Government in Council saying "the settlement you consider eminently moderate, it is in fact identical with the proposals of the Bengal Government and I am prepared to agree."[61]

Accordingly the percentage of revenue was fixed at 53 in Cuttack, 59 in Balasore and 58 in Puri or 54 per cent for three districts[62] as shown in Appendix 'A'.

As a result of this settlement, the Zamindars received less amount as their incomes, when percentage of revenue was raised on the assets. The Zamindars were allowed to retain their shares amounting Rs. 17,62,527 against their income of Rs. 20,25,710.[63]

4. Duration of the Settlement

Controversy took place on the term of the settlement. Sir Anthony Mac Donnel, the officiating Lt. Governor of Bengal was of opinion that unless thorough, proper investigation on the material development of the lands to which part the settlement would be applicable and the possibility of future development by roads and railways would be made available, it would not be advisable to determine the term of the settlement. He again reiterated that if Orissa would be connected

60. Maddox Report, Vol. II, Appendix No. 12, Government of India to Government of Bengal, No. 2397-192-Z, October 13, 1897.
61. BRP, February, 1898, Secretary of State for India to Governor General in Council, No. 20 (Revenue), February 3, 1898.
62. RAB, 1901-1902, p. 121.
63. BRP, July, 1900, P.C. Leyon to Board of Revenue, No. 1549S, July 24, 1900.

with Calcutta and Bombay by rail links, a prosperous time would come into the economic life of the people of this country. The prices of the products would definitely rise and as a result of which the increase of rent rise might be thought of. Under the above conditions he recommended that the ensuing settlement should only be for a period of 15 years. In January 1897 a conference was held where this question was carefully discussed. It was suggested by Alexander Mackenzie that the period of the settlement should be fixed at 20 years. On this question the Government of India was of opinion that it would be most unwise to fix the demand of Orissa for a long term of 30 years when Orissa was provided with a new lease of life with a heavy expenditure from the public treasury. They approved the proposal for a term of 20 years.[64] This was referred to the Secretary of State.

The Secretary of State did not concur the suggestions laid down thereof. In his reply he argued that the province had already enjoyed 2 successive 30 years' settlement, the present settlement should expect to yield an increase of 56 to 68 per cent revenue. He found no justification in reducing the term of settlement. The term of the settlement was thus fixed for 30 years as per the direction of the Secretary of the State.[65]

5. Incidence

The incidence of the new revenue as per the settlement of 1897 increased moderately in comparison to the incidence of the old revenue of the settlement of 1837 as given below.[66]

District	*Settlement of 1837* *Rs. An. P.*	*Settlement of 1897* *Rs. An. P.*
Cuttack	1 — 2 — 5	1 — 5 — 5
Balasore	0 —12 — 3	0 —14 — 6
Puri	0 —15 — 6	1 — 0 — 2

64. Maddox Report, Vol. II, Appendix No. 10, Government of India to Government of Bengal, No. 2397-192-Z, October 13, 1897.
65. *Ibid.*
66. BRP, July, 1900, P.C. Leyon to Board of Revenue, No, 1549S, July 24, 1900.

6. Results

The settlement of 1897 yielded an assessment of Rs. 38,57,600 against the assessment or assets of Rs. 21,38,200 that gave the Government a net revenue of Rs. 21,05,073 against Rs. 13,84,190 in 1837. Out of the total assessment of Rs. 38,67,600 the balance of Rs. 17,62,527 deducting the revenue was left in the hands of the Zamindars of the temporarily settled estates as their income. As a result of this the income of the Zamindars was reduced by Rs. 2,63,183 or 13 per cent. The Zamindars who were enjoying the privilege of higher income when pushed into a lower income, were in terrible apprehension of further reduction of their income. The period of 60 years from 1837 to 1897 was very important from the point of the relation of the Zamindars and raiyats or tenants. This settlement was regarded as a proper step to enhance the rights of the tenants at the cost of the prestige of the Zamindars. Due to lack of proper education and training the raiyats did not have the courage to take any drastic step that would reduce the status of the Zamindars. Rather they continued to be the obedient servants of their old social masters as they were not well equipped either with wealth or unity among them to meet the challenges of the Zamindars. The relation between the Zamindars and the tenants thus became uncongenial as a consequence of this settlement, but it could not be tuned to such an unhealthy situation to dislocate the social behaviour among them as in other parts of Bengal. This settlement of 1897 had virtually welded the rights of the tenants with their lands. This can be said as a development on the extension of Bengal Tenancy Act of 1891. The exaction of illegal *abwabs* or cesses by the Zamindars on the tenants were discovered by the officers engaged in the operation of the settlement and reported to the authority.

On report the Commissioner of Orissa suggested for the total abolition of the cesses that the Zamindars were collecting from the tenants, to the Board of Revenue.

7. Illegal Abwabs

On investigation it was discovered that the Zamindars of

Balasore were in habit of exacting illegal *abwabs* or cesses from the raiyats. They enumerated some twelve cesses which were levied regularly and as many as twelve others which were demanded as irregular *abwabs*. The *abwabs* sometimes reached the limit of serious oppression.[67]

Tar Kharcha or a rate of payment for telegraph expenses, *Iskool Kharcha* or to cover the Zamindars' subscription to the Government School; *Tikkus* or Income tax; *Sunta Salami*; *Maharir Kharcha* or present to the Maharirs; *Babarta Rasam* or present to Zamindars' head agent; *Basanta Panchami* or present at the Festival; *Salami* or annual present to the Zamindars; *Khurrapani* or present to inferior Maharirs; *Digwar Kharcha* or present to Zamindars for the establishment of rent collection, were some regular important *abwabs* collected by the Zamindars.

Rassud Kharcha or a general levy for supplies to camp of Magistrates on visit; *Baruni Asan*, a sum raised when a Zamindar goes to bath at the festival of Jajpur; *Hathbara Mahaprasad* or to pay some tax when the Zamindars return back from Puri taking a handful of sacred food called Mahaprasad; *Rahadari Kharcha* or levy for costs of supplies to regiments marching through districts; *Gasta Kharcha*, cost of Zamindars' visit to any part of their estates; *Hathi Kharcha*, the cost of the maintenance of elephants; *Ghura Kharcha* or cost of Zamindars' horses; *Kanungo Kharcha* or cost of Kanungos; *Amin Kharcha* or expenses for sending amins for local investigation and *piada fandkar*, a fee levied to meet the salary of peons of the Zamindars were some important irregular cesses exacted by the Zamindars of Balasore in particular which were also accepted by the Zamindars of other districts as a source of additional income.

The district officers viewed that the record and the settlement of fair rents had largely enhanced the status of the tenants and as such they were no more left on the mercy of the Zamindars after the settlement of 1897.

67. BRP, No. 242-244, November, 1872; RAB, 1871-72, p. 30.

The 1897 settlement resumed the *Jagirs* of *Patwaris* and assessed at full rates. They were footed with the *Thani* raiyats and ceased to be liable to extend their service to the state village or Zamindars. The assessment of the *Jagirs* of *Patwaris* numbered 245 in 3 districts covering an area of 3,950 acres on a rent fixation of Rs. 5,860. As regards the *Kanungos* the settlement did not abolish their posts and they continued to work on local enquiries of civil nature and to help in the collection of Government dues and in other miscellaneous revenue works.[68]

Patwaris belonged to a class of public servants since the Hindu period.[69] This class existed at the time of British conquest. The *Patwaris* remained as a subordinate to the *Kanungos*. The *Patwaris* were required to keep the detail account of the *Mauza* to which he was attached and to make the raiyats informed about the payment of rent and to file the annual statement of demands, collections, and arrear of rent in the office of the *Kanungos* for onward transmission to the collector. In accordance with the provisions of Act X of 1859 the practice of having *Patwaris* engaged in the Government work was discontinued and hence the *Patwaris* remained as the servants of the Zamindars. The *Patwari* system was again revived in 1875[70] under Sir George Campbell. The Collectors were asked to use the services of *Patwaris* and to place them under the Zamindars. In 1885 the question of imposing a cess for the cost of *Patwaris* was opposed by Baboo Baikunthanath De on the ground of an arbitrary addition of extra burden on the people.[71] The bill after this was abandoned in 1892 as the Secretary of State did not approve it. The *Patwaris* were given training in the Survey Schools at Cuttack and Puri with a view to be absorbed in the settlement work but the idea of using them in Government works was dropped.

68. Maddox Report, Vol. I, p. 230.
69. GAROD, 1878-79, p. 37.
70. RAB, 1882-83, p. 67.
71. BLCP, February 14, 1885.

Kanungos remained as agents of the Imperial Government in the estates of the Zamindars. The *Kanungos* became the supervising officers. Due to unscientific work in 1872 a set of rules of conduct for *Kanungos* were framed. Consequent upon this the *Kanungos* formed the only agency in supplying information to the collectors pertaining to revenue matters after making due enquiries. They were described as serviceable and efficient and were accepted as useful a class of public servants.[72] In view of this work the posts of *Kanungos* were not abolished in the settlement of 1897.[73]

8. Defects of the Settlement

The settlement of 1897 was marked by a number of defects. The revenue demand was increased to the extent of 52 per cent. The incidence was fixed at Re. 1-0-9 pie per acre in the *Thani* and *Pahi* raiyats, the fixed incidence for other classes of raiyats became Rs. 2-2-6 pie.[74] During the last 60 years the number of sale of estates increased due to the defective procedure of the Sale Law. The settlement did not take much initiative in any manner as a result of which the old sale law was allowed to continue. But due to the new rates of the settlement the sale of estates slightly decreased.

The permanently settled estates of Orissa differed from the temporarily settled estates in many respects besides that of fixity of revenue.[75] In fact the question was raised whether a special legislation would be necessary for temporarily settled estates in which the relative incidence of land revenue was naturally higher than permanently settled estates in Bengal. Most of the permanently settled estates of Orissa had not been cadastrally surveyed and no record of rights had been prepared on them whereas in the temporarily settled estates there had

72. GAROD, 1882-83, p. 41.
73. Maddox Report, Vol. I, p. 230.
74. BRP, July, 1900, P.C. Leyon to Secretary, Board of Revenue. No. 1549S, July 24, 1900.
75. Malley, S.S.O., *Bihar and Orissa Gazetteer, Cuttack*, p. 185.

been two such surveys by the end of this settlement. Therefore though the customary rights of the tenants in the temporarily settled estates were well known this was not the case in the permanently settled estates. Certain provisions were made to apply only in the temporarily settled estates and in this respect the permanently settled estates were still regulated by the custom. The discrepancy created by the settlement thus easily differentiated the status of the tenants in temporarily settled estates and permanently settled estates. The Zamindars of course considered the provisions applicable for temporarily settled estates advantageous for them and initiated the application of these provisions to their economic benefit. The right to remission was denied and the regular collection of Government dues was always enforced with rigidity.

D. SETTLEMENTS IN THE KHASMAHAL ESTATES

Besides the temporarily settled Zamindari estates in Orissa there existed some estates directly managed by the Government called *Khasmahals* or Government estates. The number of such estates varied from time to time. The estates were reserved under the management of Tahasildars. These *Khasmahals* were subject to periodical assessment like temporarily settled estates. In small *Khasmahal* estates collections were made by *Pargana Kanungos* on a commission basis at the rate of 5 per cent. The number of acquisition of these estates varied from place to place according to circumstances present at the time of acquisition. The Government estate of Khurda, the biggest estate of the province had been forfeited for State offence. The other estates mostly were acquired by *Khas* management due to the denial of revenue payment by the proprietors. Noanund became the interesting example of this type. It belonged to one of those 266 estates which were sold only in 1807. The estate was sold only for Rs. 5,013 against the Sadar *Jama* of Rs. 9,456 and was again sold for arrears in 1818 and purchased by the Government for one rupee.[76] The number of Khasmahal estate thus could not remain in fixity.

76. Final Report on the Settlement of Balasore, 1899.

1. Khurda

The biggest Government estate was Khurda having an area of 1,000 sq. miles of the area of 6,000 sq. miles of the province under temporary settlement. Killa Khurda was annexed and held *Khas* by British Government in 1805 due to the rebellion of the Raja in the year 1803. A summary settlement was made by Major Fletcher in October, 1805[77] but was found to be impracticable. He apparently had taken the gross value of the crop of Rs. 5,75,000 as the amount of revenue demandable by the estate.[78] His valuation moreover of the crop appeared to have been over-estimated. Golam Kadur, the Tahasildar in 1806 made a settlement. This appears to have been more detailed one. Some lands were set aside for religious endowments and *jagirs* at low quit rent or *Tanki* rents. The general average came to merely 8 annas per *man* or Re. 1 per acre. The revenue obtained was Rs. 1,14,320. A part of this estate was made over to Rani Mukuta Dei of Sambalpur by an Government order but the fixed revenue of Rs. 12,000 could not be realised as fixed by Golam Kadur for this new Mahal known as Panchgarah. She finally relinquished. The experiments continued upto 1817 when the rebellion of Bakshi Jagabandhu Mahapatra put an end to the ruined estate and parts of Khurda were almost depopulated. All revenue work came to a standstill. In 1818 W. Forrester was appointed as a Deputy Collector for Khurda to be in independent charge of Khurda revenue. His settlement continued to be in operation upto 1821. In 1820 Mr. Wilkinson relieved Mr. Forrester and inaugurated a system of settlement approaching that of *raiyatwari*. However he retained the rates of his predecessor and assessed a new rate for new cultivation and directed the *Sarbarakars* to give *pattas* to the raiyats for their lands they held as a proof of record of right.[79] Wilkinson reported in 1823 the completion of 5 years' settlement of Khurda which should have expired in 1828 but there was no increase of

77. Settlement of Khurda, p. 34.
78. *Ibid*, p. 1.
79. *Ibid.*, p. 35.

demand upto 1836. The demand was Rs. 1,04,025 or an increase of Rs. 32,142.

Measurements were commenced in December, 1854 and were completed in February 1856 but the *nayabadi* settlement (new cultivation) was not reported for confirmation till July 7, 1857.[80] Mr. Schaleh, the senior member of the Board recommended the cadastral settlement in 1871 that was confirmed in 1875. It took five years time to complete the work and rates were fixed and calculated at "nominal fourth" of the value of the out-turn. The term "nominal fourth" was accepted as a basis of collection.[81]

The mufasil *Jama* with cesses settled and confirmed by Government amounted to Rs. 3,63,931 out of which half was collected in 1880-81 and the whole was collected in 1882-83. In 1883 on petition filed by some professional agitators and a few tenants Government reduced the rates of the cultivated land by 1/5 not because the rate was high, nor the lands were unable to bear the rent but because the special committee on Bengal Tenancy Bill had come to the conclusion that 1/5 of the produce of the land should be collected by a proprietor from a tenant.

The estate was divided into 12 parganas known as *Zillas*. The table on page 35 will give a clear picture about the *Zillas* with the area they covered making an increase of 14,424 acres in the settlement of 1897 in comparison with the settlement of 1837.[82]

With the exception of *Zilla* Rameswar and Banpur the reason for the difference was merely the increase of areas, the outer boundaries remaining the same. The increase of 11,311 acres in *Zilla* Rameswar was chiefly due to the omission of a tract of Chilka and mud flats laying between *Zilla* Rameswar

80. *Ibid*, pp. 36-37.
81. BRP, July, 1880, Pr. 55, Government Resolution No. 2361-1348LR, July 23, 1880.
82. Settlement of Khurda, Pr. 3, p. 1.

Name of the Zilla	*Area as recorded in the last Settlement*	*Area as ascertained in the present Settlement*	*Difference*
Dandimal	1,29,822	1,29,782	—40
Tapanga	32,704	32,704	
Khurda	50,351	50,353	+2
Haladia	4,986	4,986	
Kuspalla	43,791	43,790	—1
Manikgora	22,535	22,534	—1
Panchgarah	26,648	26,645	—3
Rameswar	1,04,452	1,15,763	+11,311
Kuhuri	44,683	44,779	+96
Banpur (including Mala)	1,48,411	1,51,409	+2,998
Balabhadrapur	24,175	24,236	+61
Mughalbandi	1,172	1,173	+1
Total	6,33,730	6,48,154	+14,424 or 23 sq. miles

and *Pargana* Serai of the district of Puri at the last settlement.[83] This tract under the name of village Subhadrapur with an area of 11,271 acres was added to the estate in 1890. Some raiyats made engagements for a mud flat tract covering an area of 315 acres in the hope of reclaiming them for paddy cultivation in the same year 1890. A mufasil *Jama* of Rs. 252 with an addition of Rs. 13 as cesses was added. The raiyats however proved unsuccessful in earning some crops out of this tract as the salty water of Chilka had been inundating the tract every year and to that effect annual remission of the rent had been granted. The reason for the increase of an area of 2,998 acres in Banpur was due to the fact that the areas of Khandahana hill of 2,522 acres was omitted in the last settlement.

83. Settlement of Khurda, Pr. 4, p. 1.

The main portion of the estate comprising *Zillas* was bounded on the South East by Chilka *Pargana*. Daya and Kooakhai rivers formed a part of the boundary line. The Northern boundary of the estate formed the boundary of Puri with *Killas* Patia and Sarangarah. The South Western boundary of the estate was the boundary between Bengal and *Zilla* Ganjam of Madras presidency. Khurda comprised about 2/5 of the area of the district of Puri, the main portion of the estate formed the Sub-Division of Khurda.

According to the settlement of 1897 the Khurda *Killa* or estate was composed of *Khasmahal* villages, *Khandayiati* villages, Revenue free villages including *Ekhrajats* and *Tankibahal* villages.

Type of villages	*No. of villages*	*Area*
Khasmahal villages	1,377	5,65,356 acres
Khandayiati villages	10	9,710 acres
Revenue free villages including Ekhrajat	164	72,659 acres
Tankibahal villages	1	429 acres
Total	1,552	6,48,154 acres

The *Lakhraj Bahaldars* including *Brahmottar* and *Debottar* or *Pirottar* were preserved directly under the control of the Collector, Puri. Their work were always subject to be assessed by the Collector. If they were found negligent in their duties of worship, they were liable for dismissal by the Collector. The Board of Revenue retained the power under the Act XIX of 1810 to arange for the management of all other endowments in Khurda including the lands of Bhagabati Thakurani of *Zilla* Banapur and lands of Lingaraj Mahadev in Bhubaneswar.

However due to the ineffective management of the Committees established under Act XX of 1863, the Committees were dismissed by the order of the Judge at the commencement of the present settlement of 1897.

Khandayiat tenures were held in good conduct. *Khandayiats* or Commander-in-Chiefs like *Dalabeheras* and *Dalais* of the old Raja families were allowed to hold free lands for their duty to defend the country. It was decided in the present settlement as per the order of the Commissioner to declare their holdings null and void for their misconduct if so noticed.[84] Further they were required to pay road cess at the rate of 6 pies in the rupee not on the quit rent but on a valuation of the collection made by the *Khandayiats* from their tenants. This cess amounted to Rs. 182 per annum.[85]

Bahal Tankidars were maintained undisturbed in the settlement of 1897. They paid an annual rent of Rs. 976.[86] *Bahal Tankidars* were also required to pay road cess at the rate of 6 pies per rupee, banker in the same rate of road cess and *Chaukidar* cess at the rate of 10 pies per rupee.

Rafa Tankidars who agreed at the decennial settlement to periodical enhancement in proportion to the enhancement of rents applicable to the ordinary raiyats were retained in the new settlement.[87]

Ordinary tenure holders obtained a new status in the settlement of 1897 in accordance with the provision of Bengal Tenancy Act. The reclamation areas in Banpur Malas were assessed at the rate of annas 14-10 pies per acre for *Sarad*, annas 9-11 pies per acre for *bazefasal* and annas 8-4 pies per acre for orchards against the old rate of 8 annas per acre for all categories of lands. The larger tenure granted in 1295 to

84. BdRP, August, 1879, Smith, Commissioner to Board of Revenue, No. 1885, August, 1879.
85. Settlement of Khurda, Pr. 207, p. 53.
86. *Ibid*, Pr. 208, p. 53.
87. *Ibid*.

Raghunath Rajguru, Syamsundar Rajguru Mohapatra and Balavadra Dewan Pattanaik consisted of 2.094 acres of lands in the forest lands in the villages of Banpur Malas were measured and rents were settled in the settlement of 1897. As per the terms of the settlement of 1897 the lease holders were made *Sarbarakars* and allowed to an allowance of not less than 25 per cent of the *mufasil Jama*.

All tenants with occupancy rights were recorded as settled raiyats. *Chandinadars* who had acquired arable lands since the last settlement, *Hinayat Jagirdars* whose lands were resumed in 1897 settlement and occupiers of Government lands were assessed for a rent of Rs. 3,23,222 in the settlement of 1897 against a rent of Rs. 2,52,548 in the last settlement.[88] The holders of these *jagirs* were paying road cess at the rate of 6 pies in the rupee, banker 6 pies in the rupee and *Chaukidari* cess at the rate of 10 pies in the rupee as decided in the settlement of 1897.

Nayabadi tenants or non-occupancy tenants who had acquired lands during last few years had been included in the settlement provisions. An amount of Rs. 5,098 at an incidence of Re. 0-9-1 pies were recorded in this settlement. They were also subject to the payment of road cess of 6 pies in a rupee, banker 6 pies in a rupee and *Chaukidari* cess at the rate of 10 pies in a rupees.

Rent free homesteads of *Dalai*, *Chaukidars*, *Tandakars* and other Government servants were re-assessed in this settlement with an increase of rent of Rs. 264.

Biranarasinghpur was held by the Brahmins under the Puri Rajas on a quit rent of Rs. 1,520-8-6 pies of which a sum of Rs. 1,253-5-4 pies was hypothecated for the religious duties in the temple of Lord Jagannath and Rs. 266-10-8 pies for the services of Kanaka Durga, the family Goddess of Puri Raja, in this settlement.[89]

88. Settlement of Khurda, p. 57.

89. *Ibid*, p.54.

The Government was not prepared to vest the propriety rights of the *Sarbarakars* as a regular practice to continue in this settlement of 1897.[90]

The revenue of the Khurda Government estate varied from time to time. In the settlement of 1856 the demand was Rs. 1,76,004 out of which a portion yielding a rent of Rs. 16,827 in 1858 and some villages with a revenue of Rs. 6,889 were made over to the superintendent of Puri temple. The revenue demand was again increased in 1880 to Rs. 3,63,931. On petition filed by the tenants the demand was reduced to Rs. 2,44,036 in 1883. The demand could not maintain its rigidity till 1897 but there had been the addition of revenue demand due to new cultivation of lands and before the settlement of 1897 it amounted to Rs. 2,50,901. At the settlement of 1897 the demand was raised to Rs. 3,05,842[91] making the burden of revenue demand on the tenants too heavy. Parity could not be maintained on the fixation of rents between the rich and poor lands that had pressed the tenants into hardship. The principles of fixing the revenue at the rate of 1/5 of the produce was not strictly followed in the settlement of 1897. The tenants of Khurda Government estate were certainly better off in comparison with the tenants of Zamindari estate. In spite of heavy assessment the average incidence per acre in Khurda was Rs. 1-10-6 pies whereas the settled *Pahi* rents in other parts of Puri district fell to Rs. 1-15 annas. The arrangements provided for the Khurda Government estate became the best possible system, the system that combined the advantages of *Zamindari* and *raiyatwari* settlements.

Besides the demand of revenue on land tenures Khurda Government estate yielded revenue from other different sources like Fishery or *Mechhadia* of Tua and Satpara and orchard

90. BRP, November, 1868, H.L. Dampier to Secretary, Government of India (Home), No. 3354, October 22, 1868.

91. BRP, November, 1899, P.C. Leyon to Board of Revenue, No.1889S, November 14, 1899.

growing Poonang and Coconut and Mangoes.[92] Thus the increase of gross revenue at the settlement of 1897 amounted to Rs. 75,230 or 21.81 per cent over the gross revenue of the last settlement.

Similar terms of settlement were prescribed for other small Government estates. The most important *khas* estates were Noanand and Birso in Balasore, Bazarhai, Buldeo and Banki in the district of Cuttack.

2. Banki

Banki was a tributary state—the property of the Raja of Banki until 1839. Raja was accused of a murder and was sentenced to imprisonment for life. Consequent upon this he was dethroned and the tributary state of Banki was confiscated by the Government. Banki remained under the management of the Superintendent of Tributary Mahals from 1839 to 1882 and had been treated as a Government estate since then. It was in charge of a Deputy Collector vested with Second Class magisterial powers and with those of Deputy Collectors for the trial of rent suits.[93] The settlement was extended to this *Khas* estate following the year 1882 when it was annexed to Cuttack district.[94] The principles for the settlement of Khurda was made applicable for this *Khas* estate. The increase of rents amounting Rs. 1,370 over the former settlement was made after 1890.[95]

3. Angul

As regards the Government estate of Angul assessment was made in all 623 villages in the settlement of 1897. According to the settlement the rent at full rate was fixed that

92. Settlement of Khurda, Pr. 380, p. 104.
93. Malley, S.S.O., *Bihar and Orissa Gazetteer, Cuttack*, p. 222.
94. BRP, Nos. 3-5, August, 1882.
95. GAROD, 1889-90, p. 16.

amounted to Rs. 1,11,336 against the previous assessment of Rs. 39,199.[96]

4. Other Khas Estates

The total number of *Khas* estates under the direct management of the Government at the close of the year 1899-1900 was 28 against 35 in the year 1895-96. The decrease of 7 estates was caused due to the sale under the order of the Board of Revenue.[97] The gross demand on these estates in the year 1899-1900 remained at Rs. 7,54,495 against the demand of Rs. 4,40,840 in 1895-1896 an increase of Rs. 3,13,655 due to the revision of settlement and the transfer of estate Kotdesh in Puri district into the management of the Government owing to the recusancy of its proprietor.[98] The number of *Khas* estates was 29 in 1881-82 against 26 in 1880-81.[99] Hence the demand and collection of revenue from Government estates remained always fluctuating due to the increase and decrease of *Khas* estates. Sale of estates became a feature in the case of the Government that had been parcelling out the estates and the tenants as well into the hands of the Zamindars bringing them into the category of temporarily settled estates.

E. WARDS ESTATE

Permanently settled estates sometimes were placed under the control of the Government. In accordance with the Court of Wards Law, the Court of Wards had been assuming charge of the property of proprietors paying land revenue. When female successors were declared incompetent to manage their own property or successors declared as minors or persons adjudged by a competent Civil Court to be of unsound mind and incapable of managing their affairs or persons adjudged by a competent Civil Court to be otherwise rendered incapable by

96. *Ibid.*
97. GAROD, 1899-1900, Pr. 85, p. 21.
98. *Ibid.*
99. *Ibid*, 1881-82, Pr. 131, p. 31.

physical defects or infirmities of managing their own property or persons who having ceased to be subject to the jurisdiction of the Court themselves preferred to remain under protection or persons to whom the local Government after due enquiry declared them disqualified for public interest were liable for management under Court of Wards so long as changes for the interest of the estates and the tenants as well would occur by the successors of the estate.[100]

Kanika, Madhupur and Kujanga were the wards estates in Cuttack in the year 1899-1900. Kujanga belonged to the Burdwan Raja and was under the general management of Raja Banabehari Kapur. There remained a local Sub-Manager over whom the Collector was exercising supervision. In Balasore there was no wards estate in the year but during the quinquennial period therer emained the estate Jamkunda which was releasedon May 7,1897 when the minor Raja attained majority. Roranga and Malighti were the two wards estate in the district of Puri. The proprietor of Malighati being a minor had been remaining in Midnapore where the major property was situated.[101]

The Collector had been in charge of the persons of the minors of Kanika, Madhupur, Rorang and Jamkunda during the quinquennial period. The ward of the Rorang estate attained majority. On an appeal made by the Raja, Government had agreed to remain in charge of his estate for a period of 3 years more. The former minor of Kanika died on July 29, 1896 at the age of 14 years 8 months. Consequent upon this the next minor was allowed to receive training in the affairs of the management of his estate.[102]

Patia was an attached estate since May 15, 1878. It was kept under the control of the Civil Court for debt. The Jagir

100. BRP, March 7, 1891.
101. GAROD, 1899-1900, p. 25.
102. GAROD, Pr, 100, p, 26.

Mahals in Puri also were attached to the group of wards estate under the order of the Civil Court.[103]

F. PERMANENTLY SETTLED ESTATES

Besides the temporarily settled estates the permanently settled areas of the East India Company constituted mainly of the estates having importance. They were being dealt with lenient treatment by the Government. When the English conquered the province they found a few land owners of a superior class. They were the descendants of the noble families or of high officials to whom large estates had been assigned for their maintenance. They were liable for the payment of a quit rent.[104] Such were the Rajas of Kanika and Kujanga who belonged to the royal family of Mayurbhanj (Moharbhanj). They established their *Killas* in about 13th century A.D. under the Gajapati dynasty. The Raja of Patia and Aul were confirmed in their estates by Todarmall. There existed a number of estates along the sea-coast denominated as *Garahs* or *Killas*, which were held by Khandayiats. They paid light peskash or quit rent like other powerful Rajas of Aul, Kanika and Kujanga. They had been keeping band of *Paikas* to defend their *Garhas* and to render military service when called upon to do so. A few of them had succeeded in maintaining the privilege of paying only a quit rent whereas most of them had been reduced to the position of ordinary Zamindars in the course of events. These petty Chiefs made vigorous attempts to defend the country at the time of British conquest. On the approach of British force on the vicinity of the province they had liquidated their *Paikas* and surrendered before the British force. From then Government had tried to secure their loyalty and pardoned them. Government through Regulation 12 of 1805 had confirmed them in their *Killas* with propriety rights with the settlement of tribute. The Sanands were granted to the Khandayiat Zamindars of Darpana, Sukinda and Madhupur and the Government by doing so, had secured the revenue

103. *Ibid*, Pr. 99, p. 25.

104. Malley, S.S.O., *Bihar and Orissa Gazetteer, Cuttack*, p. 184.

from them. The Chiefs of Darpana, Sukinda and Madhupur were the adventurers from the North-West and though equally independent were of inferior rank to the Chiefs of the sea coast. They received Sanands and executed 'Qubuliyats' for the payment of revenue while the Rajas of Aul, Kanika and Kujanga etc. executed agreements.[105]

Most of the permanently settled estates of Orissa had not been cadastrally surveyed and no record of rights had been prepared. Though the main provisions of the regulation had been applied to all classes of estates, certain provisions were made to apply only in the temporarily settled estates. Hence the permanently settled estates were regulated by customs.[106] The proprietors of the permanently settled estates however had not been slow in taking advantage of the provisions meant for the temporarily settled estates.

In the case of big estate like Kanika, Kujanga and Aul the law of primogeniture was strictly adhered to. In view of giving practical training in the affairs of estate administration land tenures were provided to the younger members of the family. Accordingly villages were assigned to such type of members of the family of the Chiefs and the other near relatives known as *Baradaranjagir*, *Khorakposak nijkar* etc.

The list of such type of permanently settled estates with the area is as follows :

Cuttack District	*Area*
Kanika	440 sq. miles
Aul	135 sq. miles
Kujanga	370 sq. miles
Patia	53 sq. miles
Madhupur	79 sq. miles
Harispur	60 sq. miles
Sukinda	37 sq. miles

105. Malley, S.S.O., *Bihar and Orissa Gazetteer, Cuttack*, p. 184.
106. *Ibid*, p. 185.

Darpana	100 sq. miles
Bisnupur	17 sq. miles
Dampara	83 sq. miles
Kalkala	19 sq. miles
Chhedra	83 sq. miles

Puri District	*Area*
Marichpur	53.29 sq. miles
Parikud	67.52 sq. miles
Jagirmahals	72.58 sq. miles

In Balasore there were 148 such estates which covered an negligible area of 23.22 sq. miles only.[107] The major portion of these big estates remained unsuitable for cultivation. The largest estate Kanika in the revenue roll was deltaic.

1. Kanika

Kanika is situated along the sea coast on both sides of the estuary of Dhamara extending about 20 miles inland. It was bounded with Akhura and Bhera of Balasore district in the North, by the Bay of Bengal and *Killa* Kujanga in the South and on the West, by Parganas of Utikan and Damarpur of *Killa* Aul in the East. Its lower parts close to sea coast consisted of low marshy and dense jungles which became thinner as they receded from the sea. Higher up were arable plains, the lower portion was subject to salt water and flood during cyclone. A very small amount of lands were exempted either from flood or cyclone.

From a brochure published by the guardian of the late Raja in 1884, it appears that sometimes in 1200 A D. a brother of the Chief of Mayurbhanj, Bhujabala Bhanja acquired by conquest this tract known as Kanika, when he found no suitable place in his paternal *Killa* due to the fraternal quarrel.

107. Maddox Report, pp. 420-421, Note by Finance Director, Department of Land Records and Agriculture, Bengal.

The place at that time was inhabited by aboriginal tribes and ruled by a low caste Raja. Bhujabala having subdued this Raja established a reign of his own in the name of Bhanja Raj of this *Killa*. The status of this new dynasty was recognised by the Gajapati kings of Orissa. The last Chief of Kanika Raja Balabhadra Bhanja was ruling the *Killa* Kanika when the East India Company conquered the province in 1803. On December 7, 1803 the Sanand was executed (*ekrarnama*) by the Raja of Kanika with the financial engagement. The Raja agreed to pay Peskash of Rs. 20,407-13-4 pies or 84.840 Kahan (28,840 Kahan in Chaita, 28,000 Kahan in Jaista and 28,000 Kahan in Asara) to the Company besides other obligations by the Raja.[108]

The status of the Raja of Kanika was more or less that of a semi-independent ruler of small principality. Following the date of the conquest the status of the Chief gradually declined. In the Regulation 12 of 1805 the Raja of Kanika was described as a Zamindar and his Peskash or tribute was converted into land revenue. Against the loss of sovereign right the Raja was assured of all kinds of protection from external danger to which it used to have been humiliated prior to 1803.

The history of the estate from 1803 to 1845 has been fully described in the Persian *ruidad* of the settlement of this estate which was made under the supervision of the Collector Mr. Glimore. On report of some malpractice the Government took immediate note of it and the *Killa* was placed under *Khas* Tahasil.[109] The Raja was taken as a prisoner for some time and on the appeal made by the Raja the Government took a favourable decision on the matter and the Raja was reinstated on July 17, 1807. The *ekrarnama* and *kistbandi* were duly executed for the payment of Peskash of his *Killa*.

After the death of Raja Balabhadra Bhanja his 2 sons Jagannath and Harihar pressed their demands for the right.

108. Settlement of Kanika, 1889-94, pp. 45-46.
109. *Ibid.*

The suit was referred to the Provincial Court of Appeal. In the meanwhile they came to an agreement to divide the estate among them which were to be entered in the records of the Collectorate, Cuttack. Jagannath Bhanja died leaving no heir to succeed his share and consequent upon this Harihar Bhanja having signed the *ekrarnama* and *kistbandi* was declared the sole proprietor of the estate. Harihar Bhanja died in 1830. His son Binayak Bhanja was a minor at that time. Under this situation his mother Satyabhama Pattamahadei was accepted as a guardian of her minor son as per the approval order of the Commissioner in his letter of October 25, 1830. On the attainment of majority a possession *parwana* was granted to the Raja Binayak Bhanja when he was only 18 years old. He was said to have been an oppressive Raja unlike his parents. Hence the estate could not pay the required *Peskash* as the servants and the tenants would not co-operate with the Raja in the rent collection. The Raja appealed the Government to take a note of his servants and to set them right. In 1843 the estate was brought under the regular management of the Government officials. In 1845 Binayak Bhanja died leaving 2 minor sons Tribikram Bhanja and Padmanav Bhanja on whose behalf the charge of the estate was retained by the Government and subsequently it was brought under the Court of Wards on April 13, 1846 and remained till 1849.[110] During this 6 years time under the Government managament a settlement was affected for 4 years (1845-1849). The total rental obtained in the settlement amounted to Rs. 82,548-12-6 pies.[111] Having attained majority Tribikram Bhanja assumed the charge of the estate with the sanction of the Board of Revenue in their Memo No. 53, May 4, 1849. The Raja hardly had established himself over the estate when his brother Padmanav Bhanja initiated a suit claiming his right over the estate. However in 1857 after the death of Tribikram Bhanja, Padmanav Bhanja succeeded him. The estate faced a great economic setback that compelled the Raja for an appeal before the Government for the manage-

110. Settlement of Kanika, 1889-94, p. 49,
111. *Ibid.*

ment of the estate which was in debt of arrears to the extent of Rs. 9,00,000 for a period of 10 years. The estate thus came under the direct management of the Government for the second time with the Government approval.[112]

The Collector was asked to arrange the second settlement and a few *amins* were sent out from Cuttack. Baboo Nabin Kishore Sarkar, S.D.O., Jajpur was required to take up the work of settlement in addition to his own work. Harish Chandra Ghose and Jagamohan Ray both Deputy Collectors completed the works within 3 years. In the meanwhile the Raja was declared insane by the district Civil Court and the charge of his estate was assumed by the Court of Wards in 1865.[113] A fresh arrangement was made for the completion of the settlement. The work was completed in 6 years from 1865-71 by Sapneswar Das which was disturbed during the period of Famine. The whole estate was measured with 22 *dasti padika* rod. The status of all class of tenants were determined and rents for all holdings were recorded in par with the rates fixed in the neighbouring estates. The total land revenue demand as per this settlement was fixed at Rs. 1,08,728-6-1 pie.[114] In 1871 a 2 years' settlement was made within *mustagirs* which was executed by Macpherson, the then Collector that remained valid upto 1874. This was followed by a 5 years' settlement completed by Beams under Board's order.[115] The new settlement started commencing from 1879-80 which was fixed for a period of 10 years by the Board.

The tenures of *Thani* raiyats, *Pahi* raiyats, *Chandina* raiyats, *Debottar* tenures, *Pirottar* tenures, *Khairat* tenures, *Datta Anugraha* tenures, *Nelak* tenures and Service tenures were recognised in the settlement of 1865-71 and their rights and status were determined too. Subsequently in the records of the settlement of 1882 the tenants in the categories of

112. BRP, April, 1862, Government of Bengal's approval No. 2524, April 4, 1862.
113. *Ibid.*
114. Settlement of Kanika, 1889-94, p. 50.
115. BdRP, March, 1874, Board's Letter No. 254, March 2, 1874.

Chandina, Thani, Pahi, Tanki and *Baziaftidar* had no rights to the lands leased to them than that of occupancy. They were allowed to hold their rents to the estate. No excess demand of rent at any enhanced rates would be exacted from them till the expiration of the settlement period.

A class, regarded as the superior servants of the estate which belonged to the same caste of the raj family was required by the Rajas to work during the time of social and religious ceremonies. They were locally identified as *Samantas* and were granted with service tenures known as *Rajkumar Jagir*. *Rajkumar Jagirs* were all resumed in the settlement of 1865-71. Twenty-four of such *Samanta* families existed in the estate by 1894.[116]

Dewan, Bebarta, Chaudhurys were working under the Rajas for revenue collection work. All such revenue officers were merely the servants at pleasure of the Raja.[117] The settlement did not pay any attention to these revenue officers.

Cultivable lands were classified into first class, second class and third class according to the fertility of the soil.[118]

The total rent was fixed in the settlement of 1893-94 at Rs. 1,36,063-14 annas against the rental of last settlement of 1881-82 of Rs. 1,12,632-11-6 pies from the raiyati lands.[119] Besides land revenue the collection of miscellaneous revenue was regularly made by the Raja. Such revenues were usually collected from fisheries, river, creak, forests, fruits, honey and wax, markets and ferries.[120] In spite of the rental increase the Rajas of Kanika were not able to remain clear from the debt caused by non-payment of revenue due to natural calamities passing over the estate with short intervals.

116. Settlement of Kanika, 1889-94, p. 54.

117. *Ibid*, p. 61.

118. *Ibid*, p. 61.

119. *Ibid*, p. 83.

120. *Ibid*, pp. 123-35.

2. Aul

Killa Aul consisted of 2 complete blocks covering 2 *Parganas*, Derabis and Ulihar Kotabsahi. They were about 6 miles apart from each other stretched wholly within the local limits of the Kendrapara Sub-Division of Cuttack district. *Pargana* Derabis is situated on the North-Eastern side of irrigable loop formed by Pattamundai canal and Gobari canal and Gobari extension canal and with an exception of one Mauza Basupur included in thana Pattamundai, the whole of it was located within the jurisdiction of thana Kendrapara. *Pargana* Utihar Kotabsahi lies on the North-Eastern part of the Cuttack district and was included in the triangular delta formed by Brahmani and Kharsua rivers. It stretched between thana Pattamundai and thana Aul. The total area of the estate was 134 sq. miles.[121]

Killa Aul was a permanently settled estate on the revenue role of the Cuttack district bearing *Tauzi* No. 23. The Raja of the *Killa* agreed to pay an annual revenue of Rs. 28,139-2-7 pies as confirmed by the Board of Revenue in accordance with the Resolution 12 of 1805. Previously this *Killa* was granted by Akbar to the descendants of the Hindu King Telenga Mukundadev. At the time of British conquest this *Killa* was held by Ramakrishna Deo. His son Prataprudra Deo was an useless successor. Following this the estate was preserved by the Court of Wards till 1847. On the attainment of majority Padmalav Deo, son of Prataprudra Deo took over the charge of the estate with a vast accumulated treasury. In 1868 the Raja was found to be wayward and the estate had accumulated heavy debt. As a result of this the estate remained under the attachment and administration of the Civil Court for 16 years from 1866 to 1883.[122] Again Jadunath Deo, the son of Padmalav Deo followed the footprint of his father whose highhandedness and rigorous oppression attracted the attention of the Government that led the Government to initiate a

121. Settlement of Aul, 1892-1901, p. 1.
122. *Ibid*,

settlement. In 1900 on the death of Jadunath Deo his son Pitamber Deo succeeded over the estate. The estate was never thrown into any controversy of partition and continued to be in possession of the oldest and respectable family of Orissa.

The estate was held by the actual cultivators of the soil under the direct control of the proprietor. There were very few intermediate tenure holders interposing between the proprietors and the raiyats. On attaining age each used to get a plot of land for his dwelling house. These grants either were rent free or assessed on quit rent. The rent free tenures were locally called *Bardaran Khorak Posak Niskar* and those of quit rents were called *Bardaran Khorak Posak Ghenan*. These tenures were heritable but not transferable and the proprietor had the right of resumption on the failure of a direct heir. There were a number of rent free tenure holders in the estate. They were generally granted for the religious and charitable purposes. These tenure holders were identified as *Sebait Jagir* who had their origin from the pre-British days. The validity of these grants had never been determined and recognised by the Government. The quit rent tenancies were known as *Ghenan* corresponding to the *Baziafti* tenure of the Mughal Bandi. This type of tenure holders used to designate the proprietor of the estate as *Maharaja*,[123] which was never conferred on the family by the Government in the settlement of 1900. *Chaukidari Jagir* was allowed to the servants. The lands of this category were resumed and assessed with the consent of the propietor under the provision of the Chaukidari Act. The *Jagirs* were retained and the rights of possession were confirmed in the settlement. There was no trace of *Thani* raiyats in the estate and no such right was recognised in the settlement records.[124]

Sunia Bheti, *Bibhachina*, *Magon*, *Salami*, *Dakhilkharaj Kharcha*, *Khorapani* and *Bisodhuni* etc. were the types of cesses or abwabs exacted by the proprietor or Raja on tenantry. The

123. Settlement of Aul, 1892-1901, p. 11.

124. *Ibid*, p. 12.

Raja who exhibited himself as despotic in his dealings with the tenants, claimed to utilise the services of the tenants free of cost or sometimes giving them one meal per day. Washermen, Barbers, Carpenters and Potters used to get contributions from the tenants for their village service. Except the village *Chaukidars* and *Mukaddams* the proprietor did not extend any privilege of rent free tenures in the form of *Jagirs* other than the persons engaged for his personal services.

The settlement yielded an increase in the proprietors rental of Rs. 7,170-2-10 pies or 71 per cent. The rental fixed in the settlement of 1892 amounted to Rs. 1,07,532-15-8 pies against the old rental of Rs. 1,00,362-12-10 pies.[125] The major portion of increase was caused from the assessment of *Ghenan* tenancies being resumed into rent.

3. Darpan

Killa Darpan was bounded with Madhupur, Kalkala, Tributary State Dhenkanal, Kerualkhand, Jeypore and Alti and some others. Just after the British conquest, *Killa* Darpan including *Killa* Kalkala was permanently settled in accordance with the Resolution 12 of 1805 with Raja Gulzar Hussain for 30,000 Kahans of Cowrees. In the same year *Killa* Kalkala was made a separate estate with an engaged tribute of Rs. 6,853-11-10 pies that continued till 1836 which was converted into current rupee and was fixed at Rs. 3,310-10-2 pies. This was paid under *Tauzi* No 18 of Cuttack Collectorate. In 1823 Raja Gulzar Hussain was succeeded by his son Akbar Hussain. On his default the estate was sold at Rs. 64,000 to Gopinath Pandit on June 30, 1843.[126] On the death of Gopinath Pandit in 1860 *Killa* Darpan was preserved by the Court of Wards as his son Baidyaṇath Pandit was a minor at that time. This remained under the Court of Wards for 6 years. On the attainment of majority Baidyanath Pandit got back the estate in 1866 and remained in possession till 1899.

125. *Ibid*, p. 13.

126. Settlement of Darpan, 1901, p. 7.

Prior to the year 1860 Gopinath Pandit initiated a private settlement but of no use. During the period when it remained under Court of Wards a settlement was started forthwith and was expedited in 1865. This settlement was locally called as "1268 Settlement".[127] This settlement of 1865 was not welcomed and accepted by some tenants on the ground of illegal resumption of high assessment. Most important of these cases subsequently formed the matter of several disputes between the proprietor and the people. The proprietor for whose interest the Court of Wards took initiative for the settlement did not agree to the proceedings of this settlement of 1865.

Niskar Bahal, *Debottar*, *Baziafti Jagir*, *Chandina*, *Chaukidar Jagir*, *Paika Garnayak Jagir*, *Zamindar Dih Jagir* and *Zamindar Dih Niskar* were the main categories of tenants confirmed in the 1865 settlement. The old rent of the *Tanki Bahaldars* was changed and resumed as *Pahi* raiyats with the same rate of rent as fixed by the Musalman Raja.

Raja entrusted the work of revenue collection to *Sarabarakar* who was assisted by a Zilladar, 2 Muharirs and 3 Peons in 1 *Diha*. In all the 8 *Dihas* there were 8 sets of officers working under 1 *Sarbarakar* for the purpose of rent collection. The rents were collected from the raiyats in 3 instalments or Kists, first in Kartik (November), second in Baisakh (April) and the third and last Kists in Soonia (August). The Raja was always in habit of exacting different types of cesses alongwith the regular rents from the raiyats.

The settlement that commenced in 1891-92 and was completed in 1899-1900 confirmed all the land tenure holders. In this settlement in 286 villages covering an area of 63,942 acres survey work was operated and after the attestation rents were fixed on a total cost of Rs. 17,299.[128] The new settlement rent amounted to Rs. 49,243 or 24 per cent increase

127. *Ibid.*

128. *Ibid*, p. 14.

on the old rent of 1865 and the incidence varied from Rs. 1-11 annas to Rs. 2-7 annas. Tenants numbering 10,354 were assessed in this settlement.[129] Government besides land revenue was getting a revenue from irrigation sources of Rs. 15,410 from Darpan estate.[130]

4. Kujanga

In the case of Kujanga, the estate was kept under the Court of Wards due to the inability of the Raja to manage the administration of the estate smoothly. The estate being situated on the sea coast was yielding a very low revenue to its proprietor. Settlements were affected resulting in the increase of revenue due to new cultivation of lands. Land tenures like the tenure holders in Kanika were confirmed by the settlement of 1891-92. By the time of the great famine the estate was in a high debt by not paying the regular annual *Peskash* to the Government as per the Resolution 12 of 1805 and the engagement made thereof amounting to Rs. 2,44,415-11-5½, the interest of which reached at Rs. 31,280.[131] As per the balance sheet the net revenue left in the hands of the Raja became Rs. 46,916 deducing the annual tribute which became meagre to meet the expenses of the Raja and the interest accrued thereof.

The total Government revenue demanded on the permanently settled estates in the year 1896-97 was Rs. 1,51,701,[132] against the demand of Rs. 1,46,805 in the year 1881-82[133] with an increase of Rs. 4,896 in about 15 years duration.

The other permanently settled estates of Orissa continued to pay the fixed quit rents in perpetuity as per the *ekrarnama*. As most of the permanently settled estates were subject to the

129. *Ibid*, p. 17.
130. *Ibid*, p. 5.
131. BRP, December, 1866, T.E. Ravenshaw to Board of Revenue, No. 1253, November 29, 1866.
132. GAROD, 1896-97, Pr. 7, p. 3.
133. *Ibid*, 1881-82, Pr. 131, p. 31.

humiliation by natural calamities, the Rajas were always under heavy debt. It became a regular feature with the proprietors of estates to face the financial burden by not being able to realise the full rental amount even though they had exercised their authority in a despotic manner.

G. TRIBUTARY STATES OR MAHALS

Treaty engagements were executed with the Chiefs of the hilly tracts of Orissa apparently when the country was ceded to East India Company. These Chiefs were often irrregular in payment of tribute to the Maratha Government being secured in their forts, being surrounded by dense forests. Occasionally they showed the spirit of insubordination to the supreme Maratha Government in Orissa. Even before this during the Mughal rule, particularly in the beginning of the rule of Aurangzeb most of the tributary Chiefs of Orissa refused to pay tribute. They had the courage to declare war against the Mughal Governor of Orissa Khan-i-Dauran.[134] Making a careful study of these incidents of insubordination by the tributary Chiefs and non-payment of regular tribute, the East India Company Government thought it proper to execute *Sanands* with the ruling Chiefs with a permanent and fixed income for them annually.

In accordance with the provisions of Sections 36 and 37 of Regulation 12 of 1805 the Chiefs agreed to pay a regular tribute to the Company as fixed in the *Sanands*. Further all the Chiefs except the Chief of Keonjhar promised to depute contingent force to assist the Government against any opposition by the enemies of the Company Government. The Government was assured of the amount of the tribute every year from the Tributary States as entered in the *Sanand*. The tribute was not subject to any revision, as it so happened in the case of the Rajas of *Killas* or permanently settled estates, under any circumstances by the Government. These Tributary Mahals

134. Roy, B.C., *Orissa under the Marathas*, p. 129.

did not form any part of the British India.[135] The Feudatory States—Athagarah, Athamallik, Boud, Baramba, Dhenkanal, Duspalla, Hindol, Keonjhar, Khandpara (Khundeipara), Moharbhanj (Mayurbhanj), Nilgiri, Narasinghpur, Nayagarh, Pallahara, Runpur, Talcher and Tigiria were ceded to the East India Company by the Maratha after their defeat. The status of these Chiefs were identified as Rajas. They were allowed to maintain their independence in the matter of administration internally but in some matters, their hands were regulated by the Government, involving the social humiliation to their subjects.

These Feudatory States were kept under the supervision of the Superintendent of Tributary Mahals, the office which was created in the year 1814. The Superintendent of the Tributary Mahals used to regulate the Chiefs through the Political Agents appointed by the Government to be stationed in each Mahal.

A very important duty of the Political Agent was to establish cordial relation with the Chief where he was posted. He was required to make supervision over the administration of the Chief and not to give any order or advice on his own accord to the Chief, not to receive any complaint against the Chief from the people and not to forward the petition of allegation of any serious nature, to make enquiry on the complaint so made by subjects and was always required to be vigilant about the breakdown of the administration. The Political Agent was never maintained as the superior to the status of the Chief in any case. He was however to receive the place of honour on ceremonial occasions when the Commissioner or the Superintendent was not present as the representative of the Government. Hence the Political Agent was always required to make the Company Government informed about the conduct of the Rajas or Chiefs of the Feudatory States.

In States under direct administration the Superintendent occupied the place of the Chief and was supposed to exercise

135. Selection Records (Feudatory States), Pr. 2, p. 2, O. Kinealy's Letter No. 961, May 26, 1874 (O S.A.).

his powers as these were delegated to him. The Commissioner could however limit or extend these powers with due sanction of the Government.[136]

The only State in which the powers of the Chief had been extended was Mayurbhanj, a most advanced Tributary Mahal of Orissa. All such extensions of powers were conferred as strictly personal favours. The Raja was permitted to cast sentence of imprisonment for a period of not exceeding 5 years. The Chief was also permitted to delegate the higher power conferred on him to the State Judge with the approval of the Government.

In the case of 5 Sambalpur group of States (Patna, Sonepur, Kalahandi, Bamra and Rerahakhole) powers were extensive. They had full powers of administration in Criminal, Civil and Revenue matters except that in the case of capital sentence.

The financial settlement became permanent and Government was realising the fixed amount as tribute from the Feudatory Chiefs as shown in Appendix-'B'.[137]

In the case of Athagarah, Milla revised the Government tribute as it was originally fixed at a higher rate due to the wrong calculation.

At the time of British conquest Angul and Banki belonged to the group of Tributary States. Their tributes were fixed at Rs. 1,550-6-4 pies and Rs. 4,162-4-7 pies respectively. Subsequently Banki was declared as a *Khasmahal* in the year 1882[138] Angul due to maladministration was declared as a Government estate in the year 1848.

The Commissioner of Cuttack became the ex-officio Superintendent of the Tributary States of Orissa. Sometimes

136. *Ibid*, p. 20.

137. Selection Records (Feudatory States), Bengal Government, 1851.

138. Malley, S.S.O., *Bihar and Orissa Gazetteer Cuttack*, p. 22.

the Magistrates of districts were required to assist the Superintendent in the capacity of Assistant Superintendent.[139] The Chiefs were allowed to administer Civil and Criminal justice under the control of the Superintendent. The States under this category were exempted from the general regulation system applicable for the rest of the British territories.[140]

In connection with the *nuzrana* system which was in vogue in almost all the Feudatory States, a change was introduced in the year 1870. As per the new *nuzrana* rules of 1870 the Bengal Government excluded the Chiefs from paying any *nuzrana*. The Government of India in their communication to the Government of Bengal made some specific directions to the Superintendent of Tributary Mahals of Orissa to realise *nuzrana* in the case of successors who would be distantly related than of the third degree. The *nuzrana* in that case should be equal to one year's tribute.[141] This new system was yielding a good income to the Government Treasury without having any colateral responsibility.

H. RESULTS

The results of the settlement proceedings became far reaching. Settlements were aimed at ascertaining the area of each estate and equalising the assessments. These settlements resulted in tremendous economic setback to some poor Zamindars who had to accept sale laws to clear up all arrears of land revenue due for payment to the Government. Additional *Jama* was imposed on the newly cultivated lands between the periods of 2 settlements of 1837 and 1897 and new *pattas* were distributed among the estate holders. These new assessments were yielding heavy revenue to the Government.

139. Selection Records (Feudatory States), p. 1 (O.S.A.).

140. Aitchison Treaties, Vol. III, p. 98.

141. BRP, April, 1874; Selection Records (Feudatory States), Secretary to Government of India (Foreign Department) to Government of Bengal, No. 850, April 11, 1874 (O.S.A.).

By the end of the 19th century the total revenue income from all sources was Rs. 25,26,700.[142]

The individual rights of *Mukaddams, Sarbarakars, Padhans, Khariddars* and other village tenure holders in large number were separately ascertained. This allowed the poor cultivators to save themselves from the oppression of the revenue officers of the Zamindars to a great extent. Mills was of opinion that "operation which have conferred such permanent blessings on the people and will be also beneficial to Government in fiscal and judicial point of view have not been dearly purchased".[143] Settlements also fixed the percentage of allowance for the under tenures like *Mukaddams, Sarbarakars* and others. The village service tenure holders like barbers, washermen, blacksmiths, etc. were confirmed with the possession of their petty *Jagirs*. This in a way could introduce a healthy relation of the service tenure holders with the villagers as they were not subject to humiliation through the exaction of extra financial burden by the Zamindars. In many estates the village accountants were remunerated by the grant of lands through the settlement proceedings and in some other cases the accountants were not remunerated who were living on contract with the Zamindars.

The settlements thus provided all possible measures for the security of the people from the oppression of the Zamindars. The social value of this settlement became outstanding in comparison to the conditions prevailing in Bengal as realised by the British officers. Yet the British land policy was not completely free from any curse to the agricultural population. The regular collection of land revenue as fixed by settlements were enforced with rigidity by the Revenue Collectors. The Government was not paying any heed to the remission of rent when demanded by the people even during the period of the presence of natural calamities. The regular

142. Maddox Report, Vol. I, p. 384.

143. Selection Records (Settlement), January 23, 1847, Minutes of Mills.

rent collection without being denied or delayed by the cultivating population clearly signalised the capacity of payment by the tenants. As such the question of remission of revenue was not considered by the Government at any stage. There was also no popular clamour for remission by the cultivators. This posed a healthy sign of the material prosperity of the cultivating population in general even though in some cases it harassed the landlords for their extravagancy.

The Zamindars were facing extreme losses and were placing high demands on the Government for remission for no reason. The Government knowing this fully well was always neglecting the clamour of the Zamindars as the settlement of 1897 gave a new lease of economic stability to the Zamindars.

The comparative prosperity of the economy of the people of Orissa was thus marked by moderation in comparison to the earlier British Land Policy. The people felt secured in their economic turnover as they were not subject to any economic humiliation either by the Government or by their Zamindars. Consequent upon these blessings of the settlements the economy of the State gradually had its upward tendency. The blessings of 1897 settlement particularly were felt everywhere, by the cultivating class, by the Zamindars, by the tenure holders and by the officials engaged for the purpose of revenue collection. This new revenue policy on the whole improved the economy of the people and the economy of the State of Orissa as the rights of the tenants were welded to their lands by the Government with careful consideration.

2

Agricultural Problems and Colonial Policy

A. AGRICULTURE

Agriculture was the main occupation of the people of Orissa. It was the fundamental basis of the rural economy. Almost the entire population of Orissa was associated with the land for earning their livelihood as they had no other source of income due to inadequate industrial growth. The Oriya raiyats (cultivators) cared only to grow sufficient quantity of rice to support themselves and their family for the whole year whose landed properties were their only protection against robbery, extortion and oppression. This types of agrarian economy in Orissa continued from ancient time till the days of Maratha misrule. The Maratha misrule led to the decentralisation of the Governmental responsibility thus giving a trend to the overgrowth of a non-productive, parasite class in the agrarian economy of Orissa.

1. Agricultural Prudence

The period witnessed the rising conflict of the landed proprietors that virtually led to the anxiety of the money speculators particularly the *Sahukars* and the *Gossain Mahajans* who became indispensable persons to the agrarian economy. In the year 1803 the British conquest of Orissa marked a turning point in the agrarian economy of Orissa. The agrarian Orissa faced a challenge from the Bengali middle class '*Baboo*' society, the society which was based on money speculation in the land tenure system having a negative result on the economy.[1]

The gradual elimination of Oriya and Maratha revenue officers from the British administration and their complete ignorance of the revenue system in Orissa during the period of Company rule compelled them to introduce short term revenue settlements. Thus there came an economic dislocation in the social heirarchy. Large scale sale of landed estates, replacement of native officers by Bengali speculators, resumption of non-revenue paying lands and enhancement of *Jama* became the features of the revenue administration. Neither the Government nor the speculative cultivators desired for large scale capital investment for the agricultural improvements because of the short term land tenures. The traditional land holders also could not undertake large scale capital investment due to lack of their saving capacity. Thus in the early years of 19th century the agrarian economy of Orissa was neither prosperous nor encouraging.

The poverty of the tenants forced them to remain under the control of the paddy dealers. They were in habit of borrowing either paddy or cash at high rate of interest to meet the contingencies of cultivation. They exhausted themselves for the whole year for better outturn but in some years they were deceived by the silent industry of nature. The greatest single climatic rhythm dominated the cultivation of rice and other crops as well. Cyclones, storms too contributed to the periodical role in destroying the standing crops that ultimately exhausted the energy and purse of agriculturists. Statistically speaking, out of the annual crop one-tenth was destroyed by

1. Orissa Records, Vol. V. 1965, Bhubaneswar, pp. 54-77.

flood and one-tenth by drought.[2] The balance left with the cultivators naturally became insufficient to meet the arrears of interest due on them.

2. Methods of Agriculture

The technique and methods followed by the Indian agriculturists varied in nature depending on the nature of the soil and the crop. The same thing happened in the case of the cultivators of Orissa. The methods they usually followed were almost primitively simple retaining the same pattern since ancient times. The cultivators with the pair of animals (bullock or buffalo) and a few village made tools used to give their lives throughout the year for the purpose of earning a good harvest. The main implement for cultivation was the plough and for harvesting the sickle. Cultivation in Orissa, though very simple in its type, required hard physical labour. The raiyat regulated his routine of work with the keen observation of the climate which sometimes yielded him severe oppression. The prime need of the agricultural life was thus the regulation of water at every time through canal system to save the agriculturists of Orissa from their economic depression. Besides water supply there existed other difficulties from which the peasants suffered. The main support of agriculture was cattle, their number and condition. Short supply of food for cattle was a general drawback that terribly affected agriculture. Cattle mortality was a staggering factor due to non-availability of medical aid to the animals at the door of the cultivators. Rent burden added fuel to the miserable plight of the peasants of Orissa. With all these odds, the peasants of Orissa struggled on and on but 19th century Orissa could not facilitate the cultivators much upto the years of 1868 when the canal project inaugurated a new lease of life in agriculture. A prosperous agricultural life thus became a myth due to the hammering of the natural calamities on crops, lack of irrigation facilities and the heavy rent burden on agricultural holdings and other corollaries of social evils.

2. Maddox Report, Vol. I, p. 91.

3. Class of Agricultural Fields

The lands were divided from agricultural point of view as follows:[3]

(*i*) *Kala*

The kala lands consisted of homestead garden plots attached to dwelling houses and orchards growing vegetables and fruits.

(*ii*) *Jala*

Jala lands were all rice growing fields in almost every part of the country.

(*iii*) *Pala*

Pala lands being enriched with silt deposits of the flood water were generally utilised for growing rabi crops, tobacco and other vegetables. Amongst pala lands those adjoining the water edge were used for growing tobacco that yielded highest rates but as soon as the river receded the fertility of pala lands diminished.

(*iv*) *Gora*

Gora, situated in high lands closed to villages, better cared of and manured yielded two crops in a year and those close to the jungle were frequently barren that yielded very poor crops.

(*v*) *Taila*

Taila, the high dry lands receiving the ashes of leaves for its nutriment could not retain more water for better cultivation. Taila was a fresh clearing of jungles and after which the lands were ploughed up with the ashes that added more fertility for growing more crops. These lands were not fit for permanent cultivation except for three to four years only.

3. Maddox Report, Vol. I, p. 44 and p. 54; Settlement of Keonjhar, pp. 42-43,

(vi) Dalua

Dalua lands were the part of river lands (low lands drained by the rivers) that generally used for spring rice and ordinary lands like Balichar, Balia, Goria, Matala, Dahi Matala, Talia Matala, Sudh Matala, Chaulia Matala, Panisa Mahala (Ash colour), Kimbhiria Matala, Telia Balia, Dhaulia Matala, Nalia Matala, Haladia Matala, Janha Matala, Hadua Matala, Kulthi Matala, Chikita Matala, Kala Matala, Nunia Matala and Nunia were usually identified as third class lands from agricultural point of view. These lands could not be made available for crop purposes due to non-availability of irrigation facilities till the canals were brought for operation after the Orissa Famine.

4. Crop

Dr. Cheng Hang Seng divided India into 16 regions on the basis of topographical situation, agricultural facilities, crop system and tenure system and general economic division.[4] Eastern wet (rice) region included Bihar, Orissa, Eastern U.P., Andhra Pradesh and Eastern Tamilnadu etc.[5] Orissa thus was mainly a rice growing region during nineteenth century. Besides rice, the cultivators were taking much pain in producing tobacco, jute, sugarcane, pan and rabi crops from their fields.

(i) Rice

Sarada or winter rice sown in June and July were ready for harvest in November and January. Biali or Autumn rice shown in May and June were harvested in August and September and Dalua or Spring rice sown in November and December were ready for harvesting in March.[6] Sarada was divided into

4. Seng, Cheng Hang, *Agrarian Regions of India and Pakistan*, 1950, p. 11.
5. Memoria, C.B , *Agricultural Problems of India*, p. 15.
6. Maddox Report, Vol. I, p. 5; Malley, S.S.O., *Bihar and Orissa Gazetteer, Cuttack*, p. 17.

Baradhana and Laghudhana. The following table will show the yielding capacity of varieties of rice in an acre of land.[7]

Biali	20 to 120 gauni average per acre
Chhot Laghu	50 to 60 gauni average per acre
Medium Laghu	100 to 120 gauni average per acre
Bara Laghu	140 to 160 gauni average per acre
Sarada	200 to 220 gauni average per acre
Baradhan	200 to 240 gauni average per acre

(*ii*) *Tobacco*

Tobacco was an important and valuable crop usually grown in lands covered in silt of flood water specially on the basin of the rivers. This crop was yielding a good earning for the cultivators.

(*iii*) *Rabi Crop*

After harvest of paddy, in the fields rabi crops like Mug, Birih, Kulthi and Harhar were sown in many parts of Orissa.[8]

(*iv*) *Sugarcane*

Sugarcane became an important crop in the irrigable fields as it required heavy water supply for its growth. Even though irrigation facilities were not amply provided the cultivators used different types of hand-made instruments to get river and jheel water into their fields for this purpose. This crop was usually grown in many parts of Puri district and some parts of Cuttack district.[9]

7. Maddox Report, Vol. I, p. 70.
8. *Ibid*, pp. 5, 44 and 70.
9. *Ibid*, pp. 5 and 70; Settlement of Darpana, p. 6; Malley, S.S.O., *Bihar and Orissa Gazetteer, Puri*, p. 174.

(v) *Oilseeds*

Oilseeds like Sorisha and Til were grown as second crop in some paddy fields in Puri district mainly and in some places in Cuttack district.

(vi) *Pan*

Pan or betel leaf is an important crop in Orissa. It was grown in high lands. This crop was treated as very valuable crop as this was a commodity of export to Calcutta.[10] In many parts of Puri, Cuttack and Balasore Districts the crop was found to have grown plentily. Narsinghpur occupied a good place among the Pan producing regions for which the crop was named after the name of the place as Narsinghpuripan.[11]

(vii) *Fruits*

The principal fruits and fruit bearing trees were Mangoes, Jack, Papeya, Custard Apple, Pine Apple, Coconut, Pulango and Plantain. Out of these fruits Mango was the best that served as an important part of food supply of the people.[12]

(viii) *Vegetables*

Vegetables were grown generally by every cultivator for their own use and to earn something for the purchase of some commodities of daily use. Tailas and Pala lands were also used for cultivating vegetables. Orissa was producing all types of vegetables throughout the year.

(ix) *Other Crops*

Mandia, Cheena, Dhania, Juani, Panmahuri etc. of less important type were grown in limited parts of the country.

10. Malley, S.S.O., *Bihar and Orissa Gazetteer, Puri*, p. 171.
11. *Ibid.*
12. *Ibid*, p. 174.

(*x*) *Jute*

Cultivation of Jute took a major share in the agrarian economy of Orissa. After rice this cultivation was taken up. Cuttack district occupied a good position in Jute production.[13]

(*xi*) *Wheat*

Wheat was never grown by the cultivators of Orissa as the inhabitants were very much reluctant to take Wheat as one of their main food-stuffs even at the time of scarcity. For this reason Wheat cultivation was never tried by the cultivators of Orissa.

B. AGRARIAN ECONOMY AND THE BRITISH COLONIAL POLICY

The agrarian economy of Orissa before the British rule was in a distorted form. Little attention was paid for the development of agriculture. Large tracts of lands were left uncultivated as most of the cultivators did not have the confidence of the out-turn due to the vagaries of nature. The first half of the 19th century Orissa witnessed the rapid growth of monopoly in agriculture that replaced the diversified agriculture, producing all necessities of daily use for the people in a self-sustained village economic unit. The growth of village population led to the concentration of manpower on land and agriculture.[14] This resulted in the decline of the cultivation of non-food crops like Cotton for rural weaving industry to meet the village requirements. The old age traditional Cottage Industries in villages which had been maintaining the balance in the agrarian economy by utilising the maximum manpower thus came to an end. On the other hand the craze for lands and cultivation for the subsistence of the villagers resulted in the extension of cultivation in the Taila lands in the hilly regions. But due to the non-fertility of the Taila lands after a few years the harvesting

13. Malley, S.S.O., *Bihar and Orissa Gazetteer, Cuttack*, p. 172.
14. RCF, pp. 102-0, 63-68.

was abandoned leading to large scale relapse of lands to jungles particularly Sal jungles after 1875.[15]

The growth of rice cultivation did not have impact on the economic growth of Orissa. The export of rice was harmful to the internal economy of the village units. The pressure from above compelled the cultivators to sell their crops at cheap rates without any marginal profit for their annual subsistence. The minimum profit they received sometimes became insufficient to meet the cost of cultivation due to the rise in price of seeds and wages of labour. Thus the conditions of the peasantry became worse day by day.

The British Colonial Policy indicated no immediate benefit to the agricultural community. The Britishers were basically the commercial group and their main aim was to increase the commercial activities. They realised that their commercial interest in Orissa was mainly connected with agriculture. The officers, on realisation, were deeply attracted towards the agricultural problems of Orissa. They thus adopted a new agricultural policy to cripple the local industries and to establish their own industrial projects.[16]

Land was used as an instrument to win the loyalty of the natives. A landed aristocracy was created. The *Mahalwari* system of settlement gave rise to a lot of evils against the agrarian economy following the year 1837. It produced the new feature of absentee landlordism which did not exist more or less since 1818. The landlord proprietors were transformed into a rent collecting agency, the main aim of which was the regular payment of land taxes to the Colonial Government. They were further induced to purchase the foreign goods with the surplus that they had with them from the tax collection of the peasantry.

15. Beams John, *Notes on the History of Orissa under the Mahammadan, Maratha and English Rule*, Vol.II, Edt., N.K. Sahoo, Calcutta, 1956. pp. 302 6.

16. Senapaty Fakir Mohan, *Fakir Mohan Granthabali*, pp. 630-33.

A new class of parasites depending on land thus grew. They were favoured by the Government. They had little interest for the local people. They had the monopoly of land and the majority of the people depended on their charity. As a result of this the speculators from Bengal played a very unpleasant role in determining the price of land according to their choice. The poor Orissan peasantry could not withstand the competition of the Bangali speculators at the time of settlement. The Government were aware of the situation but a very little was done to improve this.[17] This condition virtually impaired the agricultural community as a whole.

The agrarian economy of Orissa was further exploited by the Colonial Government by the introduction of salt monopoly. The natives were not allowed to prepare their own salt from the sea water though Orissa possessed a vast sea line and one of the largest saline lakes of the world.[18] This salt monopoly forced the sizeable inhabitants to remain unemployed and for which they opted for their alternative employment in agriculture.[19] The skilled workers like ship-builders, when thrown out of their employment, rushed into agricultural fields to earn their livelihood.

Colonial policy neglected the policy of industrialisation for which urban markets remained static for the agricultural product. Agricultural products remained confined to the local market. It yielded no profit to the cultivators. The rural credit gradually developed and intensified its exploitation when the raiyats and the Zamindars surrendered themselves before the money lenders.[20]

This new agrarian economic policy exposed the exploiting nature of the British Rule which was very keen in rent collection from the lands through agencies and the increase of colonial commercial activities at the cost of the wretched agrarian economy of Orissa throughout the 19th century.

17. Guha, A.C., *Land System in Bengal and Bihar*, p. 15.
18. Senapaty Fakir Mohan, *Fakir Mohan Granthabali*, pp. 642-43.
19. Agarwal, S.C., *Salt Industry in India*, pp. 231-32.
20. Mamm, H.H., *Social Framework of Agriculture in India, Middle East and England*, 1967, pp. 104-17.

In this deplorable state of agrarian economy of Orissa, the Zamindars and the peasants clashed with each other. The Government became particular to the security of land revenue from the Zamindars.[21] An increase of *Jama* was affected by the Government during the short term settlements, the 30 years' settlement of 1837 and the settlement of 1897. During the period from 1837 to 1897 the Government revenue increased by 52 per cent and the income of the Zamindars diminished by 13 per cent.[22] The Zamindars were apprehensive of their fate due to this increase of Government *Jama*. They felt insecured when their estates were sold in auction by the Government for non-payment of revenue. As an immediate result of auction sale a large number of landed aristocracy became landless. This high pitch of revenue demand disheartened the revenue farmers. This had eliminated the native as well as Bengali land proprietors before the competition of sale of landed estates. The crisis was also experienced by the destitute peasantry including the wage earning labour class. The absentee land-lords did not pay any interest to the qualitative development of the lands or to the material prosperity of the peasants. They collected the maximum rent from the cultivators. The minimum left with the cultivators was not sufficient for their annual subsistence. The Zamindars collected much more what they paid to the Government. The Government failed miserably in keeping up the promises to offer protection to the peasantry from excess exaction of revenue. Vital points to help the peasants were not properly considered even at the time of assessment.[23] In this conflict between the Zamindars and the peasants to which the Government was the silent spectator, the economic growth in Orissa was denied.

1. Zamindars

The existence of absentee landlords mostly Bengalis had the worst impact on the agrarian economy of Orissa. They expressed their disinterest in the material prosperity of their

21. Hunter, W., *Indian Administration*, pp. 227-32.
22. RAB, 1899-1900, p. 44.
23. Maddox Report, Vol. I, pp. 160-64.

estates. They were only interested in rent collection through their *Goomastas*. Most of them spent the surplus they had with them lavishly. At the time of natural calamities like flood, famine and cyclone, when they were not able to collect rent from the cultivators, their estates were auctioned by the Government for default of revenue. Consequent upon this their lands were divided into small plots for easy sale. Number of the landlords increased. Towards the close of 19th century there remained 6346 landlords in Orissa.[24] Landlords with their low income and small margin of balance after payment were not encouraged for the capital investment for better production. Without any committed obligation to the estate by the Zamindars there could be hardly any chance of agricultural prosperity. The Zamindars had their arguments against their disinterest in capital investment. They alleged that the Government did not allow any remission of rent during the years of natural calamities.

Under this economic hardship the landlords did not even repair minor irrigational embankments. For this negligence there could be number of breaches through which flood water had its easy flow over the crop fields damaging crops. On account of the great Orissa Famine the Government had spent huge amount of canal projects for better irrigation facilities to the cultivators. But the landlords expressed their reluctance to use canal water. It was feared that any increase of production might ultimately mean higher assessment of rent.[25] The agricultural output thus could not increase and became a positive harm to the economic development.

The Zamindars of Orissa treated their raiyats very badly, even they did not show any sympathetic consideration towards them at the time of distress either in suspending the demands or subsidising them through food-grains. In spite of giving charity the Zamindars who had stock of rice lent it to their tenants with high rate of interest as a matter of speculation

24. Revision Settlement, Pp. 36-37
25. BRP, No. 93, May, 1 8(.

that aggravated the severity of their distress.[26] Enquiries of 1871 revealed that the Zamindars in majority of cases did not grant remission to their tenantry even though Government granted remission during the period of Famine. Some had granted 4 annas and some 6 to 8 annas but they had recouped themselves by realising excess rent in the following years.[27]

The *Taqavi* loan advanced by the Government to reestablish the raiyats after the famine had been kept back by many Zamindars. The Lt. Governor Sir George Campbell expressed his grave concern to the Government of India over the arbitray dealings of the Zamindars with the tenants. The Secretary of State agreed with the proposal of the Governor General that no special measure against the oppression of the Zamindars on the cultivators was necessary.[28] The Government failed miserably to help the raiyats in protecting them from the rapacity of such type of notorious Zamindars.[29] This oppression of the Zamindars continued to exist in Orissa till 1885 when the Bengal Tenancy Act was brought for enforcement.[30] The Zamindars' attitude thus was a negation to the development of agrarian economy of the province in the whole of 19th century.

2. Peasants

In this state of callousness of the Government and the notorious character of the Zamindars it was quite but natural that the peasantry would pay for it. The independent peasant community gradually degraded into a class of dependent peasantry. The declining economic position was distinctly found with the agricultural communities. Consequently 3 types

26. BRP, Nos. 160-61, August, 1867, T.E. Ravenshaw to Secretary, Government of Bengal, No. 469, July 15, 1867.
27. *Ibid*, January, 1872, T.E. Ravenshaw to Secretary, Government of Bengal, No. 620, November, 1871.
28. BRP, January, 1876, Secretary of State's Despatch, No. 61.
29. BRP, February, 1875, H.J. Reynold, Officiating Secretary, Government of Bengal to Government of India, No. 351, February 12, 1875.
30. *Ibid*, Nos. 31-32, June, 1894, Resolution of Government of Bengal.

of peasants were noticed—peasantry with lands but no stock, peasantry with stock but no land and a class of landless labourers including day and seasonal wage earners. The landless peasantry cultivated the lands with the stock of the owners of the soil for half share of the produce (Bhaga). In fact the landless peasants were better off than the peasants having land and no stock. Capital and labour remained in separate hands. There was no controlling power to bridge the gap. Exorbitant rate of interest discouraged the cultivators damaging their initiative to work. The trend in the increase of capital with the community other than agricultural was marked with the loss of interest for agricultural improvement among the peasantry.

The defective administration had worsened the economic conditions of the peasants. Due to non-payment of rent by the peasants the lands were auctioned and at that time the officers participated in the bid and purchased the lands in ghost names. The poor peasants did not have the economic audacity to stand by this loss.

Against these odds there manifested a tendency with the tenants to complain against their Zamindars for high rate of rent.[31] The raiyats ultimately failed to display organised resistance in a combined manner against their oppressive Zamindars. Lack of able leadership and their timidity did not help the peasantry to shout against their Zamindars. However there occurred the Paika Rebellion in the early part of the Company Administration mainly against its agrarian policy through short settlements. The settlement of 1837 removed the hardship of the Zamindars and relieved the peasants to some extent but the behaviour of the Zamindars forced the peasants to revolt against the economic inequality of the society. In 1872 in *Killa* Dampara, a permanently settled estate in Cuttack district there appeared a minor peasant revolution against the Zamindar.[32] But all these peasantry

31. BRP, March, 1875, Minutes of the Lt. Governor Richard Temple, March 16, 1875.
32. *Utkal Dipika*, Part IV, No. 2, January 24, 1874.

uprisings were suppressed within no time. As a result of which the peasants could not assert their rights for their subsistence.

Patwaris acted as an officer of check and balance between the revenue payee and the revenue collectors or landlords. The abolition of the *Patwari* system in Orissa by the Government on the pretext of the economic burden acted against the economic prosperity of the peasants. There was none to present the case of the cultivators before the Government that aggravated the misery of the peasants.

The peasants were subjected to a number of extra cesses or abwabs by the Zamindars on such items like growing grass, betel-nuts, mango and cotton, feasts and marriage. The total burden on the peasants became heavier than ever before.[33] Many penalty taxes were also imposed. Excess exaction of these taxes compelled the raiyats to migrate to other places to earn their livelihood on wage earning labourer basis. This became more common on *Pahi* raiyats. When the *Pahi* raiyats deserted the villages the burden of exaction was shifted over the *Thani* or resident or *Khudkast* raiyats.[34]

In this deteriorating agrarian economic condition the peasants suffered the worst putting the agrarian economy of Orissa static.

3. Clash of Interest and its Consequences

Under the prevailing condition it was unfortunate that the Government was never attracted throughout the 19th century to the improvement of agro-economic conditions of the province. In the beginning the Government was very much hopeful for the economic and commercial growth of the province but contrary to that there was anly 52 per cent growth in trade in Bengal-Orissa whereas it was 153 per cent

33. D. Pingle, Acting Collector, Cuttack to Hunter, Commissioner of Cuttack, October 28, 1833, Vol. 364, File No. 116, 1833-34, p. 79 (O.S.A.).

34. RevisionSettlement, p. 25.

in Bombay and 118 per cent in Madras.[35] The Government improved the economic status of the Zamindars in every settlement ignoring the peasants with the hope of the security of the *Jama* permanently. On the other hand the Zamindars did not spare the peasants for the economic growth of the peasantry. It was calculated that the Zamindars were getting 27 per cent of the total produce in 1822, 35 per cent in 1840 and 46 per cent in 1897.[36] On this increased profit of the Zamindars the Government should have directed them to invest a part of it on the lands but nothing was done. The Zamindars instead of helping the people in general and the peasants in particular at the time of distress, were busy in exporting rice to Calcutta. As most of the Zamindars belonged to Calcutta as the absentee landlords in Orissa they were very much keen in the material prosperity of Calcutta at the cost of Orissa. According to the Famine Commission's Report 33,000 tons of rice were exported to Calcutta from Orissa in 1865 when scarcity of rice was very much felt by the people.[37] It is interesting to note that in 1865 when rice was sold at the rate of 18 seers a rupee in Cuttack it was sold at the rate of 30 to 35 seers a rupee at Calcutta.[38] This could have been checked easily by the Government only by introducing some restrictions on the free export of rice from Orissa but nothing was done. Agriculture was a way of life to the cultivators in absence of any other alternative means to live and when agricultural products were drained to Calcutta market at a low rate the condition of the peasants in Orissa became miserable.

The peasants were hard pressed for excess payment of rent and other taxes to the landlords. They resorted to loan from the *Mahajans* with a high interest and with a promise to sell the agricultural products to them only on the rate to be dictated by the *Mahajans*. Moreover they had no other alternatives to sell their products in the markets at a high rate as there were no markets available nearby. Consequent upon

35. Starchey J., *India*, pp. 106-12.
36. *The Imperial Gazetteer of India*, Vol. III, p. 266.
37. RIF, 1889, Part I, p. 41.
38. Mukharjee, P., *History of Orissa*, p. 361.

this the peasants sustained a great loss that could barely afford their annual subsistence. The poverty of the peasants day by day increased. The interest of the peasants thus clashed with the interest of the Government and the Zamindars.

After much of prolonged correspondence by the Commissioner of Orissa with the Government of India and the Secretary of State, Bengal Tenancy Act was passed in 1885.[39] This was extended to Orissa in 1890.[40] This Act could not help the peasantry of Orissa much as the conditions prevailed then were not taken into consideration at the time of drafting the Act. On this ground the Commissioner of Orissa opposed to the extension of this Act to the province.[41] However this Act was brought into force. This was a revolutionary attempt by the Government though lately for the welfare of the peasants but the Act failed to produce the desired results in Orissa as the peasants were illiterate to understand the meaning of the Act. They took the help of the lawyers who hailed from Calcutta also. They tried to exploit the illiteracy of the peasants. The peasantry in Orissa was thus to fight against the Zamindars remaining under the control of the lawyers. Ultimately the consequences were disastrous.

It was under this underdeveloped rural economy, controlled by a few giving misery to millions of peasants of Orissa throughout 19th century the exploitative nature of the British rule was exposed, the rule which failed to attain the economic growth through industrialisation and the increase of the volume of the agrarian products. This tendency led to the constant poverty of the people. The agrarian economy thus remained unhealthy throughout 19th century.

39. BRP, Nos. 31-32, June, 1894, Resolution of the Government of Bengal.
40. *Ibid*, October, 1891, E.C. Buck, Secretary, Government of India to Secretary, Government of Bengal, No. 1421, June 22, 1891.
41. *Ibid*, Welsey, Commissioner, Cuttack to Secretary, Board of Revenue, No. 1568, September 17, 1891.

C. IMPACT OF NATURAL CALAMITIES

Orissa was subject to the evils of natural calamities like inundation, cyclone and famine that reflected the failure of the agrarian economy of the province. The disastrous consequences of the famines arising out of drought were on some occasions accentuated by the devastating floods and cyclones. The historic famine and its intensity was aggravated by the flood of September, 1866. Throughout the 19th century natural calamities played a vital role in disturbing the economic conditions of the people of Orissa.

1. Flood

Heavy flood at intervals in almost all the rivers of Orissa destroyed the crops in the fields. The main land plain of Balasore, Cuttack and Puri districts were rich in fertility often interspersed with navigable rivers. These rivers like Baitarani, Brahmani, Mahanadi, Kathojori and Kooakhai were liable to ruinous inundation from the sudden overflow of the accumulated rain water in the Chhotanagpur Plateau. Floods were more frequent in Orissa than in any other divisions.[42] The people of Orissa were accustomed to such inundation. They were in habit of taking shelter for the time being in comparatively high lands with their property and cattle and after subsidence of the water they used to repair and rebuild their huts and transplant new seedling in field where the crops were damaged.[43] In some years the floods were so heavy and so prolonged that the whole country remained under water for weeks together damaging crops seriously. The damages caused by flood water in some years could not be recouped by the peasants that ultimately caused hardship for the poor people and sometimes caused famine. Due to heavy flood in some years Orissa was cut off from outer world. High floods in

42. Selection of Papers (Famine), Vol. I, October, 1896, p. 305, R.C. Dutta, Commissioner of Orissa to Secretary to Government of Bengal, No. 17 PT, Camp Puri, September 21, 1896 (O.S.A.).
43. *Ibid.*

Orissa not only caused damages to crops but also took away lives of people and animals.

In 36 years from 1831-32 to 1866-67 floods' disasters necessitated the remission of Government revenue in the districts of Cuttack due to damage of crops in the fields. Subsequently the floods caused considerable injury to the state economy in 1868, 1872, 1879, 1881, 1892, 1895 and 1896. In 1885 there were about 89 breaches on the embankments and flood water entered into the paddy fields and in 1896 flood, considerable areas of Balasore, Cuttack and Puri districts were submerged in flood water that practically disturbed the economic conditions of the people.[44] Flood in Orissa with short intervals played disappointing role in shaping the economy of the people. It was after the famine the Government thought it necessary to regulate flood water through irrigation projects to protect the province from the twin evils of inadequacy of water or drought and inundation. But permanent source of protection against flood could not be afforded during 19th century.

2. Cyclone

Cyclone played no less important role in the agro-economic life of the people of Orissa. In the years when there was no flood or drought the ripe crops were damaged by cyclone that caused scarcity of food. Cyclone not only destroyed the crops but also destroyed the property of the Government and the people. In 1867 cyclone passed over Balasore district that caused sufferings to the people. The Government directed the balance of the Famine Relief Fund with the Commissioner, to the District Charitable Society for the people affected by cyclone of November, 1867.[45] Again in the year 1872 a cyclone affected the Balasore district that damaged both houses and crops. Remission of town tax was granted by the

44. *Narrative of the Principal Events, Chapter XXVI*, p. 53.
45. BRP, Nos. 199-200, November, 1867.

Government.[46] In the year 1874 a terrific cyclone passed over the whole of Orissa Division causing casualties in cattle and men. Government collected information about the damages done due to this cyclone and extended help to the people.[47] Orissa was devastated by the cyclone of June 25, 26 of 1887 that virtually collapsed the economic life of the people.[48] Thus Orissa was subject to the economic humiliation caused by cyclone with short intervals.

3. Famine

Large part of India had experienced famines in 19th century. Orissa could not escape from these devastating famines. A great famine visited this country in the year 1866 that had virtually disturbed the economic life of the people of Orissa. It was of greater magnitude that had confidently pushed a third of her population to death.[49] This catastrophic event hammered the backbone of the economy of Orissa. The area most affected by this famine was about 12,000 sq. miles with a population of about 4 millions. Of this only 3 districts comprised an area of 8,000 sq. miles containing a population of about 3 millions. This intensive famine is commonly known as the "Orissa Famine".[50] This famine is regarded as a turning point in the history of Orissa as well as her people.

Early Famines

Orissa in various times suffered from terrible famines. Great famines are said to have occurred in the 14th, 15th and 16th centuries. In the reign of Raja Kahil, Indra Deo, Raja Rai Ooriya and Raja Pratap Muda Deo famines came into this land. The great famine in Bengal of 1770 was felt grievously in Orissa and a few years later in 1774-75 another great

46. *Ibid*, Nos. 118-120, September, 1872.
47. *Ibid*, No. 49, January, 1875.
48. BRP, Nos. 2 and 3, June, 1887.
49. RIF, 1880, Part I, Pr. 51, p. 27; Buckland, C.E., *Bengal*, Vol. I, p. 330.
50. *Ibid*, 1901, Pr. 3, p. 1.

scarcity is stated to have occurred. The last famine of traditions visited Orissa in the native year 1200 corresponding to 1792-93.[51] After which no famine of that magnitude had ever humiliated the people of Orissa. The famine of 1866 surpassed everyone of the previous famines in its character. The ghastly nature of this historic famine exhibited the defects of the Bengal administration and the callousness of the Government for the development of Orissa.

Causes of Famine, 1866

(*i*) *Cessation of Rain*—The main cause of the outbreak of the famine caused by the scarcity of food was the premature cessation of rain in 1865. Much rain fell early in the season before the usual time of sowing in the fields. While the later rain was expected usually in the later part of September and early part of October miserably failed, it had caused widespread damage to the rice crop and tuned the coming of the famine.[52] There were 36.3″ of rain in Puri and 51.5″ and 52 6″ of rain in Cuttack and Balasore respectively in the year 1865.[53]

(*ii*) *Heavy Export*—The food stocks in the preceding year was quite inadequate to meet the challenges of the grievous injury to humanity by the famine when the price of grain had been increasing considerably day by day and when the people had expressed their inability to purchase foodgrains at higher price, the *Koomtees* of Madras territory were busy enough to collect Orissa grains for sale to a enterprising French House (Messers Robert Chariol and Co.) exporting through false point. The quantity of export of rice from Orissa amounted to 937,528 maunds only in the year 1864-65. Prior to that regular export of rice was on the way. The table on page 82 shows the export of grain by sea upto the year 1864-65 when the rate of export was too high.[54]

51. RCF, Vol. I, p. 15.
52. *Calcutta Review*, Vol. XLIV, 1867, "Orissa Past and Present".
53. RCF, Vol. I, p. 16.
54. RCF, Vol. 1, Part I, p. 13.

Years	Balasore (Maunds)	Cuttack (Maunds)	Puri (Maunds)	Total
1860-61	3,50,074	23,049	83,936	4,57,059
1861-62	3,27,504	60,880	46,780	4,44,164
1862-63	4,07,622	36,696	4,816	4,49,134
1863-64	5,20,052	29,464	—	5,49,516
1864-65	8,06,576	72,128	58,824	9,37,528

The crop in 1864 was good in Cuttack and excellent in Balasore though very poor in Puri. The heavy drain over the stock of foodgrains through export had tremendous impact of the economic life of the people. Orissa could be identified beyond British possession mainly due to the export of rice of good quality and in large quantities by the French and American ships.[55] The rise in price was caused due to the increased demands on the stocks. Hence the position of a man of Orissa solely depending on money wages had by no means improved.[56] Rice was sold 7 to 8 seers a rupee at that time that could not allow the wage earners to get rice for consumption.[57] Before the outbreak of this Famine rice was sold in many parts of Orissa at a very low rate. According to Dr. Hunter's Statistical Account of Bengal, 43 seers of coarse rice, which the labourers used to consume were sold per rupee.[58] During the period of famine the rate of rice gradually increased. A rupee could only fetch 4½ seers of rice from the bazar of Cuttack town,[59] that afforded no facility for the wage earners to go for rice at that high price. The price rise of rice became imminent due to the fact that when the people of Orissa were crying for food and the Government was trying to import rice for relief, at that time the people were exporting rice to neighbouring

55. GAROD, 1876-77, p. 10.
56. RCF, 1866, Vol. I, Part I, Pr. 17.
57. BRP, No. 197, June, 1867.
58. GAROD, 1878-79, Pr. 39, p. 13.
59. RCF. 1866, Pr. 282, p. 89. T.E. Ravenshaw, Commissioner, Cuttack to Government of Bengal, Telegraph, May 28, 1866.

places. They were exporting rice to Calcutta to sell to Government for the purpose of importing it back again to Orissa for relief work to the distressed persons. The administration was not able to check this type of imprudent exportation of rice from Orissa.

(iii) *Unemployment Problem*—Unemployment problem aggravated the miserable plight of the people. Apart from the scarcity of food there appeared a mass unemployment among the wage earners engaged in salt factories (*golas*) when the manufacture of salt was abandoned in Orissa.[60] They were thrown out of their employment and consequently, they had tried to be engaged in agricultural fields to earn their subsistence but they were denied of that privilege when agricultural fields became barren. The purchasing power of these types of men naturally diminished. The cultivators also suffered from the same deficiencies.

(iv) *Lack of Irrigation*—The waters of the rivers had not been used for irrigation till the years of famine. The whole country was not provided with any irrigational facilities except tanks and *jheels* which became insufficient to cater to the need of the cultivators on the eve of the famine. The success of crop therefore depended solely on the rain, the failure of such timely rain led to the total failure of rice crops in Orissa that had virtually threatened the life of millions of people.

(v) *Impact of 30 years' Settlement*—Thirty years' settlement added fuel to the fire. This settlement was just then expiring and new arrangements were yet to come. As a result of this there prevailed a shadow of uncertainty in the minds of the cultivators who were afraid of any further extension of their land than to contract the assessable area of cultivation.[61]

60. BRP, November, 1865; RCF, Vol. II, p. 16, T.E. Ravenshaw, Commissioner, Cuttack to Secretary, Government of Bengal, No. 280, November 14, 1865.

61. BRP, November, 1865, T.E. Ravenshaw, Commissioner, Orissa to Board of Revenue, No. 249, October 30, 1865.

(vi) *Poverty of the People*—Poverty of the people of Orissa had played no less important role to play with this calamity. The Zamindars were poor and improvident. The rents of the raiyats were very high. There was no trading class. Thus the wealth could not be accumulated to be used at the time of distress.[62] The raiyats did not feel it wise to keep the reserve stock for more than 2 years. They had also no storage capacity to meet the challenges of these natural upheavals.

(vii) *Communication*—Lack of communication became another factor for this Famine. In Orissa at that time there were no good roads for wheeled vehicular traffic. The whole province was isolated from the rest of India.[63] The only road that connected Orissa with Calcutta through Medinapur crossed over many bridged rivers and was unmetalled that could not allow even bullock carts during rainy seasons what to speak of speedy vehicles. Hence the undesirable conditions of communication could not inspire the trading class of Orissa and outsiders to procure foodgrains for the people. The Government in the beginning remained unalarmed to the situation and could not initiate anything for the timely importation of rice to Orissa as it became a difficult task to import rice through roads. There was very little communication by sea too.

(viii) *Defective Administration*—To add injury to this the entire administration of British-Orissa was defective. There were lack of viamedias between the Government officials and the people. The Executive officers were busy in attaching importance to the principles and orders of the Government. They did not like to go into reality as they had no knowledge either about the material conditions of the people or the economic status of the country. The Civil officers present at that time at the helm of the affairs were new to their own assignment. Musprat joined in early 1865 as Magistrate and Collector, Balasore. The new Collector Cornell joined in Cuttack in February, 1866. The Commissioner T.E. Ravenshaw

62. RCF, Vol. I, Part I, Pr. 47.
63. RIF, 1880, Part I, Pr. 51, p. 17.

himself had joined his office in July, 1865. Barlow who had a standing account of brilliant service for the last 10 years was the Collector of Puri on the eve of famine. He did ample justice to his duties till his departure in the year 1866.[64] In addition to the ignorance of the British officers about Orissa and her people, they lacked foresight. They could not foresee the approach of the impending danger to the humanity.[65] Towards the last part of October 1865 the signs of food scarcity were experienced by the people and this was brought to the notice of the Government. The administration however could not realise the intensity of the coming famine and remained unconcerned till it became severe.

(*ix*) *Defective Trade System*—The Commissioner, Mr. T.E. Ravenshaw did not interfere in the course of the trade when the grain dealers were consensus to earn good profit out of the trade at that time of scarcity. He had thorough idea about the food scarcity in the coming year but did not like to express his deep concern and to declare the apprehension of the famine.[66] He was of opinion that the stock of foodgrains in the hands of the grain dealers would be more than sufficient to meet the demands for 2 years and rice would be sold at higher rate in the bazar.[67] On getting the information from the Commissioner, the Board of Revenue and the Bengal Government remained confident on the food stock of the Orissa grain dealers and the Government did never try to procure foodgrains for the people during the early days of famine when the casualties were increasing.

The calamity came into light. The Government of Bengal and the Commissioner of Orissa Division did not feel it wise to interfere with the process of trade of the grain dealers. In

64. RCF, Vol. I, Part I, Pr. 61.
65. BRP, May, 1867, Minutes of the Governor General, April 20, 1867.
66. BRP, September, 1867, T.E. Ravenshaw, Commissioner, Cuttack to Board of Revenue, No. 523, July 29, 1867.
67. *Ibid*, November, 1865, T.E. Ravenshaw, Commissioner, Cuttack to Government of Bengal, No. 407, October 27, 1865; RCF, Vol. II, p. 24.

lieu of that the Board arranged for the declaration of retail prices of foodgrains that would afford purchasing capacity of the people at large. The officers became reluctant to make any departure from the principles relating to the distribution of foodgrains in the bazar even though many incidents of forcible entry of starving people into the shops of the grain dealers were reported to the Government.[68] Importation of foodgrains was requested by the Commissioner much lately and importation of rice to Orissa was immediately ordered by the Lt. Governor.[69]

(x) *Lack of any Agency*—The famine began but there was no agency to inform the outcoming of the impending danger to the Government. The distress appeared at first at Puri (Pooree) district but there was a very lamented delay in submitting the report to the Government.[70] The European settlers other than Government officials particularly the missionaries were busy in sending information to England.[71]

(xi) *Education*—Education was not properly handled by the Government. Orissa remained extremely backward in education. There was a general need of enlightened people who could throw light on the Government about the prospect of a famine and to call upon the Government for a remedy against it. Lack of public consciousness thus allowed the famine to come unnoticed with all its impacts to shatter the economy of the country.

Thus several unfortunate factors combined together to invite the great Orissa Famine and to disrupt the healthy economic life of the people of Orissa.

Course of the Famine

In order to study the gradual rise and fall of the famine, the entire period may be divided into 3 phases. The

68. RCF, Vol. I, Part I, Pr. 283.
69. *Ibid.*
70. *Ibid*, Pr. 235.
71. *Ibid*, prs. 19-20.

period when the approach of the famine was noticed but no attempt was made to assess its nature and to know the position of foodgrains to meet the demands of the people in the first instance continued from October 1865 to November 1865. The next prolonged period that spanned from November 1865 to May 1866 when Government expressed its deep concern other than importation of rice from other parts of India or outside India forced the province to enter into widespread disasters. The last period started from May 1866 when food was imported to avoid crisis and virtually put an end to the famine.

(*i*) *Approach* : In August 1865 rice was selling in the bazar at normal rates of 30 to 35 seers a rupee in Cuttack and 18 seers in Puri. The first alarm was felt from Puri in about the middle of October 1865. Till September 1865 the people were never alarmed over the cessation of rain but after which everyone became terribly afraid of the situation. That state of affairs continued till the middle of October. Consequent upon this a countrywide panic over the loss of agricultural products was felt. The rice trade came to a standstill. Villages refused to export rice to towns. On October 26, rice shops in the towns of Cuttack and Puri were closed.[72] Everywhere the inconvenience of food shortage was realised by the people. Symptoms of a famine was experienced by everyone but the Commissioner regarded it as a food scarcity of milder nature. The Commissioner Mr. T.E. Ravenshaw informed the Bengal Government that the grain dealers took it as an advantage combining themselves to earn greater profit due to the short supply of foods and that would be easily averted if there would be no Government interference on their trade.[73] The view of the Commissioner was accepted by the Bengal Government.[74]

72. BRP, November 1865, T.E. Ravenshaw, Commissioner, Cuttack to Government of Bengal, No. 407, October 27, 1865; RCF, Vol. II, p. 24.
73. *Ibid*, T.E. Ravenshaw, Commissioner, Cuttack to Government of Bengal, No. 7A, October 22, 1865; RCF, Vol. II, p. 22.
74. *Ibid*, Government of Bengal to Commissioner of Orissa, No. 5969, October 23, 1865.

On October 26, 1865 the scarcity of rice was experienced severely as rice was selling at 6 seers per rupee at Puri.[75] Ramakhya Chatterjee, Deputy Magistrate, Puri reported to Mr. G.N. Barlow about the acute scarcity of food in almost all the places of Puri including mufasil areas.[76] According to the report of Mr. Chatterjee the inhabitants of mufasil areas were mainly living on the fruits and roots of different kinds of trees. In many cases they had left their houses along with their children to mainly Cuttack in the hope of getting work under the Irrigation Department. People lived without food for days together. The Magistrate of Puri Mr. Barlow accounted for the deplorable conditions of the whole district of Puri particularly of the localities of Nubbah, Gope, Pipili and around the border of Chilka lake like Boosonpore (Bhusandapur), Malud and Parikud.[77] Mr. Barlow recommended for immediate importation of a ship load of rice to Sardeighat at Malud directly from Calcutta but this was not supported by the Commissioner who considered the relief work to the distressed persons as the bounden duty of the Zamindars.[78]

Musprat, the Collector, Balasore informed the Commissioner about the worst conditions of the cultivators and the Zamindars. He forwarded the application of Zamindars who had prayed for time concession for the payment of their rents due to the conditions prevailing all over Balasore.[79] The Commissioner of Orissa over the petition of the Zamindars (Pudholochan Mandal and others, October 25, 1865) recommended for the rejection on the ground that the improvidence of the raiyats should not be the consideration for any con-

75. *Ibid*, W.C. Lacy, S.P. to D.I.G., October 26, 1865.

76. RCF, Vol. II, p. 10, R. Chatterjee to G.N. Barlow, No. 68, October 25, 1865; BRP, November, 1865.

77. RCF, Vol. II, p. 14, G.N. Barlow to Commissioner, Orissa, November 8, 1865; BRP, November, 1865.

78. *Ibid*, p. 14; BRP, November, 1865, T.E. Ravenshaw to Government of Bengal, No. 280, November 14, 1865.

79. *Ibid*, p. 18; BRP, November 1865, Musprat, Collector of Balasore to Commissioner, Cuttack, No. 217, October 26, 1865.

cession in regard to the payment of rent in time.[80] Thus the Board of Revenue rejected the petition as inadmissible.

Prices of foodgrains in Balasore had gone up. The vessels of Vizagapatam and Madras were forced to return from the river mouths as they found no prospect of getting cargo full vessels as usual due to high price of foodgrains.[81] The rice was selling at 16 seers per rupee at that time.[82]

Cuttack district experienced the famine in the same degree. Rice was not available for consumption in the open market. On getting the news of the approach of the famine the grain dealers had closed their shops with the hope of getting good profit from the stock in their hands. The shops of the dealers were surrounded with half famished crowd clamouring for rice. At that time very small quantities could be obtained at price that varied from 6 seers to 8 seers per rupee.[83] The price of rice was exorbitantly high that put the wage earners into task to procure the required quantity of rice for consumption. Shops were resumed opening but could not sell rice when ransacked and a good deal of rice was carried off by the crowd without payment. Food scarcity became so acute that complaints from different quarters were hurled to the Commissioner Mr. T.E. Ravenshaw. Troops were not getting their share of ration regularly. The Judge complained that the *Vakils* of the Court were unable to fetch rice. All the *Amalahs* and *Vakils* (Lawyers) attached to the Court were not able to procure rice except 2 *Amalahs* who could get it through difficulties. When the Government officials failed to get their rice quotas including the cantonment officials the miseries of others could be well imagined. On November 11, W.J. Money, Collector, Cuttack reported that large portion of the crops had

80. BRP, November 1865, Commissioner of Orissa to Board of Revenue, No. 249, October 30, 1865.
81. RCF, Vol. II, p. 18, S.P., Balasore's Report, October 26, 1865.
82. BRP, November 1865, Musprat, Collector of Balasore to Commissioner, Cuttack, No. 217, October 26, 1865.
83. *Ibid*, T.E. Ravenshaw to Secretary, Government of Bengal, No. 407, October 27, 1865.

failed for which petitions for enquiry for remissions were pouring in.[84] In comparison to Puri and Balasore, Cuttack district escaped slightly from the danger till April 1866 as many people were afforded employment facilities under the Irrigation Company. The Company was giving rice to their labourers in part payment and the people seemed to have relieved from their miseries. That could not last long as the rice stock of the Company was exhausted due to heavy load of labourers on it and the relief afforded by them greatly diminished.[85]

The Board of Revenue on the proposition of the Zamindars and the recommendation of the Commissioner ordered for no remission of rents that had added fuel to the distress of Orissa.[86]

(*ii*) *Continuity* : In December a temporary halt on the continuity of the famine was felt when price of rice was gradually decreased due to the harvest of small crop. Towards the close of December rice was selling at 14 seers per rupee at Puri and 15 seers a rupee in Cuttack and Balasore against the sale price of 7 seers and 8 seers per rupee respectively. Acute distress in Puri was reported continuously by the Collector Mr. Barlow. Consequent upon this it was decided to import 250 bags of rice from Burmah by steamer.[87] Rice however could not reach Puri as the Steamer Company expressed their reluctance to take that small despatch to Puri. Distress in Puri thus was doubled. Barlow submitted a scheme of the construction of roads that would afford employment to the famine stricken people. The scheme included the prospect of payment of wages through food and the storage of foodgrains by

84. RCF, Vol. II, p. 27, W.J. Money, Collector, Cuttack to Commissioner, Cuttack, No. 201, November 11, 1865.
85. *Ibid*, Vol. I, Part I, Pr. 253.
86. *Ibid*, Vol. II, p. 43, Extract of the Paras 2 and 3 of Board's Letter No. 10A, January 10, 1866.
87. RCF, Vol. II, p. 51, Lt. Governor to Board of Revenue, November 25, 1865.

imports.[88] The Bengal Government allotted a fund of Rs. 69,000 for the construction of roads but however rejected the proposal of payment of wages in rice.[89]

At the grievous moment the Commissioner Mr. Ravenshaw left Cuttack for Tributary Mahals on a tour to assess the intensity of the famine in the hilly region. His absence for 2 months from November 20, 1865 to January 31, 1866 added problems for the Government to initiate new policies in respect of the famine.[90] On the other hand the communication between the Commissioner and the Government of Bengal remained paralysed.

In January 1866 the situation became injurious. Rice could not be procured in any quantity in Puri. Barlow requested the Executive Engineer for the purchase of rice for the labourers engaged in the Government work.[91] This suggestion was not affected as the matter of payment of wages in foodgrains could not be decided.

On return Mr. Ravenshaw informed the Board about the acute scarcity of rice in Puri and recommended for the importation of rice to Puri all at once but the Board on February 1, refused to import rice to Puri pressing the famine stricken people of Puri to live on charity.

The Lt. Governor Cecil Beadon arrived at Cuttack on an official visit along with the Secretary, Public Works Department and the Member Board of Revenue Mr. Cockburn in February to investigate the distress in Orissa.[92] At his grand

88. BRP, December, 1865, Barlow, Collector of Puri to Commissioner, Cuttack, November 29, 1865.
89. RCF, Vol. I, Part-I, Pr. 151, p. 46.
90. BRP, December, 1865, Ravenshaw to Secretary, Government of Bengal, No. 160, December 2, 1865; RCF, Vol. I, Part I, Pr. 154, p. 48.
91. BRP, February 1866, Barlow, Collector, Puri to Nolan, Executive Engineer, No. 324, January 15, 1866.
92. RCF, Vol. I, Part I, p. 55.

Darbar at Cuttack at Lalbag on February 17, Rajas of Tributary Mahals, 80 Zamindars and many officers attended with high hopes of getting concrete suggestions and advice to meet the challenge of famine. He left the province without having received from local officials or non-official public any clear impression about the extremity of the distress.[93] He in his statement in the *Darbar* openly said that the duty of relieving individual distress rested on the Zamindars and the Government had provided ample facilities to thousands absorbing them under the Irrigation Company and in the Public Roads.[94] On his return to Calcutta he in a personal interview with the Governor General explained that the circumstances in Orissa arising out of famine did never require importation of rice.[95] Under the above circumstances importation of rice to any part of Orissa was abandoned.

In April mortality and distress became very severe in Puri and Balasore and famine came into Cuttack.[96] Cholera broke out in Puri and Balasore causing many casualties.[97] The attention of the European Press and public began to pour in as the distress became more and more severe. The 'Englishman' in the editorial said "though we have more than half the year to pass through before we can procure any considerable addition to our present stock of staple food famine prices already prevail and are steadily increasing. It is a question whether we shall pay now to save the living or hereafter bury the dead".[98]

Orissa became completely empty of food by the end of May. Rice was not even procurable at 4½ seers per rupee in any part of the province. The troops and the officials were

93. *Hindu Patriot*, March 5, 1866.
94. RCF, Vol. I, Part I, p. 57.
95. BRP, May 1867, Government of India Despatch to Secretary of State, No. 71, April 22, 1867.
96. BRP, June 1866, T.E. Ravenshaw, Commissioner to Government of Bengal, May 18, 1866.
97. RCF, p. 151 and p. 179, Extract of D.S.P., Puri, February 27, 1866.
98. *The Englishman* (Editorial), April 28, 1866.

starving. The relief work organised by the parties and the missionaries remained standstill for want of food.[99]

On May 28, Mr. Ravenshaw telegraphically informed the Lt. Governor at Darjeeling about the alarming situation prevailing over Orissa.[100] Lt. Governor Cecil Beadon on receipt of the telegram ordered the Secretary in Calcutta to call on the Board of Revenue to send down rice immediately to False Point at Cuttack and Dhamara at Balasore through Aracon steamer or through any other steamer available.[101] On receipt of the order the Board promptly despatched the steamer Court Heg with the cargo of 3,000 bags of rice to False Point[102] This cargo was placed under the disposal of the Commissioner for sale at a cost price of Rs. 5 per maund to different. Government Departments. He was further authorised to sell the surplus if not required by the Government Departments in full, to Relief Committees and even to the general public provided that such sale would not disturb the Tacques Fourestier which was sent down on private account. Simultaneously 2,400 bags of rice were sent to Balasore in native sloops to be accompanied by steamer Namesis. For the above step it was said that the intensity of the famine was not realised fully by the Government.[103]

Relief Committees

District Relief Committees were formed and subscription raised for the relief of the distressed poor in all the districts, Cuttack, Balasore and Puri.[104] Relief Committees were constituted of respectable individuals and some Government officials to help the distressed poor and the orphans.

99. BRP, June 1866, T.E. Ravenshaw, Commissioner to Government of Bengal, Telegram, May 28, 1866.
100. *Ibid.*
101. RCF, Vol. I, p. 89.
102. RCF. Vol. I, Pr. 1, p. 183, Cuttack Narratives.
103. BRP, June 1866, Lt. Governor's Telegram to his Secretary at Calcutta, May 29, 1866.
104. RCF, Vol. I, Part I, Pr. 269, p. 85.

Puri—The distress in the town of Puri had reached such a pitch that it was no longer possible to leave it to the unorganised charity and mercy of the *Matha Mahantas*. W. Miller a Baptist missionary Bishop volunteered himself to the rescue of the poor and expended Rs. 5,000 which was placed under his disposal by Sykes and Co.[105] Relief house was opened in the town at which cooked food was supplied. Mr. Miller took the active charge of this. About 300 paupers were being fed daily. On receipt of a grant of Rs. 10,000 from the Government at the end of May the Committee appointed Lacy to superintend the mufasil relief operations on a salary of Rs. 100 and Rs. 50 as his travelling allowances.[106]

Balasore—Balasore at the end of January witnessed the gathering of the poor famished people. The Famine Committee resolved to invite subscriptions and to purchase a store of rice. From February 13 distribution of food began at the pilgrim rest house known as *Dharmasala.*[107] In March and April the number of starving people increased in the town. People were living on roots, herbs and leaves. People in large number were dying of Cholera. Relief operation became insufficient. The starving crowds were beyond control and the cry of the famine stricken people shouted louder and louder every day to which the Commissioner Mr. Ravenshaw was a witness. He was almost trampled underfoot by a starving mob on the roads of Balasore town. So uncontrollable was the attack of the paupers on the pots of the cooked foods that the Relief Committee was forced to distribute uncooked rice to the mass. About 5,000 pieces of cloths were distributed in May at the charity of Syamananda Dey.[108] Soon after learning the state of affairs in the district the Government of Bengal in the middle of May assigned Rs. 10,000 for the relief operation in Balasore from the balance

105. RCF, Pr. 2, p. 219.
106. *Ibid*, Pr. 4, p. 219.
107. RCF, Vol. II, Part II, p. 234.
108. RCF, Vol. I, Part II, Pr. 4, p. 234.

of North-Western Province Famine Relief Fund.[109] On May 26 the Superintending Engineer receiving the allotment of Rs. 60,000 for works reported to the Bengal Government Public Works Department that the allotment of funds became useless for Balasore as the labourers were leaving the works due to non-availability of rice to procure in exchange of money.[110] Importation of rice to Dhamara and False Point by the merchants virtually stopped. At this time importation of rice by land from Medinapur and Hidgelee was carefully considered to the North of Balasore but sufficient quantity of rice could not be procured to meet the demands of the district. The traders tried to import rice from Calcutta through the Hidgelee river and then to Balasore on pack bullocks but this could not continue beyond middle of June due to rain that made the unmetalled roads closed.[111]

Cuttack—Upto the end of May there opened no Government relief work in the district. The Irrigation Company afforded employment to a great number of distressed people but gradually the number of labourers decreased due to scarcity of food. Government of Bengal sanctioned Rs. 44,000 and the Superintending Engineer was asked to start the work on Cuttack-Ganjam road and Cuttack-Puri road.[112] On January 1866 the Commissioner requested the Board of Revenue for permission to provide foods to the labourers, which was denied by the Board. In consequence of this the Commissioner directed that the wages on relief work must be paid in cash but not in grain. Even if the officers realised the necessity of providing food to the labourers at this distress, they failed to help them as directed by the Board of Revenue.[113] Colonel

109. BRP, June 1866, Government of Bengal to Board of Revenue, No. 632T, May 21, 1866.
110. RCF, Vol. I, Pr. 8, p. 235, Narratives of Balasore.
111. *Ibid*, Vol. I, p. 236.
112. BRP, December 1866, J.E.T. Nicolls, Secretary, Works Department, Government of Bengal to Superintending Engineer, No.6062, December 19, 1866; RCF, Vol. II, p. 73.
113. BRP, February 1866, R.B. Chapman, Secretary, Board of Revenue to Commissioner, Orissa, No. 16A, January 26, 1866.

Rundall, Officer of the Irrigation Company strongly affirmed that the severity of the distress in Cuttack was very much present but the Commissioner and the Collector did not attach any importance to this situation. By the end of May the district went entirely bare of food and the relief operation till that day was never affected.

(*iii*) *Zenith and Decline*

It was towards the end of May when the intensity of the distress was at its height the Government expressed its concern over the issue and consequent upon this the Board in about the middle of June threw themselves into sincere work. But it was till September any sufficient quantity of food had reached the centres of demand.[114] The Government machinery remained callous and the district authorities maintained their silence as they thought the existing policy of dealing with the famine had been settled permanently. But the period gradually preferred the intensity of the famine to grow into its highest dimension. Mortality gradually increased. The centres of relief turned to be temporary homes of houseless crowds. The recipients of relief lived in a manner which must have been demoralising and debasing.[115] There was acute caste prejudice and many were compelled to remain away from the feeding centres due to this insuperable native feelings waiting for death. There can be no doubt that all these causes exercised a very deterrent effect.

Mortality

Mortality became highest in August as a result of heavy storm and rains. The people were exposed to cold and wet. Fearful number of men died during this period.[116] The flood in August that followed the rains washed away the nearing ripe crop and aggravated the misery of life of the people.[117] Disease

114. RCF, Vol. I, Pr. 317, p. 98.
115. *Ibid*, Pr. 311, p. 97.
116. BRP, September 1866, T.E. Ravenshaw to Board of Revenue, No. 604, August 30, 1866.
117. BRP, No. 37, Janaary 1867, Minutes of V.H. Schalch, Junior Member, Board of Revenue.

forced into the arena of distress. Cholera, Fever, Dysentery and Plague carried off the lives of many even though medical assistance was provided with the means at the disposal of the local officers.[118] Cholera became very much destructive in the towns of Puri and Balasore. Every morning about 12 to 15 persons were found dead lying on the streets of Puri. Accounts of death in Cholera from mufasil areas of Puri district continued to be grave day by day.[119] About 2,10,866 or 35.81 per cent of the total population died of different diseases in Puri district.[120] In Balasore the figure of death from June to October became 8,900 caused by Cholera in the town only.[121] Many fell into the water through sheer debility and were drowned. The loss of lives in Balasore increased rapidly. In Cuttack about 37 per cent of the total population died of starvation and different diseases.[122]

Role of Zamindars

The Government for mitigating this evil relied upon the landlords to fulfil their obligation rested on them. They were required to assist their people with charities but as the majority of the proprietors were non-resident Bengalis and the minority of them were the Oriyas, the reliance of the Government could not be proved fruitful. The rich Bengali proprietors thought it wise to contribute their share in the big cities but not in their own Zamindari. There were exceptions to this. Nine Zamindars in Cuttack, 3 in Puri and 15 in Balasore extended their liberal and charitable hands towards their raiyats.[123] Raja of Parikud

118. RCF, Vol. I, Pr. 72, p. 207.
119. RCF, Vol. II, p. 151, Extract of the Report of the D.S.P., Puri, February 27, 1866.
120. *Ibid*, Vol. I, p. 232.
121. *Ibid*, Pr. 95, p. 256.
122. *Ibid*, Raghunath Chaudhury, Examined at Puri by Famine Commission, Evidence No. 6, December 19, 1866.
123. BRP, September 1867, Secretary of State's Despatch, No. 99, July 25, 1867.

stood pre-eminent in the matter of charities also.[124] Among the Garhjat Rajas, Raja Bhagirathi Mahendra Bahadoor of Dhenkanal was fully engaged in extending charity not only to his own subjects but also to the famished crowd coming from the coastal areas.[125] In many interior areas where the Zamindars could not think of it as their bounden duty the death rate gradually increased.

Intensity of Famine

Intensity of the famine was well marked in almost all the places of Puri. Nubbah Sub-Division, Gope, Khurda, Tanghy, Malood and Parikud suffered severely in the famine.[126] In Cuttack, Kendrapara received major injury in the famine. Jagatsinghpur, Pattamundai, Jajpur and Salipur received slightly milder intensity of the famine.[127] In Balasore, Bhadrakh, and *Pargana* Bhera, Byung Ayar, Katnah, Dalgram and parts of Ancoorah experienced the miseries of the famine and the death caused by starvation was more.[128]

Even canibalism was reported to have occurred in many parts of Orissa. In July 1866 the story of canibalism was reported by the *Chaprasis* and *Burkundzas* to the Deputy Collector Doorjadhan Das Kendrapara. The story was that a Hindu of low caste had seized the corpse of the child which was floating on the river Gobaree, cooked and devoured it. Low caste Hindus also ate cows commonly sometimes raw.[129] As

124. *Ibid*, December 1865, G.N. Barlow's Telegram to Secretary, Board of Revenue, December 25, 1865.
125. RCF, Vol. I, Pr. 330, p. 101.
126. BRP, November 1865, Lacy, S.P., Puri to D.I.G., November 1, 1865.
127. RCF, Vol. I, Evidence No. 1 by Doorjadhan Das, Deputy Magistrate.
128. BRP, October 1866, Musprat, Collector of Balasore to Commissioner, No. 350A, October 11, 1866.
129. RCF, Vol. I, Evidence No. 1 by Doorjadhan Das, Deputy Magistrate.

per the statement of Nursingha Charan Das, Deputy Magistrate, Puri a man while going towards Puri was engaged in eating the arms of the corpse raw.[130] Men were mainly living on grass and various types of trees.

Relief Operation

Under these compelling circumstances the Government decided to import rice to Orissa towards the end of May 1866. The actual operation started in about the middle of June. An amount of Rs. 6,00,000 the balance of North-West Province Famine Fund was placed at the disposal of the Bengal Government. On June 25, 1866 an additional grant of Rs. 20,00,0C0 was also placed at their disposal for Orissa Famine.[131]

Importation of rice was found to be a difficult task due to the outburst of the monsoon. There were no good harbours in the coast line except False Point. The Light House and the port at False Point are situated in a isolated spot above 60 miles from Cuttack. The depth of water did not admit ships coming closer to Light House and thus the passage of 7 miles was to be linked with boats. Even if the ships brought rice to the port at False Point it was difficult to unload it. There was also the greatest difficulty in carrying the cargoes to the interior due to the defective communication. In these difficult situations the Government could have done something by spending lovishly on importation by engaging small steamers to carry the grains near the boats.[132] Hence the importation made by the Government till September 1866, was insufficient.

The rice so imported was sold to the public and distributed to the Relief Committees for the purpose of gratuitous relief. As per the resolution of the Government of India

130. *Ibid*, Evidence No. 5, Nursingha Charan Das, Deputy Magistrate; Examined, December 19, 1866.

131. BRP, August 1866, Extracts from the Proceedings of the Government of India, No. 2217, June 25, 1866.

132. RCF, Vol. I, Part I, Pr. 293.

importation of rice would continue so long as famine prices would continue to be higher. It was directed in that resolution that sufficient care should be taken to see that sales are made at such prices as may not discourage private traders to import foodgrains to the famine stricken areas.[133] Rice was sold at market prices. The first supply of rice that reached Orissa in June was greedily purchased by the hungry population at the rate of 5 seers per rupee. The British Indian Association urged upon the Government to sell rice in Orissa at a fixed rate of 10 seers per rupee.[134] The Relief Committee of Cuttack strongly protested against this price and suggested that the Government rice should be retailed to all coming for the purchase at a price not higher than 6 or 7 seers per rupee.[135] The Commissioner ruled out the proposal with the view that if Government rice would be retailed lower than market price the grain dealers would close down all the shops leaving the impossible task of procuring rice for the whole province.[136] The price continued to remain high till September 1866 and the rice was sold at a rate of 6 seers per rupee at that time.[137] A further supply of 3,69,000 maunds of rice was ordered by the Board after the flood of August 1866 but the consignment could not be made available for sale till November 1866 when it was of little use. The order of importing this additional quantity of grain was made on the basis of the recommendation of Schalch, Member Board of Revenue.[138] However rice was imported in large quantities but it was not sold at less than the market price. The total quantity of foodgrains imported to Orissa till the November 1866, amounted to 10,000 tons.[139] The rice was brought partly from Calcutta and partly from Burmah.

133. BRP, August 1866, Resolution of Government of India (Home Department), No. 2043, June 20, 1866.

134. *Ibid*, J.M. Tagore, Hony. Secretary, British Indian Association to Government of Bengal, June 28, 1866.

135. *Ibid*, Narrative No. 46.

136. *Ibid*.

137. *Utkal Dipika*, Part I, No. 5, September 19, 1866.

138. RIF, 1880, Vol. I, Part III, Pr. 43.

139. *Ibid*, Part I, Pr. 53.

The distress continued to exist till November and December. The Spring crop was good and after the harvest of the Spring crop the market price gradually declined so also the Government price. There appeared some scarcity again towards June 1867 and the Government did not reduce the price of rice during that period as a result of which Government rice could not be of much use when it was barely needed by the people.[140] The Autumn crop was unusually good. The rate naturally fell down and it became very difficult on the part of the Government to exhaust the whole stock in Orissa till 1869.

Public Works

Government resolved to adopt the principle of undertaking public works for the relief of the distress. Some were carried on by the Government through Public Works Department and some were managed by the Collectors as the managers of the Government estates. The workers engaged in different works were paid in cash but not in grain. The public works could not be useful for the distress as the Government declined to pay the workers through grains. The Irrigtion Company however was paying to their workers a part of the wages through imported grain and the other part in cash. As a result of which large number of workers were attracted towards the Company from different parts of Orissa. The average daily number of labourers employed upto the end of June as given by the officer of the Company is given below.[141]

January 1866	14,666
February	10,763
March	7,808
April	9,146
May	8,120
June	5,238

140. *Utkal Dipika*, Part II, No. 22, June 1, 1867.
141. RCF, Vol. I, Part II, Pr. 63, p. 204.

The decrease in number was mainly due to non-availability of grains to be paid as wages to the workers. The number again increased in January 1867 to 25,000. It had been estimated that the amount expended on public works became Rs. 3,00,000 in 1866 and Rs. 10,00,000 in 1867 besides the amount spent by the Irrigation Company.[142] The heavy amount expended in 1867 was mainly due to the availability of imported rice.

The detail account of the relief operation in 3 districts of Cuttack, Puri and Balasore from June 1866 to November 1866 on Government initiative throws a light about the Government initiation as shown in Appendix 'C'.

Feeding Centres (Annachhatra)

Relief Committees started collecting subscriptions. Cooked foods were distributed to the people coming near feeding centres. When rice began to be imported the number of feeding centres rapidly increased. In August and September there were 43 feeding centres in Cuttack, 23 in Puri and 22 in Balasore functioning to distribute food to the distressed persons.[143]

Light Labour Scheme

A great deal of cotton thread was distributed to weavers to earn their livelihood. A little quantity of cotton was also sold to them.[144] The charity could not afford them their subsistence as they could not stand with the imported goods. Arrangements were set on foot by the Relief Committees to

142. BRP, May 1867, Minutes of Cecil Beadon, Lt. Governor, April 3, 1867.

143. RCF, Vol. I, Part I, p. 94.

144. BRP, June 1867, Molony, Special Relief Commissioner to Shekleton, Secretary, Orissa Relief Fund Committee, No. 394, May 3, 1867.

supply cotton to women for spinning so as to provide them with occupation and earning in their homes and villages.[145]

Orphanage

Provisions were made for the care of orphans and deserted children by the Relief Committees. English and American ladies and Roman Catholics and Baptist missionaries, Mahammadan and Hindu gentlemen came forward with their charitable hands to extend help and to take care of the orphans and deserted children as the victims of famine.[146] The orphanage of Miss Crawford at Jaleswar, Philips at Santipore, Separt and Musprat at Balasore and many other missionary establishments at Cuttack, Puri and Pipili sprang up for relief operation. Money and food necessaries were provided by the Local Committees.[147] The number of orphans so deserted stood at 18,146 in the beginning but by the end of 1867 there remained a balance of 1,553 to be cared for by the Relief Committees. The Government undertook the burden of paying Rs. 3 a month for the maintenance of the orphan children upto the age of 17 for boys and 16 for girls. A total estimated amount of Rs. 25,00,000 was placed in Government security for this purpose. Marriage provisions for girls and incentive bonus for the boys after they reached the age was also fixed.[148] These provisions were declared 'judicious' by the Secretary of State.[149]

Emigration

Victims of the famine lastly adopted emigration as a part of relief to their misery. The people of this country were very

145. RCF, Vol. I, Part II, Pr. 19, p. 238.
146. *Ibid*, Pr. 86, p. 253.
147. *Ibid*, p. 283, Rules for Guidance of Local Committee, No. 6.
148. BRP, November 1867, Dampier, Secretary, Government of Bengal to Chairman of the Executive Committee of the Orissa Famine and Orphan Relief Fund, No. 4038, November 9, 1867.
149. BRP, April 1868, Secretary of State's Despatch, No. 25, February 15, 1868.

much homesick and were allergic to locomotion. But being hardpressed by the calamity they sought relief from places other than their own. The stream of migration of the famished people flooded towards Medinapur.[150] Due to the wretched condition of the people of salt tract in Orissa after the introduction of monopoly system of salt manufacture by the Government the migration of these people was encouraged to Khurda where they were provided with land and the means of cultivation.

Loans

Zamindars were encouraged for better cultivation. Interest free loans were advanced by the Government. If the *Tuccavee* loans would be detected to have been misused for other purposes the loanees were required to pay back the loan with interest within 6 months. So strictness was adhered to in the matter of promotion of agriculture. Raiyats were allowed to receive seeds free of cost who were found unable to procure seeds for cultivation. Remission of revenue *Kist* was granted in February 1867.[151]

Allowances

Employees were granted with extra allowances in view of the exorbitant price of rice from April to December 1867. The total amount of money expended in Orissa during the period of famine was about Rs. 1,45,00,000. In the famine the relief seems to have been less efficient and more costly. The Indian Famine Commission of 1880 rightly observed, "It is a melancholy reflection that while a large sum of money was spent in this Famine than had been spent before it should be associated with the memory of a greater mortality than had ever been recorded."[152]

150. Calcutta Review, Vol. XLIV, 1867, "Orissa Past and Present."

151. BRP, May 1867, Ravenshaw to Collectors, February 23, 1867.

152. RIF, Vol. I, Part II, Pr. 43.

Consequences

The great Orissa Famine became instrumental to expose the defects of the administrative system of Bengal Government. The ruling classes could get up from the sleep of self-complacency. The Famine Commission appointed by the English authority following the unprecedented catastrophe pointed out rightly that the administrative system suffered from great defect due to non-availability of correct information to shape their view on the famine. They were willingly avoiding to handle the situation quickly unless and until it became acute. After the famine the Bengal Government inaugurated a new lease of life by following an active system through direct action on the problem. The recommendations of the Famine Commission headed by George Campbell were welcomed by the Bengal Government. Following this irrigation facilities were amply provided for the well-being of the agriculturists of Orissa. Orissa was linked with Bengal through the construction of all weather road for wheeled traffic. Education was tuned in a new rythm. Schools and Colleges sprang up. Pupils of Orissa could get a new ray of life only after this great historic event. Orissa as a country was introduced to the British Crown and the public in England as well just after the famine. The modern system of administration was not the only outcome of the famine but Orissa could inhale the flavour of modernism only after the famine. The socio-economic life of the people of Orissa received a new vigour in every aspect. The recommendation of Cambell formed the foundation of a definite Famine Policy by which Orissa was not allowed to witness a famine of such an intensity even in the year 1896.

Famine of 1888-89

Temporary distress was felt in some parts of Orissa due to scarcity of foodgrains. It was in Khurda the distress was very much felt and relief work was undertaken at a cost of Rs. 1,02,836.[153] In the Government estate Banki there

153. GAROD, 1888-89, Pr. 49, p. 11.

prevailed a temporary scarcity in September and October. Relief work started on a moderate scale. An amount of Rs. 7,500 was expended to that effect.

In Balasore there was a temporary dlstress in Chandbali and Basudevpore caused by inundation in September. Employment through Public Works Department was provided as a measure to relieve the distressed persons.

Famine of 1896

All the rivers of Orissa rose after July 20, 1895 and reached the maximum level on July 24 and 25, 1895 laying practically the whole country under the flood water.[154]

The flood in the river Subarnarekha began on July 22 and reached its maximum level on July 24, 1895. The whole district of Balasore remained plunged in flood water. Subarnarekha river breached the Bhogarai embankment, the canal flood embankment, the Jamkuda embankment and the embankment No. 3 submerging the region from Bhogarai to Mirguda. The signs of high flood were visible when a number of shops and godowns under the foot of Panchpali embankment were found collapsed and the huts of the raiyats were completely found demolished by the inundation of the flood water. Eight villages in *Pargana* Bheloramchaur, 16 villages in *Pargana* Jaleswar, 35 villages in Nampochaur *Pargana* and 8 villages in *Pargana* Kamarda had lost nearly all the crops at the time of flood.[155] The second flood that appeared in August 1895 caused a great deal of damage sweeping away nearly the whole of the newly transplanted rice in Balasore district.

The district of Cuttack had suffered, from the floods of Mahanadi, Brahmani and Baitarani all of which rose simultaneously in the month of July. By the night of July 24

154. BRP, September 1896, R.C. Dutta, Commissioner of Cuttack to Government of Bengal, No. 17PT, September 21, 1896.

155. *Ibid.*

the water of rivers rose into maximum height placing a vast agricultural tract under water. The flood of river Mahanadi was within a few inches of that of 1892 which was the highest on record. While the floods of Brahmani and Baitarani were higher than ever known before. This flood virtually disrupted all communication with other parts of the country. Telegraphic communication was also disconnected by this flood. Kendrapara Sub-Division suffered most in this flood. The crop of this Sub-Division was destroyed to a considerable degree. The damages to crops as well as to the property of men were done in Jajpur Sub-Division. In the sadar Sub-Division the unprotected areas suffered terribly due to this heavy flood.

Puri district was totally submerged under the flood water of several branches of the river Mahanadi. When this district was subject to be humiliated by the flood water every year the flood of 1895 being an exception to usual floods caused great damage to the agriculture of the whole of the district.

Price of Rice

Due to damage of crops in almost all the tracts of Orissa, the price of common rice had gone up more than 20 per cent over the normal price. The price of rice commonly used by the people became exorbitantly high as per the statement given below in Cuttack district.[156]

The estimated outturn of rice varied from 6 to 9 annas in different districts. It was 6 annas in Balasore, 7 annas in Cuttack, 8 annas in Angul and 9 annas in Puri where the yielding was never more than 2 annas.

The state of affairs in certain places like Deogaon in

156. Selection of Papers (Famine), Pr. 2, p. 311, Commissioner of Cuttack to Government of Bengal, Revenue Department, No. 1 JT, November 5, 1896 (OSA).

	July	*October*	*November*
Cuttack	16 seers 2 Ch.	12 seers 8 Ch.	11 seers 3 Ch.
Kendrapara	17 seers 3 Ch.	12 seers	15 seers 2 Ch.
Jaipur	17 seers 9 Ch.	14 seers 7 Ch.	13 seers 2 Ch.

Cuttack and Malood in Puri became gloomy due to the scarcity of food.[157]

To meet the call of the distress, funds were raised for relief operation from different sources including the provincial committee. The statistical records of the funds collected and expended for relief operation are as follows [158]

	Funds raised locally	*From Provincial Committee*	*Others*	*Total*	*Expenditure*
	Rs. a. P.	*Rs. a. P.*	*Rs. a. P.*	*Rs. a. P.*	*Rs. a. P.*
Cuttack	6,535-4-3	19,000-0-0	424-7-8	25,959-11-11	15,295-12.10
Balasore	Nil	Nil	Nil	Nil	Nil
Puri	1,493-11-6	18,000-0-0	Nil	19,493-11-6	14,315-4-0

Famine Code

In the spirit of affording immediate relief to the distressed persons a Famine Code was framed and the modern policy of

157. *Ibid*, Vol. II, p. 207, Collector, Puri to Secretary, Government of Bengal, D.O. Leter, November 17, 1896 (OSA).
158. *Ibid*, Report on the Administration of Indian Famine Charitable Relief Fund in Bengal, Appendix VII (OSA).

Famine Relief Administration was determined. That policy was brought to a crucial test in the famine of 1896-97.[159] The Code envisaged the remedies through employment by engaging more work in the railway earth work, through advances by Government in accordance with the Agricultural Loans Act. 1884, through midical aid, through Agricultural Banks and through remission of rents during the years of distress.[160] In pursuance to the laws many people were engaged in the railway work that was in rapid progress and many were utilised in the District Board works.[161] The Railway Authorities afforded fair wages that had attracted thousands of steady labourers for the earth work for more than a year.

Budgets were being revised taking the famine into consideration with a view to afford more employment facilities to the famished people. The officers became extremely vigilant on the approach of a famine with their readiness to provide test relief in the areas of occurrence whenever needed. Administration was made always alert to face the challenge of the distress.

There was no importation of foodgrains to Orissa during the year 1896 but on the contrary a considerable increase of export was made in that year. Heavy stocks with the Zamindars, *Mahajans* and big cultivators helped the wage earners to a great extent during the period of scarcity. The classes that suffered most were those depending on fixed incomes, the small cultivators, the landless labourers and those who ordinarily depended on private charity. Prices of foodgrains due to heavy export became higher than in any year on record excepting that of the great Orissa Famine of 1866.[162]

159. RIF, 1901, Pr. 8, p. 2.

160. *Ibid.*

161. Selection of Papers (Famine), Vol. II, p. 207, Collector of Puri to Secretary, Government of Bengal, D.O. Letter, November 17, 1896 (OSA).

162. GAROD, 1896 97, Pr. 3, p. 1.

The intensity of the famine of 1896 could not be felt due to the alertness of the Government and the measures taken as enunciated in the Famine Code as a consequence to the enquiries by the Commission earlier. The teachings of the great Orissa Famine were used as the source of inspiration to the Government to mitigate the incoming of the intensity of the famine, 1896 saving Orissa from the economic hazards of the people.

The visit of famines at intervals virtually became stumbling blocks to the economic prosperity of the people of Orissa. Agriculture remained at the mercy of flood and famine.

The famines however helped the Government machinery to be energetic in extending their supporting hands to save the economically depressed people of Orissa. It taught the Government new lessons to draft a Famine Code, to gear up the administration for the need of the people, to keep vigilant eyes on the behaviour of the Zamindars with their raiyats and to project irrigation facilities for better agricultural output and to construct new embankments to save the country from frequent inundation. Thus the famines became lessons for future both for the Government and the people.

D. IRRIGATION

Pre-British Irrigation System

For the improvement of agriculture the Orissan peasants were acquainted with the use of artificial and temporary irrigation depending on the sources of river water, *Jheels*, *Nalas* and other water reservoirs before the construction of different canals following the years of Orissa Famine.

Artificial irrigation was carried on by the cultivators themselves. Large river waters through embankment sluices could be pushed into the fields. River water could be lifted through different means. Irrigation facilities could be procured from natural streams, tanks and wells. Of these, irrigation from natural sources was the most important comprising about 70 per cent of the whole irrigated lands. But in many cases the streams could not be used for irrigation work regularly as they were perennial. Thus the cultivators were left to the mercy of nature for timely rainfall. In the hilly regions the water flow of the spring coming out of the jungle clad was used for irrigation purposes by making small dams across the streams and leading the water to cultivated fields by means of small artificial canals but temporary, popularly known as *Pahanis.*

The 3 commonest contrivances for lifting water from a lower level to higher level were Tendas, Senas and Jantas.[163]

(*i*) *Tenda*—The Tenda consisted of 2 upright posts with a cross-bar across the posts that served as fulcrum on which a bamoo pole was used which was weighed on one end either by a mass stone or mass of mud and a rope being tied on the other end with an earthen pot or bucket to carry water from low to high level. The water then poured through the pipe which was generally the hollowed trunk of a palm tree.

(*ii*) *Sena*—Sena was used to raise water from a very few feet below the level of the field. A short of basket of split bamboo was used through a rope in either side which the user used to swing it backward and brought it down sharply into the water by the forward motion of the swing until the basket became full of water and then raised to the level of water channel when the contents were poured out.

(*iii*) *Janta*—The third popular method of lifting water from a short distance was through a scoop called Janta that was made of a piece of wood about 10 feet long hollowed out and shaped like one-half of a cone, the broad open end which was tied on the head of the water channel. The pointed closed end dipped deep into the channel could be worked by one

163. Malley, S.S.O., *Bihar and Orissa Gazetteer, Cuttack*, p. 165.

man directly or with the help of a bamboo crane. This Janta however could not pour much water from a distance than a few feet only.

Canal Project

As per the statement of Mr. Madhusudan Das (Utkal Gauraba Madhusudan Das) in the Bengal Council on April 4, 1896 the Government was more interested in the improvement of the agricultural condition of the country.[164] The great Orissa Famine enunciated the immediate execution of the Canal Project to afford irrigation facilities to the people of Orissa. In pursuance of the recommendations of the Famine Commission the Government of Bengal decided to accelerate the irrigation facilities through canals to protect the people of Orissa from twin evils of drought and inundation.[165]

Orissa was subject to economic humiliation as large tract of crop fields were laid frequently waste. Over this issue there were lot of correspondences in Government level to execute the Canal Project in Orissa. On the advice of Arthur Cotton the East India Irrigation Company was tempted to take up the work with a view to gaining much profit out of it like the irrigation work in the deltas of Godavari and Krishna. The Secretary of Madras Irrigation Company suggested the Board of Directors of the East India Company apprising them of the benefits of the construction of irrigable and navigable canals of Orissa.[166] By an Act of Parliament in 1861 the East India Irrigation Company and the Secretary of State executed a contract for the construction of works for irrigation, navigation and supply of water and other purposes in the districts confined to the delta of Mahanadi, Baitarani and Brahmni.[167] After

164. BRP, April 1896, Statement of Mr. Madhusudan Das, Member of the Bengal Council in the Council Meeting, April 4, 1896.

165. RCF, Vol. I, Part II, Pr 25.

166. BPP, No. 220, January 1861.

167. Orissa Project, Contract between the Secretary of State and the East India Irrigation Company, November 28, 1861 (OSA).

getting the work order the Company started its work. This was further accentuated by the historic famine that had pounced upon the Government to expedite the work duly recommended by the Famine Commission. This work was aimed at making a link between Calcutta and Puri.[168] This was partly completed in 1867-68. The Company however was not able to complete the work due to inadequate funds even though the Government advanced money for a time being during famine period to enable the Company to employ more labourers in order to provide relief to the famine stricken people of the distressed district.[169] Under these circumstances the Government of India represented the Secretary of State to take over the construction works of the canals in Orissa.[170] Consequent upon this the Government took over the responsibility in the beginning of 1869 for the completion of the canal project from the Company charge on a valuation of £ 990,050 s8d7 towards the cost of undertaking and £ 50,000 towards the compensation of the servants of the Company.[171] The Government management added some modifications to the original plan outlay. The work sanctioned thereon included Taladanda, Machhgan Canals for the irrigation of lands between Mahanadi and Kathajuri, the Kendrapara and Pattamundai canal for the irrigation of the area between Chitrotpala and Birupa and the 3 ranges of the High Level Canal for the irrigation of the strip of country at the foot of the hills from Cuttack to Bhadrak.[172] The canal projects that commenced from 1868-69 at an estimated cost of Rs. 3,25,15,885 including Rs. 2,94,089 for the loss of exchange was closed on March 31, 1895. Two estimates sanctioned by the Bengal Government amounted to Rs. 61,858 in 1893 and 1895. The total expenditure by the end of 1897 amounted to

168. Maddox Report, p. 22.
169. BRP, May 1866.
170. *Ibid*, August 1867, Government of India's Despatch, No. 114, July 16, 1867.
171. *Ibid*, October, 1870.
172. Maddox Report, p. 22.

Rs. 2,63,73,151.[173] There were 204-3/4 miles of canals which were navigable in addition to carrying water to the fields for irrigation, 75 miles of canals for irrigation purpose only. Besides there were distributaries of 109-3/4 miles to villages excluding village channels. The total area covered through the command of irrigation became 56,20,000 acres.[174]

(*i*) *Kendrapara Canal*—The Kendrapara Canal, the oldest canal in Orissa was opened for operation in the year 1869. Taking off from Birupa river at Jagatpur just above the anicut it skirts the northern bank of the Mahanadi and its tributary the Nun runs east to Marsaghai. The extension of the canal from Atabooah to tidal water at Marsaghai could not be completed by 1868. The agent reported that the work was pushed into execution rapidly and as such the entire length of the canal was opened for irrigation and navigation purposes in June 1869. That inaugurated water connection between Cuttack and the port at False Point giving a net income of Rs. 5,067 from duty on export and import in 1870-71.[175] This canal afforded facility for 60,000 acres of lands for irrigation.

(*ii*) *Pattamundai Canal*—The Pattamundai Canal was the branch of Kendrapara Canal. It branches off from the Kendrapara Canal just below the Birupa head work and skirts the southern bank of Birupa river and of the Brahmani river. By the of 1875-76 the earth work was only finished. The construction of this Canal was stopped by order of the authority. This Canal was meant for irrigation only.

(*iii*) *Taladanda Canal*—The Taladanda Canal starting from the right bank of Mahanadi river above the anicut at Jobra runs in the south-eastern direction upto Biribati where it gives off Machhgan Canal. The Taladanda Machhgan Canal afforded irrigation in 1870-71 for about 26,000 acres of lands

173. Maddox Report, p. 76.

174. *Ibid.*

175. RAB, 1870-71, p. 206.

only as the work could not be brought for completion.[176] The first range of this Canal was completed for 20 miles only.

(*iv*) *Machhgan Canal*—The Machhgan Canal gives a departure from Taladanda Canal only 7 miles south of Cuttack and runs along the north bank of Kathajuri river. It was originally intended to construct this canal as far as Machhgan so as to run into the tidal water of Devi river that could establish connection with the sea but this scheme was never carried out and could be brought for a small distance by the end of 1876.[177]

(*v*) *High Level Canal*—The High Level Canal was originally planned to provide a water connection for navigation between Cuttack and Calcutta. It was also aimed at irrigating the tracts through which it would pass. The progress of the canal could not be satisfactorily done and by the end of the year 1867-68 this was opened upto Nealpore, 26 miles from Cuttack where it touched the Grand Trunk Road. In 1871-72 about 20 miles of canal with distributaries for 40,00) acres were made useful for irrigation only.[178] Good progress was made for the completion of the whole project upto 1895 with modification in the original plan which was designed to connect this canal with Hoogly river across the districts of Medinapur at Ulbaria giving a total distance for navigation of 230 miles. Only 3 ranges were completed. Range I from Birupa to Brahmani river 33 miles long, Range II from Brahmni to Baitarani a distance of 12½ miles and Range III from Baitarani river to Bhadrakh. These 3 ranges of canal were brought for operation by the end of March 1881.[179]

(*vi*) *Jajpur Canal*—Starting from the head work from the bifurcation of the Baitarani and Bura the Jaipur Canal runs 6½ miles to the town of Jajpur giving protection to valuable rice growing-lands between Baitarani and Kharsua.

176. RAB, 1871-72, p. 250.
177. Revision Settlement. 1906, p. 15.
178. RAB, 1871-72, p. 250.
179. BRP, Nos. 30-32, March 1881.

(*vii*) *Gobari Canal*—The Gobari Canal is a branch of Kendrapara Canal from which it takes off at the 28th mile. It has a total length of 15 miles. Originally it was intended to be a distributary of the Kendrapara Canal but afterwards made navigable in order to facilitate communication between Cuttack and Chandabali. It gets its water supply from Pattamundai Canal and from the connecting link at Gondakia river and the Brahmani at Alba.

(*viii*) *Dudhei Branch Canal*—It was felt by the Superintending Engineer, Orissa circle that by the construction of the small project the whole tract between Brahmani and Kharsua rivers would be benefited. Accordingly an estimate of Rs. 85,000 was submitted by him. It received sanction and the construction work started immediately. After the completion of this work it afforded irrigation facility to about 12,000 acres between Brahmani and Kharsua. The length of this natural channel was 46½ miles. It was not meant for navigation and its water was little used for irrigation except in years of very bad rainfall.[180]

(*ix*) *Coast Canal*—The construction of Coast Canal was commenced in 1880 at an sanctioned amount of Rs. 44,74,941.[181] It was partially opened for traffic in 1885 and fully in 1887. It connected the river Hoogly at Goenkhali 45 miles from Calcutta with the Matai and Charbatia. It ran along the sea face at a distance varying from 2 to 10 miles from the coast.[182] Its length in Orissa was 92 miles. In the beginning it was anticipated that all the import and export trade of Orissa would pass through this Canal that would yield a net income of over Rs. 2,50,000 but due to the opening of the railway the anticipation remained in oblivion.

The canal project ensued a greater benefit to the people giving an income to the Government. The table will give a

180. Revision Settlement, 1906, p. 16.
181. RAB, 1895-96, p. 36.
182. Malley, S.S O., *Bihar and Orissa Gazetteer, Balasore*, pp. 105-106.

picture of the traffic in navigation, the cost of the articles navigated and the revenue realised from the traffic only in the year 1875-76.[183]

Name of the Canal	*Traffic Boats*		*Value of Cargos*		*Total Revenue*
	Govern-ment	*Private*	*Govern-ment*	*Private*	
			Rs.	*Rs.*	*Rs.*
High Level	220	1,806	14,775	3,57,733	3,390
Kendrapara	295	3,857	15,364	33,08,702	11,836
Taladanda	324	729	2,621	1,46,418	886
Total	839	6,392	32,760	38,12,853	16,112

Government was very much concerned on the low revenue from the irrigation and navigation through these 3 main canals. After much hue and cry the Government of India was of opinion to sanction extra funds for the construction of additional distributaries that would be effected in first instance. Every effort be made to induce the people to make the village channels at their own cost and effort. The Government further decided not to spend much on the construction of many distributaries unless direct promises would be made by the cultivators to use the canal water on lease for 5 years on contract.[184] The cultivators did pay no heed to it and exhibited no interest to utilise the water from canal as they were getting water from different sources during the normal period of rainfall. Owing to this fact the Government was not very keen in diverting much fund for the purpose.

The canals in progress of work however could be used for navigation purpose only. The statistical account of Col.

183. GAROD, 1875-76, p. 17.

184. ROC, File No. 111, 1881, p. 10, Government of Bengal to Commissioner of Orissa, No. 20541, July 21, 1879 (OSA).

Gulliver, the Chief Engineer, Public Works Department reveals the details of the canal project in Orissa and the results thereof as in Appendix 'D'.[185]

The total cost for work including all charges upto 1881 amounted to Rs. 2,53,18,197 or Rs. 122-8 annas per acre.[186]

3. Water Rates

The Orissa canals had never paid their charges, the water rate being only Rs. 1-8 annas per acre and the receipts for big navigation and irrigation barely covered the working charges and could not pay anything towards the interest. Thus it became natural that the responsible Government officers should be engaged to cast means to meet the deficit. Col. Gulliver proposed an increase of 8 annas of water rate in early 1874 for the protection of this canal project. Mr. A. Smith, Commissioner, Cuttack Division, referring to the suggestions of Baboo Jagamohan Ray, a Deputy Collector who was associated with the irrigation work suggested the Government of Bengal to increase the water rate upto the extent of 8 annas for favourably situated tracts.[187] A Bill was drafted in that light in 1877 and was introduced in Bengal Council. The Bill was designed to realise a compulsory cess from the occupants of land irrigable. Mr. Toynbee, I.C.S. was deputed to Orissa to investigate into the feasibility of imposing this overload on the cultivators of Orissa. In 1881 the Public Works Department's officers suggested for the enhancement of *Pahi* rent by Rs. 2-8 annas per acre in the ensuing settlement. The Government of India called on the Government of Bengal to impose an owners rate all atonce, when the enhancement of land

185. ROC, File No. 111, 1881, Pr. 2, p. 1, Col. Gulliver's Note, Details of canals now in Progress (OSA).

186. *Ibid,* Notes of the probable cost of the Orissa canals by the Lt. Governor of Bengal (OSA).

187. ROC, File No. 111, 1881, p. 10, A. Smith, Commissioner of Cuttack to Secretary, Government of Bengal, No. 326I, November 21, 1881 (OSA); BRP, December 1883.

revenue would not be affected till 1897.[188] From the examination of number of villages of both classes (within and without range of canals) it appeared that in the irrigable villages the rise in the 10 years ranged from 12 9 per cent to 17.8 per cent.

To encourage the general use of canal water in Orissa the Government wanted to fix a somewhat low rate. It had still been assumed that the demand for water would be so needed that the whole of the area irrigable by canals would be actually under irrigation within 10 years from the completion of the work. With much difficulties the rate could be raised from Rs. 1-8 annas 1-12 annas in 1903.

4. Impact of Rainfall

In Orissa the value of the canal irrigation was exceptionally depended on the character of the season the rainfall being ample. It was felt by the cultivators that the canal water was of no avail as a means of increasing productive capacity of the soil. Cultivators were in regular habit of accusing the Government of induction for the use of water on assurances of increased outturn which had not been fulfilled in fact. Making a comparison with the irrigation project in Madras Presidency it can be said that the Madras region did not exceed 40 inches while in Orissa it exceeded to 60 inches per annum on an average. The following table will give a picture of the rainfall in different places in Orissa.[189]

Average rainfall monthly and annual

Cuttack—Jan. 0.51″, Feb. 0.46″, Mar. 0.93″, Apr. 1.70″, May 2.30″, June 10″, July 12.15″, Aug. 10.43″, Sept. 9.49″, Oct. 6.31″, Nov. 0.93″, Dec. 0.47″-55.68″.

188. BRP, September 1883, Secretary, Government of India to Government of Bengal, No. 780R, August 13, 1883.

189. EIRF, p. 16.

Puri—Jan. 0.20", Feb. 1.19", Mar. 0.59", Apr. 1.33", May 2.45", June 7.85", July 9.48", Aug. 11.49", Sept. 9.16", Oct. 8.26", Nov. 1.78", Dec. 0.65"-54.38".

Balasore—Jan. 0.98", Feb. 1.21", Mar. 1.63", Apr. 2.70", May 4.26", June 10.45", July 11.55", Aug. 12.33', Sept. 12.68", Oct. 7.33", Nov. 0.68", Dec. 0.11"-66.01".

The land revenue system of Orissa also worked as a negation for the thirst of the cultivators for irrigation. While the tenants entertained fears for an enhancement of the land rent by the Zamindars, the Zamindars feared for an increase of land revenue by the Government at the coming settlement on account of irrigation facilities afforded by the Government.[190]

This being so the Government reached at a conclusion that as the people were not in a mood to utilise the canal water the Government could not yield a return on irrigation head more than Rs. 2 per acre. Yet it could afford a better result in future to the extent of Rs. 4 when cultivators would willingly pay such a rate availing of the benefit out of the irrigation project. There was definitely unlimited scope through which the country could be saved from famine when the irrigation project would be brought to completion. They would afford best possible protection to the agriculturists of Orissa from flood and inundation that had been causing disastrous impact on the material condition of the people. Keeping these things in view the Secretary of State unwillingly sanctioned funds for the completion of the entire system of the distributaries which were completed.[191]

The gross revenue from all sources from canals stood at Rs. 25,200 in 1875-76 and Rs. 46,466 in 1876-77.[192] Since then

190. RCC, Appendix 'G', K.G. Gupta, S.D.O., Kendrapara to Collector, Cuttack, No. 169, May 8, 1881.
191. RCC, Pr. 90.
192. RAB, 1876-77, p. 55.

it had a growing tendency upto 1897-98 when the gross revenue reached the maximum of Rs. 5,39,199.[193] After which it had a falling off due to the fact that the irrigation receipt from 1900-05 had decreased considerably by 100 per cent as the railways were opened for through communication.[194]

Results

A simple negative conclusion must not be drawn against the value of canals in Orissa. Though immediate financial benefit was very less yet the indirect benefit became enormous both for the Government and the people. It was an insurance against flood and drought through which an estimated amount of Rs. 13 lakhs was credited per annum.[195] Prior to 1866 the Government was allowing remission of revenue on an average of Rs. 89,000 (Rs. 27,000 in Puri and Rs. 62,000 in Cuttack) but since the year of famine there had been none practically due to the protective measures of irrigation through canal water which could provide incentive for the cultivators when they were actually in dire need of water during the years of unusual rainfall. The canal system was of great value to the Zamindars and the Government as well as they were provided with a better security against failure of crops of the tenants. The Government was relieved of a great burden of the future famine expenditure.[196] The Government could earn a considerable increase in the land revenue. The canal system in the long run benefited the Government to collect cesses or local funds which were made available for the wellbeing of the agricultural community. It thus relieved the Government of taking up the work which it would otherwise have undertaken.[197]

193. Inglish, W.A., *Narratives of Principal Events*, p. 55.
194. QAR, p. 37.
195. BRP (Revenue and Agriculture), January 1888, Buck, Secratary, Government of India to Government of Bengal, No. 492R-115-1, September 13, 1887.
196. RCC, Pr. 59.
197. RIC, Part I, Pr. 97.

5. Embankments

Embankments formed a part of the canal system in Orissa. The Government had no uniform and settled policy for embankments. In all the districts of Orissa some embankments were constructed since the time of Mahammadan and Maratha Governments and some were constructed by the British Government before the settlement. Some embankments made by the Zamindars were taken up by the Government for better maintenance.[198] Some of these embankments in the course of time were abandoned as they were not properly levelled. The Government thought them to be useless and wastage of lands. The annual budget after embankments was gradually lessened. Consequent upon the callousness of the Government the embankments fell into disrepair and waste. The Embankment Act of 1855 virtually failed to bring any system to regulate the embankments. Except a few major embankments the responsibility of the maintenance of these had not been defined.[199] Only after the great famine 1866-67 the question of maintaining the embankments attracted the attention of the Government. The Committee appointed the enquire into the matter of inundation and the remedy to it, came to the conclusion that the Government might safely spend Rs. 19,99,890 for Puri, Rs. 30,95,770 for Cuttack and Rs. 23,38,970 for Balasore for effective protection through embankments. It further called upon the Government and the Zamindars for the maintenance of the embankments.[200]

According to settlement records there was no specification as to who, whether the Zamindars or the Government would take care of the embankments. There was no legal obligation on either of them. For the evils of heavy flood causing damage to life and property, the Government decided to take care of the embankments by spending a part of the State exchequer

198. W.C. Taylor, Report on the Embankments, December 18, 1871.

199. BPP, July 1894.

200. BRP, October 1893, Macferson, Director of Land Records to Board of Revenue, October 6, 1893.

with the hope of the recovery of the amount from the Rajas of estates through which the embankments were stretched. After this the embankments were somehow repaired and strengthened without any scientific knowhow. The expenditure however proposed thereon by the Inundation Committee was not sanctioned as the Government was of opinion that the exchequer of the Indian Empire should not be expended after the embankments of Orissa.[201]

(*i*) *Flood and Canal Embankments*—After the high flood of 1872 a proposal was submitted to the Government on an estimated cost of Rs. 45,00,000 to construct an embankment on the Mahanadi.[202] The second proposal of 1882 to remodel the existing embankments on the rivers Kooakhai, Daya and branches of Mahanadi was placed before the Government but of no use. The Government turned down the proposals on the pretext of unpracticable financial resources. As a result of which, high floods in 1872, 1879, 1881, 1892, 1895, and in 1896 caused injury on the agriculture and life of Orissa.

The total length of the embankments on 1897 settlement was 969 miles. Again it was proposed to abandon 372 miles in that settlement and to maintain only 456 miles of embankments in an efficient condition leaving 141 miles unnoticed for.[203] The canal embankments covering a length of 293 miles 4678 ft. along the canals protected an area of 54,000 acres of lands from inundation.[204]

(*ii*) *Agricultural Embankments*—In addition to the canal embankments and flood embankments some amount had been spent on agricultural embankments following the years of Orissa Famine. The annual average expenditure on agricultural

201. BPP, October 1871, Rundall, Secretary, Government of India to Government of Bengal, No. 4671, September 9, 1871.

202. Malley, S.S.O., *Bihar and Orissa Gazetteer, Cuttack*, p. 100.

203. BRP, January 1894, Buckland, Secretary, Government of Bengal to Board of Revenue, No. 104, January 10, 1894.

204. BPP, December 1897.

embankments had been made as per the following table in Cuttack district alone.[205]

1803-1830	Rs. 17,308
1831-1845	Rs. 10,794
1846-1852	Rs. 13,700
1853-1859	Rs. 40,807
1860-1866	Rs. 59,242
1867-1876	Rs. 88,357
1877-1886	Rs. 48,813
1887-1896	Rs. 53,900

The average expenditure for the whole province on agricultural embankments from 1878-79 to 1897-98 was Rs. 1,04,600.[206] Even though there was no Government income from these embankments, these were necessary to ensure the agricultural fields against inundation and welded protection for the agricultural community.

The British Colonial Policy was a negation no doubt to the agricultural based economy of Orissa during the whole of 19th century. The colonial administration was very much negligent to the economic prosperity of the people of Orissa. The Government was busy enough to earn the fortune at the cost of the people of Orissa. The Government did not spend anything from the exchequer for the good of the people. There was stagnancy in the economy of Orissa.

The great famine of 1866-67 alarmed the Government for which, forgetting the old age traditional and defective administration, the Government switched over to a new method of

205. Maddox Report, Vol. I, p. 15.
206. *Ibid.*

administration providing all possible facilities to the people. As per the recommendation of the Famine Commission the Government on the direction of the Secretary of State took over the charge of the Orissa Canal Projects. Outdated and disrepaired embankments received due attention of the Government. Many canals, flood and agricultural embankments were constructed that afforded support to the agriculture. By 1905 the Government took sufficient initiative to protect major portion of this province against drought through irrigation and against flood and inundation.

The famine however taught good lessons to the Government that concerned them much to change the colonial monopolistic trade habits and establish a healthy and energetic administration. It was due to the intensity of the distress a Famine Code was drafted to act as a guideline to insure the life of the people against famine in Orissa.

The cultivators heaved a sigh of relief by the construction of canal system and the construction of embankments in Orissa that saved the crop fields from flood in inundation. But the frequent approach of famine in 19th century compelled the cultivators to remain always in a gloomy state of unstable economic life. In pursuance to the recommendation of the Famine Commission new ideas came with the Government that inaugurated a new lease of life in the matter of communication and inland trade through navigation.

The teachings of the famine thus restored the prosperity of the peasantry if not fully in a haphazard manner and became a source of inspiration for future for the Zamindars slightly and for the Government mainly. The Commission not only exposed the evils of the administration but also passed some censure on the conduct of the officers. The famine not only influenced the action of the officers dealing with subsequent famines but also prompted them to take greater drive in the material prosperity of the province hitherto sadly neglected. In that moment of great anxiety, the Secretary of State went beyond the recommendations of the Famine Commission in suggesting administrative reorganisation of the Government of Bengal. A new Board of Revenue was suggested by the Secretary of State for reconstitution to take better concentration of responsibility.[207] The famine thus inspired every one concerned with the prosperity of Orissa for future augmentation of the distress.

207. BRP, September 1867, Secretary of State's Despatch, No. 99, July 25, 1867.

3

Salt Revenue Policy and Administration

Pre-British System

In the Eastern Coast of India salt manufacturing industry flourished to a considerable degree. As an article of common necessity of daily life a good profit could be earned out of this trade. Before the coming of the Britishers to this country, during the Maratha period, salt was manufactured in plenty in *Aurangs* in Orissa coastal areas stretching over an area from Chilka lake to Subarnarekha river. It was a common practice in Orissa for the *Beparis* (merchants) to advance money to salt manufacturers known as *Malangis* before the commencement of the manufacture. The merchants used to purchase the salt when produced and take it to different places of business for sale. The amount of advance if could not be recovered out of the quantity they collected from the *Aurangs*, the balance amount the merchants used to collect from the *Malangis* in instalments. The Maratha Government collected only some duty from the merchants at the time of collection. The Maratha rulers did never try to establish monopoly on salt trade. Salt so manufactured in the coastal areas of Orissa was exported to Bengal, Berar, Sambalpur and other places as it was considered as the best variety of salt in Orissa Coast.[1]

The trade was extensive and the profit of the merchants was very high. It can be concluded from the example of Sambhu Bharati's business in Cuttack. Sambhu Bharati was a merchant of Cuttack who had *Kothis* (salt warehouses or golas) in different parts of Khurda Raja's territory. He stood as a surety before the Raja of Khurda for the payment of Raja's *Peshkash* to the Maratha Government throughout the Maratha period on the condition of being permitted to conduct his business smoothly free of any further duty. He was required to pay Rs. 10,000 to the Maratha ruler for that.[2]

The amount of salt exported to Berar was 3,00,000 of maunds per year.[3] The exact amount of export of salt to Bengal is not known. The East India Company was in regular practice of exporting Orissa Salt at the average rate of 68,269 maunds per year during the period of 10 years before the British conquest at the rate of *Sicca* Rs. 55-1-8 per 100 maunds[4] It is clear from a statement of Raja Ram Pandit, the Maratha Governor of Orissa that the annual income of Maratha Government from salt trade with Bengal amounted to Rs. 2,00,000.[5]

After the introduction of the monopoly on the manufacture of salt by the Britishers in Bengal they made every attempt to stop the smuggling of salt to Bengal, manufactured in the Maratha territory of Orissa. Long before the British conquest of Orissa in 1784 an order was passed and executed to the effect that no merchant except the Company would be

1. CPC, Vol. IX, No. 605.
2. BRP, No. 15, July 17, 1818, Ewer to Government of Bengal, May 13, 1818.
3. BJP(C), No. 26, September 5, 1805, Government of Bengal to Melville and Harcourt.
4. BRP (Salt and Opium), No. 3, December 26, 1817, Board of Trade to Government of Bengal.
5. CPC, Vol. VI, No. 1242.

allowed to import salt for sale at Calcutta.[6] By that the British Government wanted to exclude the merchants of Orissa in the salt trade. They further pressurised the Maratha Government to allow the British merchants to take control of salt trade in Orissa. The Maratha Governor of Orissa Raja Ram Pandit became annoyed as he thought that this system would inflict a great loss on the revenue. So he allowed the merchants of Orissa to sell salt at a cheap rate as the only alternative. The merchants were permitted to sell their salt in Bengal paying the duty of the Company.[7]

Raja Ram Pandit accepted the terms of an agreement issued by the Governor General in relation to the salt in Bengal. According to the new arrangement the merchants of Balasore only were allowed to the salt trade in Calcutta subject to the condition that the contractors would obtain an order from the British Commercial Resident of Balasore. Without the *Parwana* signed by him bearing the seal of the Company no merchant was allowed to import salt to Calcutta. However this arrangement did not function well and smuggling of salt continued. Raja Ram Pandit was again requested to extend his help in putting an end to this smuggling. In 1790 the Governor General Lord Cornwallis deputed Forster as his personal envoy to the Maratha Court at Nagpur for a negotiation and to obtain the exclusive right to purchase salt from Orissa. Raghuji Bhonsle did not agree with this proposal on the ground that this system would virtually ruin the material condition of the native merchants.[8] Thus the existing system continued till the Company monopoly in salt trade in Orissa was introduced.

During the Maratha period the duty of the Maratha Government on salt from the *Aurangs* of Chilka region only amounted to Rs. 4,500.[9] Salt was sold at a rate of 4½ maunds

6. CPC, Vol. VI, No. 1242.
7. *Ibid.*
8. CPC, Vol. IX, No. 605.
9. BRP, July 17, 1818, Ewer to Government of Bengal, May 13, 1818.

per Arcot rupee at the place of manufacture. Ewer wrote that the average sale price of salt was from 2½ to 3 *Kahans* of *Kauris* per maund in the mufasil area. Melville, the Commissioner, Cuttack said that the price of salt seldom exceeded 5 annas per maund during the whole Maratha period.[10]

A. EXTENSION OF BRITISH MONOPOLY SYSTEM

1. Monopoly from 1804-15

From the very beginning the British Government had temptation on the salt trade in Orissa due to its heavy profit. The British conquest of Orissa closely followed by the extension of salt monopoly into the whole of Orissa. A temporary regulalation was promulgated passed by the Governor General in Council for the management of Salt Department in the region between Subarnarekha river and Mahanadi river. This afforded the British Government the power of manufacturing salt. By this system the Government could yield public revenue.[11] After the introduction of this Salt Regulation, the officer-in-charge of salt and customs with his headquarters at Balasore was made the Salt Agent of Orissa. He was kept under the control of the Board of Trade, Salt and Opium Department at Fort William. He was responsible for the management of the manufacture of salt, the management of sale for local consumption and the export of surplus salt to Sulkia.[12]

The regulation restricted the exportation of salt from Orissa to Medinapur and other places by road. The export of salt by sea was also strictly prohibited except on Govenrment account. Any amount of salt attempted to be smuggled was

10. *Ibid.*
11. BJP(C). No. 26, September 5, 1805, Government of Bengal to Commissioner of Cuttack, May 4, 1804.
12. *Ibid*, Nos. 23-26, Government of Ben gal to Melville and Harcourt, May 4, 1804.

required to be confiscated alongwith the boat on which it was being carried.[13]

The Regulation declared explicitly that no exportation would be made from Orissa to Bengal until the inhabitants were provided with sufficient quantity of salt according to their requirement for consumption. It also provided facilities for merchants to carry on trade with Nagpur and other parts of India. The Zamindars, raiyats and merchants who were in possession of salt or who wanted to manufacture salt were allowed to sell the article at a rate of one rupee for 4 maunds of best variety in the Government *golas*.[14]

The Regulation included provisions for the supply of salt to merchants wishing to buy salt for consumption or resale, according to the provisions, were required to approach the *gumastas* in charge of *golas*. The *gumastas* were to grant a *charchitti* (delivery order) on payment of money which the merchant was to show to any *Jamadar* or peon in various *Chowkeys*, established under Salt Regulation as a valid passport for trade. This system was extended to salt merchants wishing to buy upto 20 maunds at the rate of one rupee per maund. Any merchant desirous of purchasing more than 20 maunds was required to apply to the Salt Agent at Balasore depositing the cost of salt at the same rate of one rupee per maund. The Salt Agent then issued 2 *Rawanas* to the merchants of which one to be delivered at one of the internal *Chowkeys* and the other to be delivered to the *Darogha* stationed in the mountain passes in the Western border of Orissa.[15]

According to the statement made by Harcourt and Melville, the British Commissioners in Orissa Government the provisions of the Regulation became a partial success. Robert

13. *Ibid*, Government of Bengal to Commissioner of Cuttack, May 4, 1804.
14. BJP(C), No. 26, September 5, 1805, Government of Bengal to Commissioner of Cuttack, May 4. 1804.
15. *Ibid*.

Ker, Collector, Cuttack stated that the net revenue as profit out of salt trade amounted to *Sicca* Rs. 1,04,894-13 annas against an advance of *Sicca* Rs. 43,000 to the manufacturers by the end of June 1805.[16] James King took over the charge of the Salt Department in 1806 and became the first Salt Agent in Orisea. He controlled the *Aurangs* numbering 11 in 1807 producing 2 types of salt.

(*i*) *Aurangs*—The salt enclosures were called *Aurangs*. The area of each *Aurang* was vast and generally was covered with tall coarse grass and scrub. The manufacture of salt was started in the month of December when the lands became dry after the rains. The *Malargis* cleared the ground, built reed-huts, furnaces, dug canals to carry the salt water from the sea in the beginning stage. John Beam described the method of preparation of salt in *Aurangs* in the words "Channels are dug from the sea to small reservoirs dug not in the sand but in the muddy soil beyond. Then a mound about 2 ft. high is made of earth and grass mixed. On the top is placed a large earthen vessel pierced with holes. A layer of grass and twig is placed in the vessel and on this again a thick layer of mud from the surrounding soil which is largely saturated with saline water from being constantly submerged by the sea. Water from the reservoir is then poured in till the vessel is full. This sea water filtering through the saline earth becomes more salt than it was before and the strong brine thus made is drawn off through a bamboo pipe into a second vessel close by is a rude dome shaped furnace consisting of a hole in the ground surmounted by a Cupola formed by fixing together with mud, a large number of egg-shaped jars with their mouths outwards. These are all filled to the brim with the brine. Then a fire is lighted inside and fed with the tall, dry grass which grows around till all the water in the jars had been boiled away. The crystals of salt are then scrapped out and piled on mats for transport to the *gola*."[17] This salt manufactured in a

16. BJP(C), No. 27. September 5, 1805, Commissioner of Cuttack to Government of Bengal, September 2, 1805.

17. Beam, John, *Memoirs of a Bengal Civilian*, p. 208.

cumbersome process was known as *panga* which was familiar in the Northern coastal region of Orissa. The other variety of salt was known as *karkatch* salt which was manufactured through an easy process of evaporation by sun rays. The persons engaged in the manufacture of salt were known as *Malangis.*

(*ii*) *Malangis*—On the introduction of salt monopoly in Orissa by the Company Government the *Malangis* were put to trouble. The *Malangis* were getting advances from the Zamindars before the British conquest. When they received advances directly from the Government, the Zamindars were deprived of their profit. They then wanted to exact more revenue from the *Malangis* as the rent of these lands used by the *Malangis* for the purpose of preparing *Aurangs.* They made unreasonable and oppressive demands on the *Malangis* who were engaged on the Government account. The exorbitant demands of the Zamindars exceeded the full value of the salt manufactured by the *Malangis.* The *Malangis* who were the real community to manufacture salt could not withstand the demands of the Zamindars and as a result of which the production of salt hampered to a considerable degree.

(*iii*) *Difficulties in Production*—James King reported to the Government about the problems he faced in the beginning stage. The *Malangis* became reluctant to manufacture salt at that rate of wage. The Zamindars became inimical to the Government. The first Salt Agent when failed miserably to get a good outturn, suggested to the Government some remedies against these problems. His first suggestion of the transfer of coastal regions from the Zamindars to the Salt Department did not receive active attention of the Government.[18] He thus continued to negotiate with the Zamindars. An agreement was arrtved at by which the Zamindars transferred their salt and fuel lands to the Government on payment of $1\frac{1}{2}$ annas per maund on the total salt manufactured within their estates. They further agreed to have no interference with the affairs of

18. CSA, Acc. No. 531, July 25, 1808.

Malangis. In addition to the amount the Government also agreed to give certain quantity of salt to the Zamindars as *khoraki* (diet) allowance. As regards the price the Government decided to rise the rate and in 1811 the *Malangis* were paid at the rate of Rs. 35 per 100 maunds.[19] Thus by 1811 the salt monopoly was firmly established in the northern part of Orissa between Subarnarekha and Mahanadi rivers. On the recommendation of the Salt Agent and the Board of Trade a new regulation was passed in 1814. The manufacture of salt on Government account was extended to southern part of Orissa. Salt Regulations of Bengal were enforced in full establishing the salt monopoly over the whole of Orissa.

2 Monopoly from 1815-28

The Salt Agent with his headquarters at Cuttack administered the salt monopoly from 1815 to 1823. The monopoly in salt manufacture resulted with the immediate rise of price of the acticle, which became the cause of the discontentment of the people. This discontentment caused the *Paika* rebellion of Khurda in 1817. Ewer was appointed as a special Commissioner to ascertain from the people about their distatisfaction. In his report he stated that the introduction of salt monopoly affected to a considerable degree the happiness and prosperity of the people of Of Orissa.[20] From the days of James King the price of salt increased. In 1814 the sale price was raised to Rs. 2 per maund throughout Orissa.

The merchants purchasing salt from *golas* at this rate were selling it at higher price adding the cost of transportation and their profits at a higher percentage. This abnormal rise of price prompted the people for rebellion. Over this issue the Government became concerned and wanted to know the real caure of the rebellion. Charles Beacher was asked to submit

19. BJP(C), No. 15, July 17, 1818, Ewer to Government of Bengal, May 13, 1818

20. *Ibid.*

his report about the salt price and its effect on the material conditions of the people. In his report he said that the average retail price of salt was 3 rupees 4 annas per maund. He submitted before the Board of Trade that the Government must not confirm this cause of rise of salt price with the rebellion. He argued that an Oriya was required to pay only 14 annas and 7 pies extra per year towards the total amount of consumption even if he consumed ½ *Chhatak* (one-sixteenth of a seer) of salt daily. He asserted that this price rise was not the cause of the rebllion. He did not consider the high price of salt with other articles of daily use. Making a comparative study of the price of salt in Orissa with Bengal he did not attribute this as the cause of rebellion.[21]

The second popular complaint against the Government salt monopoly was that the Government was selling salt only to the wholesale dealers, for which the people suffered much in procuring salt from the merchants even at a higher price. It was because the merchants were not supplied with large quantity of salt to meet the need of the people. Beacher in relation to this complaint said that an average of 1,51,035 maunds of salt was sold inside the province for public consumption during the last 3 years from 1814 to 1816.[22] This quantity was sufficient for the population of 5,37,013 at the rate of ½ *Chhatak* consumption for an individual. Richardson's Settlement Record revealed that in 1815 the population of Orissa was 14,62,500.[23] Thus it became clear that a large number of people did not get salt from the public sale *golas* of the Government. But according to Ewer's calculation the annual requirement of salt for the total population should be 3½ lakhs of maunds at the rate of 1½ *Chhatak* per day for an individual. This compelled Ewer to conclude his view that smuggling in salt was quite natural in spite of checks made by

21. Orissa Records, Vol. II, pp. 52-55, Beacher to Board of Trade, May 18, 1817.
22. *Ibid.*
23. BRP, No. 29, March 18, 1815, Richardson to Government of Bengal, December 20, 1814.

the Government.[24] William Tower, Collector, Cuttack agreed with the view of Ewer. He found the merchants collecting exorbitant price from the people when the supply was insufficient. This policy prevented the low class people from purchasing salt for daily consumption.[25]

Ewer in his report suggested some remedies. In the first place he suggested the reduction of sale price to a considerable amount. He proposed the sale price to be 1½ rupee per maund in the central *Aurangs* of Kanika and Kujanga and 1 rupee per maund as the rate near the place of manufacture, south of river Devi. For the people of Khurda he suggested the rate of 8 annas per maund. He thus suggested the graduated scale of price for the province which would fluctuate from Rs. 2 to 8 annas in different places.[26]

In 1818 the Government decided some changes in the monopoly of administration. Government appointed Robert Ker as the Commissioner with special power of general control over all Departments of the province with directives to pacify the peoples' emotion. Ker took active part in procuring more salt for supply. The uniform rate of Rs. 2-8 annas per maund was fixed as sale price throughout the province in 1818-19. As a result of which the quantity of sale of salt increased to 2,16,416 in 1818-19 against the quantity of 1½ lakhs of maunds in 1817-18.[27] Ker took effective measures in the process of smooth sale of salt. Previously salt was sold to the merchants with the limitation of 20 maunds from which merchants collected exorbitant rate from the consumers of interior places. Nine new goals were constructed at different interior parts of the province for better retail sale. Strict

24. BRP, No. 15, July 17, 1818, Ewer to Government of Bengal, May 13, 1818.
25. *Ibid*, No. 38, October 24, 1817, Tower to Board of Revenue, May 13, 1817.
26. *Ibid*, No. 15. July 17, 1818, Ewer to Government of Bengal, May 13, 1818.
27. BRP, No 25, May 19, 1820, Stirling to Blunt, February 29, 1820.

vigilance of the Commissioner refrained the merchants from charging more as the rate of sale was fixed throughout the country.[28] No merchant was ever allowed to violate the law. These measures thus improved the condition of salt monopoly administration.

In 1 19 Bengal Government reorganised the salt establishment. A new Board for the administration of sale was established, known as the Board of Customs, Salt and Opium. The Salt Agent and the Commissioner continued to remain as the controlling authority over the salt administration. Alongwith the creation of the new Board, a new regulation was also passed in 1819 in supersession to the regulation of 1814. The new regulation put much emphasis on smuggling of salt. It provided that all the native officers including the village police officers should help the salt officers in preventing smuggling and putting an end to the illicit manufacture of salt. It envisaged the punishment to the extent of dismissal to wilful negligent officers. The regulation made provisions of punishment to the merchants. According to this no salt was to be exported by land from the province to Medinapur. Salt so transported without *rawana* or *charchitti* was to be confiscated and the proprietor was to be subjected to a fine of Rs. 10 for every maund of salt. Likewise no salt was allowed to be exported from this country by sea except on Government account and any violation to this provision would lead to similar type of punishment.[29]

The *rawana* and *charchitti* system was maintained in the new regulation. The proprietors were asked to keep *rawana* or *charchitti* in their own possession carefully in order to show it before the public officers on demand. Further the merchants were required to maintain account of sale of salt daily.[30]

William Blunt succeeded Robert Ker as the Commissioner, Cuttack in 1820. He became anxious to regulate the system

28. *Ibid,*
29. ARG, Vol. IV, p. 84.
30. CSR, Acc. No. 531, Beacher to Stirling, August 31, 1820.

effectively, so that people would not be put into sufferings. In the meanwhile the quantity of salt manufactured in *Aurangs* increased amounting to 9,88,300 maunds 9 seers and 9 chhataks. This figure included both *karkatch* and *panga* salt.[31] Out of this huge quantity 2/3 was exported to the Government *golas* at Sulkia. In 1818 19 alone 6,13,753 maunds were exported to Sulkia for public sale.[32] The balance was sold in this province for consumption of the people in Mughalbandi and for transportation by land to Tributary Mahals. The Calcutta merchants became apprehensive of the fall of their trade due to the fact that salt would be smuggled to Bihar through Tributary States. Beacher, the Salt Agent denied the possibility of transportation as the quantity meant for Tributary Mahals could not exceed 47,840 maunds [33]

The rate of payment of wages to *Malangis* with a view to increasing production was raised from Rs. 35 to Rs. 40 per 100 maunds in 1820. Beacher further recommended the increase of Rs. 5 more per 100 maunds that would yield a total income of Rs. 19 per *Malangis* which would be sufficient for them.[34]

William Blunt thought of the abolition of *Chowkeys* as these *Chowkeys* were the objects of hardship to the people. Beacher argued against this proposal and was of opinion that there was no necessity to bring down the authority of the controlling officers by abolishing *Chowkeys.*[35]

In order to expedite the administration of salt monopoly the Governor General in Council decided to divide the Agency into 2 distinct divisions. By which the responsibility of one Salt Agent from such a vast region stretching from Subarnarekha to Chilka lake would be lessened. Accordingly the

31. *Ibid*, Beacher to Pakenham. Commissioner, Cuttack, December 28, 1820.
32. BRP, No. 25, May 19, 1820, Stirling to Blunt, February 29, 1820.
33. CSR, Acc. No 531, Beacher to Stirling, August 31, 1820.
34. *Ibid*, Beacher to Blunt, August 31, 1810.
35. *Ibid*.

Northern Division comprising of *Aurangs* from Subarnarekha to Dhamara and Southern Division with the *Aurangs* from river Dhamara to Chilka lake were established on October 1, 1823.[36]

(*i*) *Northern Division*—The Northern Division administration was held responsible over 8 *Aurangs* such as Bolang, Saratha, Dasmolang, Panchmolang, Ankura, Chudamani, Dhamara and Chardia.[37] This Division in the year 1823-24 after its inception made advances to the *Malangis* of these *Aurangs* for a quantity of 3,32,000 maunds of *panga* salt.[38] In return the Salt Agent was directed to invest more funds to get 4,26,000 maunds of *panga* salt in the year 1824-25.[39]

The *Malangis* in this Division were paid at the rate of Rs. 40 for 100 maunds. They were required to pay 15 maunds of extra towards the cost of revenue of the Zamindars and the loss of salt at the time of manufacture through evaporation.

Three sale *golas* were established at Balasore, Soro and Bhadrakh in 1823. These *golas* supplied the need of the people of this Division. The rate of sale in these *golas* was fixed at Rs. 2-3½ annas per maund and an extra of 3½ annas was collected as the cost of transportation from *Aurangs* to the golas. The estimate of salt was fixed at 1,20,000 maunds per year but in some years the real sale was much below the estimate.[40] In the year 1827 a new *gola* was established at Basta to facilitate the consumers. After the establishment of new *gola* the Government stopped the scale of salt at Rajghat *Chowkey* and directed the consumers and shopkeepers to go to

36. CSR, Acc. No. 575, Government of Bengal to Commissioner of Cuttack, July 24, 1823.
37. *Ibid*, Vol. XII, Beacher to Doyly, December 15, 1823.
38. BSR, Acc. No. 573, Salt Agent, Balasore to Commissioner, Cuttack, November 8, 1823.
39. *Ibid*, September 17, 1824.
40. *Ibid*, December 7, 1824.

Basta *gola* where the rate was fixed at Rs. 2-3½ annas per maund [41]

Quite a large quantity of salt was exported to Sulkia near Calcutta from this Division every year. In 1824-25 a quantity of 3,25,000 maunds was exported at the rate of Rs. 16 per 100 maunds of *panga* salt.[42]

At Sulkia the Balasore salt was sold to the merchants at a very high rate. It was sold in the year 1824 at the rate of Rs. 359 6-8 pies per 100 maunds which was raised to Rs. 411-8 annas in the year 1823.[43] Thus the salt monopoly yielded a heavy amount of Government revenue from the Northern Division.

(*ii*) *Southern Division*—The Southern Division possessed 16 *Aurangs* in total. Out of which 9 *Aurangs* were known as Cuttack *Aurangs*. They were Mundamolang, Satbhaya, Northern Kanpur, Southern Kanpur, Bardung, Northern Dhobye, Southern Dhobye, Northern Astarang and Southern Astarang. Other 7 *Aurangs* sorrounding Chilka lake were Budgergate, Malud, Parikud, Satpara, Panushpada, Haridas and Bhusandpur. Those *Aurangs* constituted the lake *Aurangs*.

The lake *Aurangs* produced only *kurkutch* salt at an average rate of 1,50,000 maunds per annum.[44] This *kurkutch* salt could not receive a good market in Calcutta due to its impurity. The Government considering the low price of the *kurkutch* salt in outside markets other than the markets inside the province, directed the Salt Agent of this Division to stop the manufacture of this variety of salt. However manufacture of *karkutch* salt was allowed according to the requirement for

41. *Ibid*, Acc. No. 582, Commissioner, Cuttack to Salt Agent, Balasore, May 11, 1827.
42. *Ibid*, Acc. No. 573, Salt Agent, Balasore to Commissioner, Cuttack, September 17, 1824.
43. *Ibid*, Acc. No. 575, Commissioner, Cuttack to Salt Agent, Balasore, April 21, 1825.
44. CSR, Acc. No. 76, Secretary to Commissioner, Cuttack to Salt Agent, Cuttack, May 12, 1825.

local consumption.[45] Consequent upon this restriction the demand of *panga* salt increased. Manufacture of *panga* salt in the lake *Aurangs* was introduced. As the general demand on *panga* salt increased, the pressure on the *Aurangs* other than the lake *Aurangs*, became heavy. The Cuttack *Aurangs* increased the capacity of manufacturer and about 4,32,000 maunds of *panga* salt were manufactured in the year 1826-27. The estimate for the year 1827-28 was raised to 4,68,000 maunds.[46]

The lake *Aurangs* were transferred from the control of the Salt Agent, Cuttack and were kept under the control of the Joint Magistrate, Khurda for administrative convenience. The *Chowkey* darogahs of Gulbye and Kalapadar and the *gola* darogahs of Puri, Pipili and Tangi were also directed to work under the Joint Magistrate, Khurda. All the papers relating to the lake *Aurangs* including accounts were transferred from the office of the Cuttack Salt Agent to the office of the Joint Magistrate, Khurda. A separate Salt Agency was thus about to be established.[47]

The discontinuance of the manufacture of *kurkutch* salt in the lake *Aurangs* put the *Malangis* into hardship as they had no other work to do to maintain their livelihood. Beacher, the Salt Agent, Cuttack suggested some alternative arrangements to engage these poor families in work. In the first place he suggested that the *kurkutch* salt should be supplied to 8 *golas* in Cuttack agency such as Deatola, Kypara, Pipili, Puri, Khurda, Tangi, Cuttack and Burrah. According to his calculation about 1,50,000 maunds of *kurkutch* salt could be sold for local consumption. This salt was to be sold at a low price of Rs. 1-4 annas per maund which would be much less than the price of the *panga* salt. By this arrangement the *Malangis* would be provided with employment and the *panga* salt would

45. *Ibid*, Acc. No. 78, Salt Agent, Cuttack to Commissioner, Cuttack, January 24, 1826.

46. *Ibid*, December 13, 1827.

47. CSR, Acc. No. 78, Salt Agent, Cuttack to Joint Magistrate, Khurda October 29, 1826.

be made available in large quantity for Bengal market that would fetch more profit for the Government.[48] The suggestion of Beacher to supply *kurkutch* salt to the Government sale *golas* was approved by the Government in 1825 and was soon implemented. To avoid dissatisfaction of the people due to this substitution of *kurkutch* salt for *panga* the Commissioner wanted the price of *kurkutch* salt to be fixed at 12 annas. Beacher argued that, since the cost price should be fixed at Re. 1 which would induce the people to *kurkutch* salt instead of *panga* salt. The rate was approved by the Government in the year 1825. The quantity of salt sold in the Southern Division increased to a great extent due to the low price of the *kurkutch* salt and the strict vigilance over smuggling in different *Chowkeys.* The following statement reveals the rapid increase of sale during 3 years.[49]

1823-24	1,78,183 maunds 33 seers 15 Chhataks
1824-25	2,26,571 maunds
1825-26	3,33,648 maunds

This Division exported huge quantity of *panga* salt mainly from Mundamolang, Hansuah and Metakua in Cuttack agency to Sulkia. Contractors were engaged in the exportation work by the help of boats. The boats were properly checked before they were allowed to load. Some amount of salt was exported from this agency through Dhamara of Balasore agency. The salt so exported were sold at Sulkia at the rate of Rs. 361 per 100 maunds and Rs. 462 per 100 maunds that fetched heavy profit as Government revenue.[50]

The Supreme Government for better arrangement decided to divide the Salt Department into 3 agencies instead of 2

48. *Ibid*, Acc. No. 441, Salt Agent, Cuttack to Commissioner, Cuttack, April 23, 1825.
49. CSR, Acc. No. 78, Salt Agent, Cuttack to Commissioner, Cuttack, October 20, 1826.
50. CSR, Acc. No. 72, Commissioner, Cuttack to Salt Agent, Cuttack, July 21, 1824.

agencies and according 3 agencies were created under 3 Salt Agents on October 23, 1828. These divisions were subsequently known as districts.

3. Monopoly from 1828-58

Orissa was divided into 3 salt agencies or districts, kept under the administration of Collectors of Balasore, Cuttack, and Puri. The activities in relation to salt administration were co-ordinated by the Commissioner at Cuttack who was further supervised by the Board of Custóms, Salt and Opium with its headquarters at Calcutta.

(*i*) *Balasore Agency*—Balasore Salt Agency which extended from river Subarnarekha to river Dhamara about 80 miles had 8 *Aurangs* in 1823. But in the year 1839 there existed 13 *Aurangs* in this Division. They were Ratai, Bolang, Sartha, Chhanua, North Dasmolang, South Dasmolang, Panchmolang, Ankura, North Chudamani, South Chudamani,North Dhamara, South Dhamara and Chardia. Out of this in 1840, 3 *Aurangs* namely Ratai, Bolang and Chardia were abolished as huge smuggling was detected from these *Aurangs*.[51] Subsequently these *Aurangs* reduced to 7, such as Sartha, Chhanua, Dasmolang, Panchmolang Ankura, Chudamani and Dhamara.[52] Due to increase in demand the Ratai Aurang was revived in the year 1854.[53]

(*ii*) *Cuttack Agency*—The Cuttack Agency with an area of 70 miles from river Dhamara to the river Debi consisted of 9 *Aurangs* in the year 1829. They were Mondamolang, Satbhaya. North Kanpur, South Kanpur, Bardung, Bakud,

51. BSR, Acc. No. 753, Salt Agent, Balasore to Commissioner, Cuttack, No. 109, September 22, 1854.
52. BSR, Acc. No. 718, Salt Agent, Balasore to Commissioner, Cuttack, September 19, 1849.
53. *Ibid*, Acc No. 753, Salt Agent, Balasore to Commissioner, Cuttack, No. 109, September 22, 1854.

North Dhobye, South Dhobye and Harishpur. The Government took a decision to abolish some *Aurangs* due to the fact that public sale decreased in Calcutta. In view of that Bardung and Bakud were united into one and named as Bakud *Aurang* and Northern Dhobye and Southern Dhobye were united and named as Southern Dhobye. Satbhaya was closed down. In the year 1852 the Bakud *Aurang* was abolished. By the close of the year 1854 there existed only 7 *Aurangs* in the Cuttack Agency.[54]

(*iii*) *Puri Agency*—There were 10 *Aurangs* in 1829 in Puri Agency out of which 7 *Aurangs* were in the shore of Chilka and was described as lake *Aurang*. By 1854 the number was reduced to 8 *Aurangs*. They were North Astarang, South Astarang, Basantpur, Haridas, Parikud, Malud, Gurubai and Satpara. Except North Astarang and South Astarang the rest 6 *Aurangs* were known as lake *Aurangs*.

In all agencies all *Aurangs* were divided into small units or Sub-Divisions known as *Bhowris*, *Bhowris* divided into *Chattis* and *Chattis* divided into *Choolhas* or fire places. Two types of salt *panga* and *kurkutch* were manufactured in all these agencies. *Kurkutch* salt manufacture was monopolised by the *Malangis* of lake *Aurangs*.

(*iv*) *Production*—The entire Orissa Salt Department was capable of manufacturing a huge quantity of salt of both varieties. The amount of production varied from year to year according to the demands both by the local consumers and the merchants of Calcutta market. Balasore Agency produced 3,99,436 maunds and 300 seers in 1836-37.[55] The average production rate of Balasore Agency from the year 1840-41 to 1845-46 was 4,94,940 maunds and it decreased to a great extent in subsequent years. From the years 1846-47 to 1851-52 the

54. CSR, Acc. No. 288, Salt Agent, Cuttack to Commissioner, Cuttack, No. 155, September 9 1854.

55. BSR, Acc. No. 649, Salt Agent, Balasore to Commissioner, Cuttack, No. 110, June 29, 1837.

average rate of production of Balasore Agency declined to an average of 3,29,810 maunds. It was due to the large importation of Liverpool salt to Bengal and the heavy stock of Orissa salt at Sulkia *gola*.[56] In Cuttack Agency the production was 5,27,165 maunds in the year 1827-28. Due to the transfer of *Aurang* Astarang in 1828-29 the production was limited to 3,00,000 maunds which was raised in 1830-31 to 4,00,000 of maunds.[57] Government thought of reducing the production further in the Orissa Agencies. When it was made clear that Orissa salt could be made available at Sulkia *gola* at a cheaper rate than the salt manufactured at 24-Pargana and Tamluk because of the low transportation cost of Orissa salt, the idea of reducing the production of Orissa salt was abandoned by the authorities. However the production capacity of the 3 agencies of Orissa was fixed at 13,00,000 maunds in 1840.[58]

The Board of Customs, Salt and Opium raised the estimate of production in 1841-42. It approved the allotment of the Commissioner of 11,60,000 maunds in all the 3 agencies. The Balasore Agency was required to produce 4,45,000 maunds, Cuttack Agency 4,00,000 maunds and Puri Agency 3,50,000, maunds according to the allotment. Beside the production of *panga* salt the Puri Agency was ordered to produce 3,00,000 maunds of *kurkutch* salt for local consumption.[59] The Board further instructed to raise the production of *kurkutch* beyond the approved quantity if it would not cost extra fund for manufucture by not paying advance to the *Malangis.* This limitation in production for some years continued since the public sale of Orissa salt declined due to the import of low priced Liverpool salt into Calcutta market. The production of

56. Selection Records, Bengal, 1853, No. XXX, Report of Henry Ricket on Balasore, 1853 (OSA).

57. CSR, Acc. No. 124, Salt Agent, Cuttack to Commissioner, Cuttack, No. 151, November 29, 1834.

58. CSR, Acc. No. 164, Commissioner, Cuttack to Salt Agent, Cuttack, No. 888, March 4, 1840.

59. *Ibid,* Acc. No. 170, BCSO to Commissioner, Cuttack, No. 990, September 19, 1842.

both *panga* and *kurkutch* salt in Orissa agencies became 16,88,564 maunds out of which Balasore produced 6,72,999 maunds, Cuttack produced 3,00,508 maunds and Puri produced 7,15,057 maunds against the estimate of 19,63,000 maunds in the year 1853-54.[60]

(*v*) *Malangis*—The Collectors as Salt Agents remained in charge of the salt agencies. But the *Aurang* darogahs were the immediate controlling officers of the worker of *Aurangs* who were known as *Malangis*. The *Aurang* darogahs were getting the salary of Rs. 40 to Rs. 70 per month according to the areas assigned to them. Under the darogahs there remained a number of *chooleas*. The Government executed contracts with the *chooleas* or contractors to supply a fixed quantity of salt. This contract was known as *taidads*. It varied from 30 maunds to 700 maunds. The *chooleas* employed a number of workers or *Malagis* who were engaged in the work of manufactured salt in *Aurangs*.[61] These *Malangis* were the real community who manufactured salt for the Government. *Chooleas* usually paid advance to the *Malangis* in 2 instalments, first before the beginning of the manufacturing season and the second in the middle of the manufacturing season. In the end of the season the accounts of the *Malangis* were finally settled. They were paid at the rate of Rs. 50 per 115 maunds. They were also allowed to take 2 pots of salt monthly for their own use which amounted to 2 maunds per *Malangi* in a season.[62]

During the time of natural calamities the Government came to the rescue of the *Malangis*. In the year 1831 severe cyclone passed over Balasore and Cuttack. About 1,889 souls drowned in Balasore Agency of which 28 were the servants of the agency and the rest were the *Malangis*. Many *Malangis* also lost their lives in Cuttack Agency. Government took immediate step to help the *Malangis* in that year. Money was

60. Report on Salt in British India, Part III, No. 3, 1856, Bengal, Appendix 'C'.
61. *Ibid.*
62. BSR, Acc. No. 753, Salt Agent, Balasore to Commissioner, Cuttack, No. 109, September 22, 1854.

distributed and rice was provided to the *Malangis* by the *Aurang* darogahs at a very cheap rate.[63] Government was paying also additional amount to the *Malangis* over the fixed rate at the time of any natural calamities. *Malangis* were paid extra during the period of distress caused by continuous unfavourable weather and loss of crops. The attitude of the Government in many ways induced the *Malangis* to come forward for hard work to produce more salt.

The rate of payment to the *Malangis* was fixed to Rs. 52-1-4 per 100 maunds in the year 1836. The *Malangis* were deprived of their *khoraki* salt from that year which also made their condition worse. In 1838 the Government further decided to reduce the rate of payment of the *Malangis* to 5 annas per maund of salt. This reduction of price put the community into a wretched condition. The *Malangis* appealed to the Secretary, Salt Board to pay them the old rate of 8 annas per maund by which they could survive.[64] The Commissoner considered the appeal and recommended for the increase of 1 anna per maund. The Government after careful consideration realised the pitiable condition of the *Malangis* and sanctioned the rate of *panga* salt at 8 annas per maund in the lake *Aurang* and 6 annas in other *Aurangs* of Orissa. The rate of payment of *kurkutch* salt was reduced from 2½ annas to 2 annas per maund. The rate of *panga* was again reduced to 5 annas by the Government in the year 1845-46. Again in the year 1853-54 when the demand increased the Government decided to pay 3 annas more on the usual rate of 5 annas on the extra quantity of salt to encourage the *Malangis*.[65] The extreme poverty of the *Malangis* could not be saved. The Government in the year 1855-56 decided to give some extra benefit to the *Malangis* by giving them 2 seers of salt per month

63. CSR, Acc. No. 447, Salt Agent, Cuttack to Commissioner, Cuttack, No. 16, February 9, 1832.
64. *Ibid*, Acc. No. 170, Petition of *Malangis* to the Secretary, BCSO, October 25, 1842.
65. BSR, Acc. No. 772, Commissioner, Cuttack to Salt Agent, Balasore, No. 95, September 25, 1855.

as *khoraki* salt. But the Salt Agents were not in favour of the continuance of *khoraki* system. The Commissioner gave his positive opinion for the abolition of *khoraki* salt distribution on the ground of its maladjustment by the darogahs and its illegal sale by the *Malangis*.

The Government was deeply concerned about the economic prosperity of their own ignoring the conditions of the *Malangis*.

(*vi*) *Sale procedure inside Orissa*—The Government made provisions to supply salt to the people at a low price than what it was in Calcutta market. The Government also decided to sell salt to the people duty free. As huge quantities of salt were manufactured in the regions of Orissa it was not desirable to extract much money from the people from salt. To facilitate the sale, sale *golas* were established in different places so that people could reach the *golas* to take the required quantities for consumption without paying any transportation cost. Salt was sold to individuals in the sale *golas* upto 20 maunds under *charchitti* or retail permit and beyond 20 maunds under the *rawana* system or wholesale permit. The *rawana* system was applicable to the sale of salt to the Tributary States. Besides this, individuals were allowed to procure their salt requirements from *chowkeys* or preventive posts. This was made to afford convenience to the villagers who were residing near the *Aurangs*. The limit of such purchase was fixed at 5 seers only.[66]

In Balasore 4 *golas* were established at Basta, Balasore, Sore and Bhadrak. There were 20 *chowkeys* also where salt was retailed to people. *Panga* salt was sold in these *golas* and *chowkeys* except 2 *chowkeys*. A uniform rate of Rs. 2-5 annas per maund was fixed. The people of 2 *chowkeys*, Rajghat and Begunia were retailed at the rate of Rs. 3-2 annas from Jaleswar *gola* under Hijlee Agency in Bengal. In 1854 the sale

66. Report on Salt in British India, Part III, No. 6, Bengal, Appendix 'C'.

of salt was made at the uniform rate of Rs. 2-2 annas per maund in 15 *chowkeys* of Balasore when 5 *chowkeys* were abolished. In 1855 Government on recommendation of the Board of Revenue abolished the sale *golas* of Sore and Basta.[67]

In Cuttack Agency both *panga* and *kurkutch* salt was sold to the people. Four retail *golas* were selling salt at Kayapara, Diahtol, Burra and Cuttack. The retail price of *panga* salt in these *golas* was Rs. 2 and a few annas and the retail price of *kurkutch* was Re. 1 and few annas. Mainly *kurkutch* salt was supplied to Cuttack Agency procured from the lake *Aurang*. Due to the introduction of *kurkutch* salt in the whole of this agency the Government was getting a heavy loss which they were getting from the sale proceeds of *panga* salt. The Salt Agent for this loss suggested for the rise of price of *kurkutch* salt to Re. 1-12 annas and that of *panga* salt to Rs. 2.[68] Government accepted the proposal in 1830.[69] The Salt Agent, Cuttack further suggested to the Government to establish a retail *gola* at Sambalpur where *panga* salt was being sold at the rate of Rs. 3-12 annas to make good the loss of the Government. Government, however, rejected the idea of establishing a salt *gola* at Sambalpur. Instead of that the Government thought of supplying superior variety of *kurkutch* salt or *abra* salt to that region to stop the sale of Ganjam salt in that region. The Government directed the Salt Agent, Puri to prod uce *ab* salt in plenty and to establish a *gola* either at Tangi or at Banpur to supply *abra* salt to the region between Cuttack and Bihar. *Abra* salt was to be sold in that *gola* not less than 5 maunds at the rate of Re. 1-4 annas per maund with *rawana*. The same rate was also applicable to the quantity not less than 5 maunds for local consumption. For the export to Tributary

67. BSR, Acc. No. 769, Secretary, Board of Revenue to Commissioner, Cuttack, No. 193, February 10, 1855.

68. CSR, Acc. No. 447, Salt Agent, Cuttack to Commissioner, Cuttack, March 26, 1830.

69. *Ibid*, May 13, 1830.

Mahals except Mayurbhanj and Nilgiri this rate was also fixed excluding the cost of transportation.[70]

In 1830 the Government made arrangements with the Rajas of Tributary Mahals for increasing the retail sale of salt in their territories and to stop the sale of smuggled salt. It was decided that the Tributary Mahals would receive their required quantity of salt from the nearest agency salt *golas*. The Rajas were asked to indent their requirements in the beginning of the year. They would be supplied at the same rate.[71] But within a few years this arrangement failed.

He 1849 the Salt Agent, Cuttack suggested to the Commissioner, Cuttack to adopt a new system of *chowkeys*' management. He referred to the system of Bengal salt trade and insisted on the Government to follow the same practice in Orissa keeping a huge storage in hand to maintain a quick supply to the *golas*. Accordingly it was decided that supply should be made to the places beyond the manufacturing regions with strict vigilance by preventing force. Sale *golas* of Cuttack were reduced from 4 to 2 at Kayapara and Cuttack. In these 2 *golas* only *panga* salt was to be sold to retailers at a fixed rate of Re. 1-8 annas per maund. This arrangement came into force from October 1, 1850.[72] The total quantity sold in this agency in 1850 amounted to 2,79,712 maunds.[73]

There maintained only 2 central depots at Puri and Tangi in the whole of Puri Agency. *Panga* salt was retailed at the rate of Re. 1-14 annas and *kurkutch* salt was sold at the rate of Re. 1 8 annas in both the *golas*. For the manufacturing areas there were 11 shops where *panga* was sold at the rate of Re. 1-8 annas per maund and *kurkutch* was sold at the rate

70. CSR, Acc. No. 105, Secretary, Government of Bengal to BCSO, December 20, 1831.
71. *Ibid*.
72. CSR, Acc. No. 260, Salt Agent, Cuttack to Commissioner, Cuttack, February 1, 1851.
74. *Ibid*, Acc. No. 288, November 3, 1853.

of Re. 1 per maund.[74] The total sale in Puri Agency in the year 1853-54 was 2,51,222 maunds only for local consumption. The increase was due to the restriction in import on Government account to Cuttack Agency.[75]

The darogahs in bigger sale *golas* in all 3 agencies were paid a fixed salary of Rs. 50 per month in the year 1853-54.[76]

(vii) Chowkeys—The salt monopoly system in Orissa required a well organised preventive system to check the illegal manufacture of salt and to check the smuggling of Orissa salt into Tributary Mahals and to Bengal where salt was being sold in high price. In view of this the Government established a number of preventive posts known as *chowkeys* in different parts of the country. The officers appointed to be in charge of the *chowkeys* were entrusted with the task of checking the illicit manufacture of salt in the areas to which they were assigned and to prevent the illegal trade in the areas under their control.[77] The Government established a large number of *chowkeys* in Balasore Agency. The *Aurangs* were not far away from the Tributary Mahals where the British Regulation was not in operation. Balasore Agency was situated on the border of Bengal where salt was sold in a very high rate that had been instigating the merchants to carry on illicit trade with Bengal. In order to check this type of smuggling in the border 5 *chowkeys* were established. They were known as Frontier *Chowkeys*. The other *chowkeys* were established in the whole manufacturing tract stretching from the river Subarnarekha to river Dhamara at a distance of 5 miles to 15 miles.[78] This arrangement became gradually ineffective. As a result of which illicit manufacture continued to grow. As a remedy to

74. Report on Salt in British India, Vol. XXVI, Part III, No. 6, 1856, Bengal, Appendix 'C'.
75. *Ibid.*
76. *Ibid.*
77. *Ibid.*
78. BSR, Acc. No. 753, Salt Agent, Balasore to Commissioner, Cuttack. No. 109, September 22, 1854.

this the Salt Agent, Balasore, Henery Ricket, submitted a proposal to the Government to appoint a Jamadar with 10 peons to assist the Jamadar near every *Aurang*. Their main duty was to check the illicit manufacture of salt in the *Aurangs*. This proposal was approved by the Government. Jamadars were also paid extra amount as reward when they seized such type of illicit salt at the rate of Rs. 2 per maund. This new system became effective. To make it more effective the Government reorganised the preventive system. In 1848 the peons were engaged for patrolling around the *Aurangs* by which smuggling was checked to a great extent. The peons, Jamadars were allotted duties by the *Aurang* darogahs. Except the 5 Frontier Agencies where more men were appointed, in other *chowkeys* there were one Jamadar, one Muharir and 10 peons. The Jamadar was getting a salary of Rs. 12, the Muharir Rs. 10 and each peon was getting a salary of Rs. 4 only.[79] This system came into force from 1849. It was reported by the Salt Agent, Balasore that the Jamadars were taking bribes from the illicit manufacturers. So he suggested the Government to appoint an European Inspector in *chowkeys* who should supervise the preventive posts or *chowkeys* frequently to check smuggling as well as to check illicit manufacture of salt. His suggestion was finally accepted and in August 1854 an officer was appointed to supervise the work of the subordinate officers of the *chowkeys*. He was to work under the Salt Agent.[80]

In Cuttack and in Puri Agencies there were less *chowkeys*. In Cuttack there were 6 *chowkeys* and in Puri there were 7 *chowkeys*. The cost of the establishment in Cuttack was Rs. 709 and in Puri it was Rs. 790 per month [81]

(*viii*) *Export and Profit—Panga* salt became the main article of export to Bengal that yielded a heavy profit to the

79. BSR, Acc. No. 695, Salt Agent, Balasore to Commissioner, Cuttack, No. 13, June 20, 1849.
80. *Ibid*, Acc. No. 753, Salt Agent, Balasore to Commissioner, Cuttack, No. 46, May 19, 1854.
81. Patra, K.M., *Orissa under East India Company* p. 172.

British Government. The amount of salt exported to Sulkia *gola*—in Bengal varied from year to year according to the requirement of Calcutta market. The quantity of salt available for export to Sulkia in the year 1853-54 was more than 12,00,000 of maunds from all the 3 agencies.[82] According to the statement of Stirling the revenue derived from the salt monopoly in Orissa exceeded the net land revenue. The net revenue the Government derived from the salt monopoly in Orissa amounted to about Rs. 18,00,000 per year[83] The net revenue the Government derived both from the local sale in the province and from the sale at Sulkia came to more than Rs. 39,00,000 annually towards the end of 1858.[84]

B. ABOLITION OF SALT MONOPOLY

The people of Orissa did not know the use of any other salt than the salt manufactured in Orissa. They regarded the foreign salt as impure. During the year 1860-61 the Liverpool salt displaced the local salt. The long prejudice vanished. The Liverpool salt could be sold freely at a very low price. The consumers gradually tempted to purchase the low priced salt. The price of Liverpool salt was only Rs. 65 per 100 maunds whereas the local salt was sold at Rs. 83 per 100 maunds.[85] The local salt thus could not withstand in the competition.

Under the monopoly system the Government was only concerned about the profit but not about the prosperity of the manufacturing community or *Malangis*. The salt monopoly put the people of Orissa to a great disadvantage. In 1854 Plowden, the Commissioner, appointed by the Government of India to enquire and to report about the manufacture and sale of salt in

82. Report on Salt in British India, Vol. XXVI, Part III, No. 6, 1856, Bengal, Appendix 'C'.
83. Stirling, A, *An Account of Orissa Proper or Cuttack*, p. 37.
84. Patra, K.M., *Orissa under East India Company*, p. 175.
85. A Earle, Commissioner, Excise, Salt of Bengal to Secretary, Board of Revenue, No. 1586, November 15, 1901 (OSA).

British India accused the monopoly system. He suggested to the Government for the introduction of the excise system.[86]

The suggestion was placed before the Lt. Governor, Sir Cecil Beadon of Bengal. He was convinced about the abolition of the salt monopoly but he was of opinion that immediate abolition would create a lot of discomfort in the minds of *Malangis* and as such it would be wise to stop work. After careful consideration in March 1863, Sir Cecil announced "the time has arrived for the Government to retire from manufacture of salt."[87] The Government thus definitely abandoned the monopoly system in 1864 which had continued to exist in Orissa for about 60 years from the days of the British conquest of Orissa. On the abolition of this trade it was left to private parties under a system of excise.[88] A set of rules for the regulation of the private manufacture was brought for execution.

Consequent upon the abolition of salt monopoly about 26,00 of *Malangis* were deprived of their earnings [89] For sometimes they were absorbed in the agricultural population. But it created a surplus of labour and before the famine they were the first to be thrown out of employment and out of food. It was because of this reason that the *Malangis* were the worst sufferers throughout the famine period.[90]

The abolition of salt monopoly caused the real decline of the indigenous industry in Orissa that had afforded food and shelter to a vast community. The flooding of Liverpool and Madras salt proved fatal to this local industry.[91]

86. Report on Salt in British India, Part III, pp. 175 83, Bengal.
87. BRP, April 1863, Resolution of the Lt. Governor, Bengal, March 25, 1863.
88. BLCP, April 23, 1898.
89. Rundall's Report, 1883, Pr. 6.
90. RCF, Vol. I, Pr. 49.
91. Agarwal, S.C., *Salt Industry in India*, Chapter X, p. 160.

The Zamindars were manufacturing salt for their own consumption and for the local consumption before the British conquest. On the introduction of British salt monopoly the British Government paid them allowances for the lands the Government occupied for the manufacture of salt. The lands were used for the purpose of establishment of *Aurangs*. The Zamindars through agreements were asked to give up their rights over their salt and fuel lands. Against this loss the Zamindars were given allowances known as *Moshaira*. This was fixed at the rate of 1 anna and 4 pies per maund of salt. Besides this allowance the Zamindars were also allowed a diet allowance popularly known as *khoraki* for the loss of their right to manufacture salt. On the abolition of salt monopoly the Government decided to stop giving such allowances to the Zamindars. Their lands were restored to them. They were set free to manufacture salt in their own lands. The Government of Bengal in 1864 confirming the proposal of the Board of Revenue declared the salt and fuel lands to have been restorted with the Zamindars permanently and derecognised the claims of the Zamindars in regard to the allowances.[92]

The manufacture of salt after the abolition of monopoly was limited to home consumption. This system seemed unprofitable due to excessive excise duty. The excise duty was being collected at the rate of Rs. 2-8 annas per maund at the time of abolition. It was raised to Rs. 3-4 annas per maund. Besides the excise duty the Government was collecting the cost of the maintenance of the Preventive Department. Salt was sold in the place of manufacture at the rate of Rs. 5 and it was sold in the market at more than Rs. 6 per maund.[93] The cost of production of salt per maund including the profit was only 13 annas. The local authorities suggested for the reduction of the excise

92. BRP, April 1864, Government of Bengal to Board of Revenue, No. 1497, April 14, 1864.

93. *Ibid* (Misc.), September 1867, T.E. Ravenshaw to Board of Revenue, No. 77, August 1, 1867.

duty to Rs. 2-8 annas due to the distressed condition in Orissa.[94] But the Board of Revenue did not approve of the proposal for any financial loss of the Government.[95]

1. Local Manufacture

Local manufactures did not come forward to manufacture salt in Orissa under excise system because they were sure that their salt would not stand the competition in the market with the Liverpool salt and Ganjam low priced salt. On the other hand the Government thought of the expediency of prohibiting the further extension of local manufacture under the system of excise duty. The Government wanted to depend entirely on the foreign salt. These factors contributed a lot to discourage the local manufacturers to produce salt even only for local consumption. The Salt Industry in Orissa continued to decline. The quantity of manufacture fluctuated In the year 1870-71 a quantity of 5,59,758 maunds was manufactured and in 1871-72 the production was 1,49,290 maunds only.[96]

The Government came forward with a scheme of graduated scale of duties in 1874. The duty under this scheme was fixed at the rate from Rs. 2-4 annas to Rs. 3-4 annas. This graduated duty beginning at Rs. 2-4 annas on the southern frontier and increasing by graduation, reached at Rs. 3-4 annas in the northern boundary. Thus salt was old near Chilka with Rs. 2-4 annas excise duty and at Balasore with Rs. 3-4 annas as excise duty.[97] This was also the old rate of duty in Orissa.

By introducing this new graduated rate the Government anticipated that salt manufacturers would come forward to

94. BRP (Misc.), September 1867, T.E. Ravenshaw to Board of Revenue, No. 77, August 1, 1867.
95. *Ibid*, R.L. Mangles, Secretary, Board of Revenue to Government of Bengal, No. 2399, August 12, 1867.
96. RAB, 1871-72, p. 371,
97. RASD, 1874-75 (OSA).

revive the manufacture but this produced a detrimental effect on the salt trade in Orissa.[98]

2. Ganjam Salt

The introduction of graduated system of salt duty was followed by the illicit importation of Ganjam salt into Orissa. The salt manufacturers could understand that the benefits which they would save from the reduction of duty be definitely less than the amount which would be earned from the low priced Ganjam salt. Consequent upon these feelings the merchants tempted for Ganjam salt business in Orissa. The import of Ganjam salt in 1873-74 was 1419 maunds. In 1874-75 it went upto 11,638 maunds and it increased further to 1,14,338 maunds in 1875-76.[99] This threatened the Cuttack salt trade. The manufacture of salt in Cuttack and Puri decreased in the proportion of the amount imported from Ganjam. In spite of the decrease the manufacturers continued to produce salt as they had no other way out to earn their livelihood. In the year 1875-76 only 67,170 maunds of salt were manufactured in Puri while the production in the previous year was 3,56,657 maunds.[100] In the year 1876-77 Cuttack district manufactured only 10,043 maunds when the district consumed 2,07,898 maunds. The deficit was imported mainly from Ganjam. It can be concluded that out of 100 maunds consumed, only 5 maunds were native production.[101]

This decrease in the quantity of manufacture in Orissa explicitly affected the Government revenue. Government was not getting any duty from the Ganjam salt as this was coming to Orissa in an illegal way. In view of protecting the interest of the Government in respect of salt revenue the Lt. Governor recommended the Government of India that either the duty of

98. BRP, November 1877, Grimley, Secretary, Board of Revenue to Government of Bengal, No. 675, September 1877.
99. RASD, 1875-76 (OSA).
100. *Ibid.*
101. GAROD, 1878-79, p. 16.

Ganjam salt should be immediately raised on the point of manufacture to the level of Orissa excise duty or the Government of Madras be absolutely prohibited to grant passes (*rawana*) for Ganjam salt into Orissa. Against this proposal Madras Government had to fight. Finally the Government of India decided that the full Bengal duty at the rate of Rs. 3-4 annas be realised by the Collector, Ganjam on all Ganjam salt coming to Orissa. The differential amount between Bengal duty and Madras duty was to be credited to the Government of Bengal. The Madras excise duty was only Rs. 1-6 annas.[102] The importation of Ganjam salt in spite of this arrangement was felt in the years 1879-80 to 1882-83 in Orissa.[103]

The illicit manufacture of salt in the coastal belt of Orissa was not the only thrashing danger in the duty paid salt in the Tributary Mahals. Ganjam salt on the other hand contributed a lot to its decline. Markets in Tributary Mahals were flooded with the Madras salt. Ganjam salt was brought for sale in the Central Province on *rawana* but on the way this was sold in Cuttack and in the Tributary Mahals.[104] The police report revealed that the low priced Ganjam salt had its way to Tributary Mahals and was exclusively consumed throughout Garhjat areas.[105] T.E. Ravenshaw, Commissioner, Orissa stated that the under taxed Ganjam salt being sold in Cuttack and Tributary Mahals became a serious threat that had been affecting the Government revenue and the morale of the people as well.[106]

In the year 1870-71 a quantity of 78,214 maunds was despatched from Ganjam for Sambalpur in Central Province but actually 52,182 maunds of salt reached its destination. The

102. Rundall's Report, 1883, Pr. 19.
103. *Ibid*, Prs. 48-50.
104. BRP (Salt), January 1866, Superintendent of Tributary Mahals to Government of Bengal, No. 164, December 7, 1865.
105. RASD, 1866-67, Pr. 49.
106. BRP (Salt), December 1870, T.E. Ravenshaw to Government of Bengal, No. 261, July 1870.

difference of 26,032 maunds could find its way into the district of Cuttack and Tributary Mahals, displacing an equal amount of Bengal salt which could have been sold in these places.[107] Under these circumstances the Government was getting a loss of Rs. 7,00,000 per year.[108]

The Government was deeply concerned over the illicit salt traffic from Madras presidency to the Cuttack Tributary Mahals. To put an end to this traffic A.O. Hume, the Commissioner of Imperial Customs in the North-Western provinces suggested for the establishment of a number of outposts at intervals of 2 miles on the route to be created through the Garhjat States. T.E. Ravenshaw, the Commissioner of Cuttack submitted his suggestion either to levy the full Bengal rate of duty on all salt coming out of Ganjam for consumption in the Tributary Mahals or for transportation to other provinces through Tributary Mahals. All such salt passed out of Ganjam into or through the Garhjat States should be transported in a particular route to be fixed by the Government. If any violation of this rule would be detected the entire quantity would be confiscated. The Rajas of the Garhjat States and the Tahsildars in the Wards States of Banki, Kandhamals and Angul should be empowered to confiscate such illicit under taxed Ganjam salt. To detect such type of illicit traffic police posts in places like Daspala, Nayagarah and Tikarpara should be established.[109] After careful consideration the Lt. Governor appreciated the proposal of T.E. Ravenshaw.

Act X of 1874 was promulgated that brought a radical change in salt trade. This Act envisaged the abolition of all restrictions on salt trade and introduced a free salt trade system. The Government of India directed the Government of Bengal to take steps in implementing the provisions of the Act.

107. BRP (Salt), May 1872, Board of Revenue to Government of Bengal, No. 14C, January 10, 1872.
108. *Ibid.*
109. *Ibid,* December 1870, Board of Revenue to Government of Bengal, No. 4534, October 23, 1868.

The Act provided that all interference, in respect of import of salt, manufactured in Madras Presidency, be ceased to exist. There should be no obstacle to the trade in salt from the coast to any part of the Central Provinces. The inland customs line which had prevented the Madras salt in Orissa salt to enter into Centeral Province without duty was abolished. These provisions thus allowed the importation of Ganjam salt into Orissa in a large scale that caused the complete ruin of the local salt industry.[110]

3. Check of Illicit Manufacture

There existed illicit manufacture of salt in Balasore. In the 1866 the Police Inspector General informed the Board of Revenue that illicit manufacture of salt continued in a rapid growth in every village on the coast of the Balasore district. The salt so manufactured was carried on by the merchants supported by a gang of armed men employed by them. This trade was in rapid progress between the coast and the Garhjat frontier. Petitions were filed by the manufacturers. They had expressed their inability to manufacture salt as long as the illicit salt was allowed to be produced. On these allegations the Member Board of Revenue made a thorough enquiry and it was ascertained that illicit salt was smuggled always in large quantities.[111] As a result of this enquiry the Government of India sanctioned Rs. 31,852 for the increase of the preventive force in Balasore district for 3 years on experimental basis.[112] At an additional cost of Rs. 16,552 the increase of number of preventive force in Cuttack district was also sanctioned by the Government of India.[113]

110. BRP (Misc.), August 1874, Government of Bengal to Government of India, No. 1729, August 1874.

111. BRP (Salt), July 1867, Board of Revenue to Government of Bengal, No. 923, April 1867.

112. RASD, 1867-68, pp. 81-82.

113. BRP, April 1868, Government of India to Government of Bengal, No. 1372, March 12, 1868.

4. Graduated Scale of Duty

To promote the local manufacture, the Government introduced a graduated scale of duty in Orissa. This was of no use. In the year 1878 the rate was reduced and fixed at Rs. 2-8 annas for the whole of districts of Puri and Cuttack and Rs. 2-10 annas for the region laying between Cuttack and Kansbans river and Rs. 2-12 annas for the rest of the Balasore district.[114] This was further reduced to Rs. 2 and this rate was applicable throughout Orissa from March 1882. With this measure the graduated scale of duty was abolished.[115]

The abolition of the graduated scale of duty relieved the burden of duty on salt trade in Cuttack and Puri districts. The manufacture and sale started to increase. In Cuttack district a quantity of 27,653 maunds were manufactured in the year 1878-79 against 10,996 maunds in the last year. In Puri the outturn was 4,01,436 against 47,839 in the year 1877-78 and in Balasore the production went upto 1,47,555 maunds in 1878-79 against 94,127 maunds in the year 1877-78. In all the 3 districts the total sale became 4,96,186 maunds in 1878-79 against 4,41,915 in the year 1877-78.[116] This rapid increase in production and sale as well was gaining while the importation of Ganjam salt was declining.[117] On the other hand the abolition of the graduated scale of duty led to the destruction of the salt industry which was in a ruined condition. *Aurangs* in Cuttack district were closed first in the year followed by the closure of industry in Balasore in 1887 and in Puri in the year 1899.[118]

5. Rawana System and its Abolition

Rawana system had its origin when the salt monopoly was in operation in Orissa. After the abolition of salt

114. RASD, 1878-79, p. 1.
115. RAB, 1881-82, Prs. 63-64.
116. RASD, 1878-79, Pr. 4.
117. GAROD, 1879-80, Pr. 41.
118. QAR, p. 16.

monopoly in 1864, the salt trade was transferred to private enterprise under the system of excise. The factories or *Aurangs* were scattered on the edge of the sea-board. In order to prevent the danger of illicit manufacture, the smuggling from the factories and the smuggling of imported salt from ships, a big preventive force was maintained at the Government cost. This preventive force was deployed in the preventive posts or *chowkeys*. Furthermore to strengthen the preventive system *rawana* system became the important line of defence against such smuggling,

Under the *rawana* system, the purchaser of a consignment of salt beyond 5 seers had to pay a duty. After the payment of duty he was obliged to obtain a permit or *rawana* to transport the salt to its destination by a specified route fixed by the Government. When the purchaser was within a defined limit, conterminous more or less with the salt manufacturing districts he had to submit his *rawana* for inspection by the inspecting officers of the pass stations or *chowkeys*. On reaching his destination he was required under this system to report the arrival of salt to the preventive officer who issued the retail *rawana* to cover the transport of any salt until the entire batch was disposed of.[119] This system worked under close supervision and served the purpose for which it was meant. After the promulgation of the new Act in 1874, as the condition and system of salt supply and trade changed, some amendments in the existing *rawana* system were felt.

The Government of Bengal concluded that the free trade in salt between Madras and Orissa would put Ganjam salt in an advantageous position due to the promulgation of the Act X of 1874. To check this the Government of Bengal called upon the Collector of Ganjam that the Ganjam salt would be permitted to come to Orissa where Bengal regulation was in operation with the Bengal form of *rawana*. After entering into Bengal territory the Ganjam salt would be subject to the Bengal regulation regarding transportation and sale. A prolonged correspondence continued. The Government of Bengal held

119. BLCP, April 23, 1898.

that the intention of the Act X of 1874 was not to give special privilege to Madras salt inside Orissa while all other salt was subjected to check and supervision. On the other hand it was argued by the Madras Government that it was the intention of the Government of India to relieve Ganjam salt from interference of the Bengal Government after the selling price being paid once. As a result of this controversy the matter was referred to the Government of India with a set of rules in connection with the Madras salt coming to Orissa. The Government of India replied that the time had come for relieving salt from all types of interference not only in Orissa but throughout Bengal during the period of transit. Finally it was announced that all interference with the internal trade and transit of salt in Orissa should cease.[120] Government of India insisted on the abolition of *rawana* system. The only vital question arose as to how the strict *rawana* rules would be relaxed without impairing the security of the Government salt revenue. The Government of India declared that even if the proposed relaxation would be resulted in a slight increase of smuggling yet the freedom of trade due to the removal of the restrictions would make good the loss of the Government when there would be the increase of the revenue derivable from the salt sold.[121] This system would grant a boon to the people of Orissa.

The Board of Revenue throught that this proposal of abolition of *rawana* should be affected in Puri first on an experimental basis for a period of 2 years.[122] The Board of Revenue said that the manufacture of salt in Puri district differed materially from those of Cuttack and Balasore due to the production of *kurkutch* salt. The process of its free manufacture in the vicinity of the warehouses need not require any

120. BRP (Misc.), October 1874, Government of India to Government of Bengal, No. 242, August 28, 1874.

121. *Ibid.*

122. *Ibid*, January 1877, Government of India to Government of Bengal, No. 353. December 22, 1876.

vigilance but in the case of *panga* salt more exhaustive preventive system was required.

This proposal was confirmed by the Government of India. According to the new law, Grand Trunk Road was declared as the demarcation line. It was adopted as the line from the coast within which the transportation of salt must be covered by *rawana* in Cuttack and Balasore districts. The *rawana* system thus declared to have ceased in Puri district with effect from April 1877.[123] The abolition of *rawana* system was strictly affected from the rest of Orissa in the year 1885.[124] Following the year 1877 there had been a tremendous increase in the sale of salt in Orissa. In Puri district the total sale was 1,70,669 maunds in the year 1877-78 and in 1879-80 it came to 3,10,999 maunds. In Cuttack in the year 1877-78 the total amount of sale was 18,882 maunds whereas the sale in the year 1879-80 amounted to 42,306 maunds. Similarly in Balasore 1,67,360 maunds were sold in the year 1877-78 and in the year 1879-80 it reached to 1,42,880.[125] These figures clearly show the rise of sale of over 50 perc ent between 1877-78 and 1879-80. In view of this increase the local officers were in favour of the complete abolition. Consequent upon these arguments *rawana* system was completely abolished in the year 1885 from the rest of Orissa. But this was too late. Had this concession been granted earlier to the people, the salt industry could have thrived for some time more to accelerate the growth of Orissan economy.

6. Panga Salt Manufacture and its Abolition

Panga salt manufacture was a very cumbersome process in comparison to that of *kurkutch*. *Panga* salt was the salt boiled out of salt earth scrapped up in saliferous soil. It was manufactured in Orissa first under the monopoly system and then under an excise system for a long time. Manufacture

123. H.E. Risley, Secretary, Government of Bengal to Government of India, No. 655. October 7, 1895 (OSA).
124. *Ibid.*
125. RASD, 1875-76 to 1879-80.

under direct system failed twice and manufacture under excise system failed once.[126]

The importation of Liverpool salt to Balasore had increased by 1884, threatening the *panga* manufacturers. Liverpool salt was imported to the extent of 36,500 maunds in 1884-85.[127] The manufacture of *panga* salt was thus a dying business and further the foreign salt would drive it out of the market due to the development of the Coast Canal that would help the supply of Liverpool salt. When salt manufacture was declining, it was discovered that illicit manufacture of *panga* still continued in a vast area. It was further discovered that in the year 1885, 28 *Malangis* were engaged to manufacture 2,46,000 maunds of *panga* salt. They knowing the fact that their sale would further diminish in the next year, were busy in their way. Trever Grant, Collector, Balasore expressed his observation in connection with the *panga* salt that the manufacture was doomed if not already dead, as a legitimate business. Knowing the fact that how costly was the production of this salt and how much its legitimate cost would be diminished, Mr. Grant could not believe that it worked even at a legitimate profit. This trade was thus maintained with the belief that it would fetch a good profit illegally to the owners.[128]

The Collector, Balasore recommended the Commissioner, Cuttack to stop the manufacture of *panga* salt from Balasore. The Commissioner of Orissa confirmed the view of the Collector of Balasore. The Government of Bengal declined to become hasty in abolishing the manufacture of *panga* salt in Balasore as the Salt Department of Bengal was likely to be placed under the control of the Commissioner, Salt Revenue, Madras. After assuming the control of the Salt Revenue Administration of

126. A. Earle, Commissioner, Excise and Salt, Bengal to Secretary, Board of Revenue, No. 1586S. November 15, 1901 (OSA).
127. GAROD, 1884–85, p. 15.
128. RAB, 1884-85, p. 269; A. Earle, Commissioner, Excise and Salt, Bengal to Board of Revenue, No. 1586S, November 15, 1901 (OSA).

Orissa in 1885 the Commissioner, Salt Revenue, Madras initiated the idea of abolition again. As the custodian of Salt Revenue the Commissioner denied to afford any further facilities to the manufacture which was meant for smuggling. According to him it was very difficult to give sufficient preventive measures to the manufacture and smuggling of *panga* salt. Ultimately the Government had to pay the penalty by losing a parts of its revenue. Under the above circumstances, the making of *panga* salt in all parts of Orissa was abolished in the year 1889.[129] The restriction of licenses for the manufacture of *panga* salt was taken to hand by Madras Government in 1886-87. The number of licenses issued by the Government fell off from 31 to 16 and from that time the decline was continuous until 1890-91 when the manufacture came finally to an end.[130]

Thus the local industry was killed that had been affording means of subsistence to thousands of people in Balasore and Cuttack districts. The Collector of Cuttack A.C. Tute held the view that the difficulty in maintaining the trade and manufacture of *panga* salt by the Government smoothly should not be the cause of its complete abolition. He argued that it must be the bounden duty of any Government to take proper measure to control the illicit manufacture in order to earn excise duty from the articie but not to prohibit the manufacturers for its production. Again he said that Orissa was the only part of the British empire where her inhabitants were prohibited to use any of the fruits of the earth, even the barest necessity of life, because the local Government was unable to excise an article. He stated further that he could not understand why the products of nature should be deliberately wasted and people punished for making use of it whether they paid duty or not.[131] These arguments went against the policy of the

129. RADSMO, 1888-89, Pr. 155.
130. H.E. Risley, Secretary, Government of Bengal to Government of India, No. 655, October 7, 1895 (OSA).
131. BLCP (Finance, Salt), November 1890, Collector, Cuttack to Commissioner, Orissa, No. 158, March 1890.

Madras Government regarding the abolition of *panga* manufacture. This new system threw 23,000 *Malangis* out of their employment. They were put to hardship. It became thus an evil in the poverty stricken country.[132] On this question, after a careful consideration, the Commissioner, Orissa suggested to the Board of Revenue that the manufacturing class must be prepared to bear the full cost of the controlling establishment.[133] The abolition of *panga* salt manufacture thus became instrumental in declining the economic conditions of Orissa.

C. ADMINISTRATIVE TRANSFER TO MADRAS

The Government of Bengal employed Fowler, the Assistant Commissioner, Madras Salt Agency to examine the defects of the salt administration. Fowler's report exposed the deficiencies of the Bengal Government in proper prevention of the illicit manufacture. He stated that smuggling was rampant without any fear of being detected.

In view of exercising better administrative control over illicit practices it was decided to place the salt administration of Orissa under the Commissioner, Salt, Madras Presidency subject to the control of the Government of Bengal. The Orissa Division was fully placed in charge of the Salt Department in October, 1888.[134]

The aim behind the transfer of Orissa Salt Department to Madras was to prevent illicit trade and manufacture inside Orissa and to increase the salt revenue of Orissa. On enquiry the Madras Salt Department ascertained that organised illicit manufacture of salt still continued to grow in Orissa. The new Salt Act XII of 1882, implemented in Orissa in supesession

132. *Ibid*, No. 2051, April 1, 1890.

133. BLCP (Finance, Salt), November 1890, Commissioner, Orissa to Board of Revenue, No. 335, April 9, 1890.

134. *Ibid*, Commissioner of Salt, Madras to Board of Revenue, No. 107, March 10, 1890.

to the Bengal Act VII of 1864, did not produce any miracle upto the satisfaction of the Government.[135]

The Government of Bengal expressed its dissatisfaction with the result achieved by the Madras administration.[136] On this point the Lt. Governor wrote to the Government of India, "there facts seem prima facie to suggest that Madras system has failed in Orissa, it has made very little local salt and that salt is bad and dear, it has failed to increase the consumption of licit salt and has done less to stop the making illicit salt than the single adjoining district of Medinapur. And in return for all this failure it had cost over 10 times as much as the system which preceded it."[137] In this respect the Board of Revenue observed that though the transfer was decided for the development of local industry and it anticipated the salt cheaper and more plentiful, they showed that only 15,000 maunds of salt were produced last year against several lakhs in former years, that the salt was bad and dear, the consumption per head was less than what it was in 1885-86, that the retail price remained stationary and was not much below the prices that prevailed in the rest of Bengal. The *Malangis* who were the manufacturers were in debt to Government. Not even a single case of illicit manufacture was detected during these years.[138] In 1894 the cost of levying less than Rs. 20,00,000 as revenue became Rs. 1,25,000 in Orissa Division. In the rest of Bengal revenue of Rs. 2,36,962 was collected at a cost of Rs. 26,778.[139]

H.G. Cook, Commissioner, Orissa Division stated that the Madras system had injured Orissa by destroying a local

135. H.E. Risley, Secretary, Government of Bengal to Government of India, No. 655, October 7, 1895 (OSA).

136. RASD, 1891-92, Pr. 10.

137. H.E. Risley, Secretary, Government of Bengal to Government of India, No. 655, October 7, 1895 (OSA).

138. *Ibid.*

139. RAB, 1893-94, p. 287.

industry. Financially it involved a loss of revenue. Cook estimated that the net profit under the old system would have been Rs. 17,27,740 against the average profit from 1886-87 to 1893-94 of Rs. 16,82,772 per year. Thus the Madras system had shown a loss of revenue.[140]

In the presence of these facts, there was justification to say that the Madras system did not operate successfully in Orissa.

The Madras Government attributed their failure to the fact that they were unable to expedite the measures to prevent the manufacture of illicit salt and their inability was caused by the differences between the Bengal and Madras Governments regarding the preventive measure. It was considered on the other hand by the Bengal Government that it was better to sacrific an unknown and possibly a considerable amount of Imperial Revenue.

The second cause of this failure was the ignorance of Oriya language of the Madrasi Officers who were engaged in the field. When the Government directed the officers for Government manufacture directly at Tua the officers failed miserably to contact the *Malangis* for better outturn.

The Government realised the fault distinctly. The Government of India observed that it was difficult to check periodical friction between the officers and the Department who were directly subordinated to the Government of Bengal and the salt establishments which belonged to a department controlled by Madras officials.[141]

Finally the Government of Bengal resumed the charge of the salt administration of Orissa on October 1, 1897.[142]

140. *Ibid*, 1894-95, p. 16.
141. BLCP (Finance, Salt), July 1897. Secretary, Government of India (Finance Department) to Government of Bengal, No. 288OSR, July 2, 1897.
142. *Ibid*, April 23, 1898; A. Earle, Commissioner, Excise and Salt, Bengal to Board of Revenue, No. 1586 S, November 15, 1901 (OSA).

D. REVIVAL OF GOVERNMENT MANUFACTURE

The year 1891 became a turning point in the history of the salt administration in Orissa. The system of direct manufacture under the Government control was abolished in the year 1863. It was partially introduced under Madras administration. The Government felt the necessity of introducing the direct manufacture system in a new model to encourage the people of Orissa and to gain much revenue for the Government exchequer. A conference was held which was attended by a number of high Government officials, Sir Charles Alfred Elliot, the Lt. Governor, Bengal; C.F. Worsley, the Commissioner of Orissa; D.D. Allen, the Collector of Puri; R. Cornish, Collector of Balasore; M.C. Master, Deputy Commissioner, Salt, Madras and Kingston, the Assistant Commissioner, Salt. It was decided in the meeting unanimously that the Government Salt Factories should be opened immediately to manufacture *kurkutch* salt in Orissa.[143]

The Salt Industry under Madras administration was in a collapsing stage. The Government came forward to revive this direct manufacture system. It was hoped that the low cost of production of *kurkutch* salt in comparison to that of *panga* salt would inspire the people for its better manufacture and would afford employment to the poor *Malangis* so as to redress the economic condition of that community. By this the salt Industry would be put into a flourishing condition.

In view of these advantages the Government established a factory at Tua on the Chilka lake in the district of Puri in the year 1891.[144] Gurubai Factory in the district of Puri also received sanction of the Government and was established on the request of the Raja of Parikud, Gaura Chandra Mansingh.[145]

143. RADSMO, 1890-91, Pr. 6.
144. Madras Board's Proceedings, No. 53, Faburary, 12, 1891.
145. File No. 125, 1892, Board of Revenue, L.P., W.S. Meyer, to Board of Revenue, No. 1296, May 20, 1892, Meyer to Superintendent, Legal Affairs, Government of Bengal, No. 1022, May 20, 1892 (OSA).

Tua and Gurubai Factories continued to work on the direct system of management by the Government. In the year 1895-96 owing to the alleged unfavourable soil, situation, climate and insufficient density of the brine the question of maintaining the Tua Factory made the Government alert.[146] Government earlier became hopeful to earn a good profit out of these 2 factories on the const of Chilka lake due to the fact that salt manufactured in this coast used to be largely consumed in Bengal even until it was oused by Liverpool salt.[147] In spite of all precautionary measures these 2 industries on the coast of Chilka, Tua and Gurubai were declining owing to the fact that salt could be brought by rail from Madras and sold following the years of the opening of the East Coast Railway. The salt manufactured in Tua and Gurubai thus faced a great setback. Finally these 2 factories were abolished in the year 1897-98.[148]

In the year 1891 a factory at Sartha in Balasore district was also established by the Government on experimental basis. In the beginning the Sartha Factory did not work upto expectation. Government of Bengal with the intention of attracting inhabitants of the sorrounding villages of Sartha, issund a notice in the year 1892. The people were informed of the advantages derivable from the factory in the following manner.[149]

"Land will be given out in Sartha Factory in plots for the manufacture of *kurkutch* salt and any person receiving a plot will obtain a license for the manufacture of such salt and such licensee will become a registered holder.

If *kurkutch* manufacture at Sartha succeeds each licensee will become a holder of valuable landed property.

146. RADSMO, 1895-96, Pr. 11.
147. K.C. Gupta, Commissioner, Orissa to Commissioner of Excise and Salt, No. 46, July 1901 (OSA).
148. *Ibid.*
149. File No. 66, Board of Revenue, L.P. Misc. Revenue Department, 1892, (Salt Branch), (OSA).

A Kudivaram of rupees 15 per garee (120 maunds) will be paid for the salt produced in all *pans* already and actually opened out in a fit state to produce salt and a tax not exceeding Rs. 3 per annum per acre to meet the interest on capital expended in their construction will be imposed.

The rest the *pans* will be marked out by the Government at a cost of about Rs. 5 per acre which will be treated as an advance and recovered in the second and third year. For these *pans* Kudivaram will be fixed at the rate of 3 annas per maund for the first year, 2½ annas per maund for the second year, 2 annas per maund for the third and subsequent years.

Advances to the extent of Rs. 5 at a time will be made to all registered holders who may ask for such to enable them to complete the preparation of their *pans* and to produce salt. Subsequent advances of Rs. 5 will be made if in the opinion of Inspector of salt revenue, enough work has been done to cover the amount of Rs. 5 as advance. These advances will be made until the industry is fairly established and will be repaid by the salt produced. If owing to unfavourable conditions of climate the manufacture does not succeed the repayment of the advances made in accordance with this and the preceding paragraph will not be rigorously insisted upon by Government so that it will be seen that the Government itself practically accepts all risks of failure.

Applications for licenses should be made to the Inspector, Balasore at Balasore or Sartha."

Under the shadow of the provisions mentioned above 2 leading Zamindars Raja Baikuntha De Bahadur and Radha Charan Das expressed their willingness to undertake the manufacture of *kurkutch* salt in their own Zamindari. This could not however be materialised for a longer period.[150]

150. BRP (Salt), June 1901, F.P. Dixon, Collector, Balasore to Commissioner, Orissa, No. *194 S, June 21/24*, 1901.

With all these facilities afforded by the Government people did not come forward to work under the system. Government considering the risk of total failure of manufacture due to unfavourable season and the consequences thereof by the financial burden on the State in the form of relief measure decided to close the Sartha factory in 1893.[151]. The same case happened in the case of the second factory Saranamooye in Balasore district.[152]

There existed a number of factors which caused the decline. Availability of adequate number of labourers became the first stumbling block to the growth of these factories. The *Malangis* engaged in the factory of Tua and Gurubai were the agriculturists. Their attendance in the early part of the agricultural season was very poor. Their attendance completely depended on the prosperity of the crop. If the crops were poor, they resorted to the alternative salt manufacture but when they felt the prosperity of the crop they were not prepared to go for salt manufacture. As a result of this problem the factory could not be maintained on a commercial basis.[153]

The persisting factor behind the fall of the factories was the decrease of sale of the Chilka salt in the market. This comparative statement reveals the quantity of sale per year.

1892-93	60,811 maunds
1893-94	15,574 maunds
1894-95	36,665 maunds
1895-96	74,635 maunds
1896-97	46,224 maunds

151. RADSMO, 1892-93, Pr. 5 of the Special Appendix.
152. S G.L. Patt, Assistant Commissioner of Salt Revenue, 24-Pargana to Commissioner, Excise and Salt, Bengal, No. 605S, June 3, 1901 (OSA).
153. RASD, 189596; J.H. Harriman, Deputy Commissioner, Salt to Secretary, Board of Revenue, Madras, No. 57, January 27, 1892 (OSA).

The decrease of sale of Chilka salt contributed the maximum share in the decline of the Salt Industries in the Chilka region.

The merchants dealing with excise salt were having huge capitals to establish trade centres not only in Puri but also in the neighbouring district of Cuttack and the Tributary Mahals. They were always ready to flow Ganjam salt and Liverpool salt into markets. Government changed its view and established direct system of mnnufacture and started establishing direct relation with the *Malangis* to compete with the Ganjam salt.

The transportation cost of Chilka salt was higher than the freight of the Ganjam salt. There continued a trade of foodgrains between Puri and Ganjam. The cart travelling on the Grand Trunk Road with grain to Ganjam returned with full load of salt from Ganjam to Puri. This could not be possible in the case of Chilka salt. Thus, when the freight charges were added with the cost of production, the price of Chilka salt increased. As a result of which this could not sustain the competition in the market.

Due to the decrease in sale of Chilka salt in Orissa markets and due to the importation of Ganjam salt easily through East Coast Railways heavy stock of salt was accumulated in the warehouses. These factors compelled the Government to close down the factories at Tua and Gurubai in 1897-98. These factors also attributed to the decline of Sartha and Saranamooye in Balasore district.

E. CLOSURE AND ITS CONSEQUENCES

After the closure of the local manufacture the Government had to depend either on the Liverpool salt or on the Madras salt to procure the requisite quantity of salt for the consumption. Orissa was linked with Madras by the East

Coast Railway. Orissa was importing Liverpool salt. After he opening of the railway line Madras salt could reach Orissa very easily.[154] It could compete with the European salt in the market which had been enjoying the monopoly for a pretty long time in the past.[155] Madras salt could easily oust the Liverpool salt from all the districts of Orissa and Tributary Mahals.[156] Thus after the closure of the factories in Sartha, Tua, Gurubai and Saranamooye Madras salt was imported for the whole of Orissa Division.

The year 1902 witnessed the last crystal of salt, manufactured in Orissa. The total amount of Rs. 5,69,589 was collected from the Chilka lake salt in the year 1902. The duty collected on the Government head of Salt Account if added to the total receipts from Orissa salt, the total revenue of the Government amounted to Rs. 27,92,301 in the year 1902 alone.[157]

Keeping the stock of Orissa salt in all the *golas* in view, the Government reduced the rate of duty on salt from Rs. 2-8 annas to Rs. 2 per maund. Again a further reduction was made and the duty on salt became Rs. 1-8 annas per maund in 1905. These reductions within a period of 4 years reduced the retail price of salt manufactured in Orissa earlier. This facilitated the whole stock to be exhausted by the end of 1905.

The Salt Industry needed more liberal and flexible consideration as the Orissa made salt could not withstand the challenge made by the imported salt. The reduction of salt duty in 1882 gave a death blow to this Industry. Government became careful to the grave economic situation of the communities depending mainly on this Industry and finally decided to establish factories in Orissa, Ultimately these industries

154. BRP (Salt), November 1897, Commissioner of Excise. Bengal to Board of Revenue, No. 125, November 11, 1897.
155. Agarwal, S.C., *Salt Industry in India*, pp. 101-102.
156. RASD, 190-102, p. 33.
157. *Ibid.*

perished. Salt Industry continued to remain as an indigenous industry even before the British conquest during the Maratha days and collapsed during the whole British Administration in 19th century due to the vested interest of the British Government. The great source of wealth and prosperity of Orissa ultimately perished. This decline also attributed to one of the most important causes of the great historic famine. The decline of Salt Industry in 19th century resulted in the decline of the economic prosperity of Orissa which remained as a neglected part of the British Administration.

4

Excise and Customs Policy

A. EXCISE

Pre-British System

The manufacture of excisable articles like opium, liquor and ganja occupied an important role to play in the economic life of the people. The source of revenue collection from excisable articles was negligible during the Maratha period.[1] The British Government after the conquest expressed their keen interest on these articles and decided to make it as an important source of revenue collection. Immediately after the conquest they established a separate department of *Abkari* in the province. In the year 1805 the net income from *Abkari* was sicca Rs. 936 against the expenditure for collection of revenue of sicca Rs. 182 per month.[2] The Government thus anticipated a good income out of this and as such decided to impose some restrictions, on the excisable articles.

1. Toynbee, G., *A Sketch History of Orissa*, p. 66.
2. BJP (Cr.), September 1805, Commissioner to Government of Bengal, September 2, 1805.

1. British Excise Policy

The management of the collection of *Abkari* revenue was in the hands of the collectors of land revenue in this province. The supervision of this branch of State revenue was reserved with the Board of Revenue at first but for better administration this Department was transferred to the newly created Board of Customs, Salt and Opium in the year 1819.[3]

In the beginning the Government was not keen to take any administrative measures on the sale of *Abkari* articles. The Government usually issued licenses to persons on a fixed rate of tax to the State revenue to open shops for the sale of spirituous liquors, opium and tari (formented juice of Palm tree). The Collector suggested to the Government to reduce the rate of tax and open more shops for the sale of excisable articles. He pointed out that many shops were closed in the year when Government was interested to issue more licenses. It was because of the high rate of tax on the articles on which the people did not have the capacity to pay. By the reduction of rate of tax at least in the mufasil areas if not in towns, there was every reason of expecting the increase of *Abkari* revenue to Rs. 15,000 which stood at Rs. 10,280 in the year 1811-12.[4] The Collector again argued that the number of shops in Orissa was much less than the number in any part of India and that there were less number of criminal offences caused by the spirituous liquors in Orissa. Hence there was no reason to restrict the number of shops in Orissa. Finally the Governor General in Council passed a regulation regarding the manufacture and sale of spirituous liquor, intoxicating drugs and tari in 1813. This Regulation No. 10 of 1813 emphasized on some new principles for the better management of the *Akbari* revenue in Bengal.[5]

(*i*) *Spirituous liquor and its administration*—The new regulation aimed at restricting the unauthorised manufacture and

3. BdRP (Misc.), No. 17, September 29, 1819, Collector, Cuttack to Secretary, Board of Revenue, September 18, 1819.
4. *Ibid*
5. ARG, Vol. IV, p. 119.

sale of spirituous liquor distilled in a primitive country process. It was provided in the regulation that distilleries should be established in every city or town at which a Collector of land revenue resided. Subsequently distilleries should be established in different places of the district with a distance of 8 miles to each other in the minimum. Such distilleries were to be called as Sadar Distilleries to be controlled by a native *darogah* or Superintendent. The *darogah* was required to keep all accounts of the distilleries to which he was attached and to work under the Collector of the district. It was further said in the regulation that no liquor was to be removed from the distillery without a regular pass issued by the Collector. The Collector was empowered to issue licenses to individuals for opening of distilleries at their own cost beyond 8 miles of Sadar Distillery. The rate of tax was to be determined by the Collector before issuing the licenses.[6] According the regulation tari was not to be sold whether in a formented or unformented process without a valid license issued by the Collector of the district or by a competent officer in charge of the *Abkari* Department. The dealer was required to pay a tax for the sale of tari to the Government every day. Similarly intoxicating drug like opium was not allowed to be sold by the dealer without having a valid license issued by the Collector or by an *Abkari* officer. This regulation did not allow the sale of *churrus*, *muddat* or *koppali* which were of noxious quality and injurious to sound health. However the sale of opium was allowed in only one or two important towns of a district. The Collector was directed to discourage the people to use opium except on some medicinal purposes.

In accordance with the provisions *darogahs* were appointed for collection of *Abkari* tax. The *darogahs* were empowered to detain a man and to send him to the Collector's Court for final punishment, who possessed any unlicensed distillery or who was engaged in the illicit sale of spirituous liquors, tari or intoxicating drug. Such detainee was to be punished with a punishment not exceeding 6 calendar months or a fine not

6. *Ibid*, Regulation No. 10, 1813.

exceeding Rs. 500. It was further required that any individual desirous of dealing with the manufacture or sale of spirituous liquor, drugs, opium and tari etc. was to give the surety of two responsible persons of the locality for the smooth execution of the engagement with the Government or was to deposit a cash equal to 20 days' tax. The license so issued after the fulfilment of the requirement was valid only for 1 year. Such license was liable for cancellation for non-payment of tax for 15 days continuously. The Collector remained in the sole charge of the *Abkari* revenue collection and the Collectors were to receive a commission of 5 per cent on the net amount realised as *Abkari* revenue by them.[7] The Regulation No. 10 of 1813 thus became the guideline for the *Abkari* administration in Orissa.

The first distillery was established at Cuttack town in 1814 at an expenditure of Rs. 800.[8] Three types of spirituous liquor from grain preferably rice and liquor from *mowah* or *mahula* were the 3 types of products. The cost of manufacture of the first type, the best variety of liquor was 7 annas per gallon that of the other 2 inferior types varied from 2 annas to 5 annas. The sale rate was fixed at 14 annas per gallon for the first variety and 4 annas to 12 annas for the 2 other varieties. The rate of tax for a retail shop was fixed at 6 annas per day in 1814.[9] Consequent upon the execution of the regulation the tari sellers were asked to pay a tax of 4 annas per day which was very low as pointed out by the Collector. The Collector said that the sale of tari was very popular as the selling price was low for which the sale of licensed spirituous liquor decreased. Hence the Collector cancelled the licenses of tari sellers and increased the tax rate to Rs. 2 per day for tari sellers only. With a view to raise the *Abkari* revenue, he argued that as the sale of tari in Cuttack town was extensive the increase of tax

7. ARG, Vol. IV, p. 119, Regulation No. 10, 1813.
8. BdRP (Excise), No. 14, April 4, 1815, Secretary, Board of Revenue to Collector, Cuttack, April 4, 1815.
9. Toynbee, G., *A Sketch of the History of Orissa*, p. 66.

either would fetch revenue to compensate the loss of revenue from spirituous liquors or induce the people to use spirituous liquors instead of tari. The tari sellers declined to take licenses at this high rate and finally tari shops were closed. The Government lost small amount of *Abkari* revenue due to the closure of tari shops. As a result of which the Board of Revenue did not approve the cancellation of licenses of tari shops with the consideration that it was illegal. That made the stand very clear. The Government did not like to encourage the sale of spiritious liquors for the sake of larger revenue.[10]

In 1815 the Collector, Cuttack proposed a small increase of tax on spirituous liquors and the inclusion of Puri town to the jurisdiction of the Sadar Distillery at Cuttack to prevent the illicit manufacture and sale of liquors at Puri. The Board of Revenue approved the proposal of the Collector in respect of the increase of tax. The Board of Revenue after careful consideration of the question of the continuance of the Sadar Distillery at Cuttack resolved in 1816 to discontinue such establishment. The Board directed the Collector to discontinue the distilleries but the distillery at Cuttack continued to function upto 1820. As regards the mufasil liquor shops the Collector suggested to the Board for the reduction of tax from 4 annas to 3 annas by which more shops would be opened and *Abkari* revenue would be increased.

(*ii*) *Opium*—Government took no notice about the sale of opium in Orissa till 1814. Opium was another important article consumed by the people of Orissa. The inhabitants were very much addicted to opium in Cuttack district.[11] The poppy was not cultivated in any part of this province. Poppy was supplied to Orissa in plenty from neighbouring provinces. Balasore district was getting it from Bihar through Mayurbhanj State. Merchants were getting poppy from cultivators of Bihar who were cultivating it on Government account at a

10. BdRP (Excise), No. 14, July 15, 1815, Secretary, Board of Revenue to Collector, Cuttack, July 14, 1815.
11. Malley, S.S.O., *Bihar and Orissa Gazetteer, Cuttack*, p. 200.

very cheap rate. They usually smuggled it through Mayurbhanj where Government regulation was not in operation. Cuttack and Puri districts were getting poppy either from Chhotanagpur or from Ganjam. The quantity of such illicit importation to Cuttack and Puri was not high as it was in the case of Balasore. So the price of opium in Puri was much higher than the price of Balasore. For this, Government was getting a very small revenue from the sale of opium. The regulation of 1813 provided some principles for the sale of opium in Orissa. The authorities were directed to open retail shops for opium sale but these restrictions were not affected immediately and illicit deal in opium continued in Orissa.[12] The Board of Revenue sanctioned the establishment of a few opium retail shops in the province in 1815. It was decided that the vendors in such retail shops be paid a salary of Rs. 5 each per month and a commission of 2½ per cent on the total amount of sale of opium. They were further to be paid Re. 1 each per month towards rent of the house occupied for the shop.[13] Opium was brought by the Government from the Board of Trade, Calcutta in August 1815 for the first time according to the new arrangement. The first allotment contained 3 chests of opium, each chest containing 40 cakes. That allotment was sufficient to meet the total requirement of Orissa for 2 months as reported by the Collector. The Collector indented for more supply of opium but immediately his requirementts were not complied with by the Board.[14] As such it was impossible on the part of the Collector to open more shops in Orissa. Only in Cuttack and Puri districts shops were opened on Government account but not in Balasore. Subsequently retail shops were opened in Balasore and Jajpur and the number of retail opium shops in Orissa increased to 13 by the end of 1816.[15]

12. BdRP, No. 9, May 26, 1815, Collector, Cuttack to Secretary, Board of Revenue, May 19, 1815.
13. BdRP, No. 10, May 26, 1815, Secretary, Board of Revenue to Collector, Cuttack, May 26, 1815.
14. *Ibid.* No. 20, August 15, 1815, Collector, Cuttack to Board of Revenue, August 7, 1815.
15. Toynbee, G., *A Sketch of History of Orissa*, p. 68.

In spite of the opening of Government retail shops the sale of opium decreased. The Collector informed the Government that the decrease was caused by the illicit importation of opium through Tributary States and the reluctance of the people to use the Government opium for its inferiority in quality. The retail shops only disposed of 10 maunds of opium against the demand of 30 maunds for Orissa.[16] Against these evils of illicit sale of opium the Collector submitted a draft proposal to the Government. He suggested that the principal vendors be issued licenses for a number of shops. Such licensed vendors were required to purchase opium at the rate of Rs. 15 per seer from the Government *gola* by which the Government would get Rs. 18.000 for 30 maunds of opium, the quantity being the total requirement of Orissa. Besides, the Government would realise Rs. 500 per maund as tax totalling Rs.6,000 per year. Hence this system would fetch Rs. 24,000 per year. The Collector requested the Government to allow him to open retail shops in the Tributary Mahals that would fetch Rs. 100 per month as tax. By the introduction of suuh system the Collector hoped to save the establishment cost of the vendors and to prevent the illicit sale of opium coming through Garhjat areas. The Government did not approve the proposals of the Collectors as it would violate the regulations of the *Abkari* administration.[17]

The other European businessmen like Danish and French were selling illicit opium through some individuals at many places. Government was reported about such practice in Balasore by the Collector. This question was taken up by the Governor General in Council and finally it was resolved that utmost care and vigilance be affected by the Collector to prevent the illicit importation of opium.

The establishment for the *Abkari* administration was also not very effective and vigilant to check such smuggling. There

16. BdRP, No 3, October 15, 1816, Collector, Cuttack to Board of Revenue, October 4, 1816.
17. BdRP, No. 12, February 12, 1817, Secretary, Board of Revenue to Collector, Cuttack, February 11, 1817.

were 8 peons at Rs. 3 each per month for that purpose who were useless according to the version of the Collector. He, therefore, proposed the Government for radical change of the *Abkari* administration. The Government confirmed the view of the Collector. Accordingly a Jamadar of circuit was appointed at a monthly salary of Rs. 10. He was assisted by 4 peons at a salary of Rs. 3 each per month. He was required to submit weekly reports to the Collector about his proceedings in the area. Furthermore the Jamadar of circuit was required to check the illicit manufacture of spirituous liquor and tari and illicit plantation of ganja. Ganja plants were detected in the compounds of houses and it became the bounden duty of the Jamadar to seize such ganja plants. For such seizure he was remunerated with a commission at the rate of 12 per cent on the value of the quantity of ganja so seized.[18] This system continued upto 1828 and the Government revenue realised from *Abkari* articles increased as per the following statistics:[19]

1808-09	Sicca Rs. 9,123
1809-10	Sicca Rs. 9,582
1810-11	Sicca Rs. 9,644
1814-15	Sicca Rs. 15,000
1824-25	Sicca Rs. 40,793
1827-28	Sicca Rs. 42,176

2. Administrative Changes and its Results

Due to this steady increase of *Abkari* revenue the Government became more interested to bring further changes in the management of *Abkari* Department. Three posts of Collectors remained under the control of the Commissioner from March 1829 subject to the further control of the Board of

18. BdRP, No. 14, September 17, 1816, Secretary, Board of Revenue to Collector, Cuttack, September 17, 1816.
19. PBCSO, No. 22, May 21, 1846, Commissioner, Cuttack to Board of Customs, Salt and Opium, May 18, 1846.

Customs, Salt and Opium. According to the new system the vendors were asked to pay their dues not in a uniform rate as before but in the rate as fixed by the Collector in the first 6 months during which period there was maximum demand. The Board supplied, after the introduction of the new system, improved quality of opium for retail sale in Orissa. This new and improved quality of opium was sold at the rate of sicca Rs. 25-8 annas against the old rate of the sicca Rs. 21-11-9 pies per seer. Out of this an amount of sicca Rs. 5 was credited to the Opium Department as the cost of production and the balance of sicca Rs. 20 was credited to the *Abkari* Department as *Abkari* revenue.[20] The terms of the *pattas* were reviewed and it was found that since the vendors were getting the nominal profit of Re. 1 per seer the illicit sale continued. As such the price of opium was raised to Rs. 30-13 annas.[21] It was expected that the rise in price would give more profit as a result of which the vendors would refrain them from illicit sale of opium. This rise in price increased the *Abkari* revenue in the subsequent years. The Commissioner submitted the retail statistics to the Board of Customs, Salt and Opium that showed the *Abkari* revenue,[22] as shown in Appendix 'E'.

The Board of Customs, Salt and Opium thought of re-establishing the Sadar Distilleries in every district and for the better consideration wanted opinions of the Collectors. Collector, Cuttack argued in favour of re-establishing the Sadar Distillery. He said that the establishment of such distillery would fetch more *Abkari* revenue for the Government if proper vigilance would be applied. However the Collectors of Balasore and Puri were not in favour of opening the distilleries as these

20. CRR, Acc. No. 93, Collector, Cuttack to Commissioner, No. 120, August 13, 1830.

21. PBCSO, No. 22, April 20, 1838, Commissioner, Cuttack to Secretary, BCSO, April 3, 1838.

22. PBCSO, No. 44, October 11, 1838, Commissioner, Cuttack to Secretary, BCSO, September 18, 1838.

were not profitable for the Government.[23] The Commissioner recommended the opinions of the Collectors of Balasore and Puri to the Board. Commenting on the opinions he said that the financial advantages were much for the Government if manufacture of liquor was owned by the individuals. After much controversy the idea of re-establishing Sadar Distilleries was abandoned by the Board of Customs, Salt and Opium in 1840.[24]

(i) *Ganja*—The Collector, Cuttack detected some irregularities in the issue of pass to import ganja to Orissa. The pass was issued by the *Abkari* Department at Calcutta without any intimation to the Collector. The Collector reported that this became a regular feature with any people to import ganja to Orissa that led to the loss of *Abkari* revenue. Further such practice allowed many for illicit importation of ganja to Orissa. On this issue he drew the attention of the Board to stop such practice and suggested that the *Abkari* Department at Calcutta be requested to inform the Collectors in advance of such pass, by which the illicit importation could be checked. His proposals were accepted by the Board of Customs, Salt and Opium.[25]

To avoid such irregularities the Commissioner A.J. Mill put a draft proposal before the Board suggesting some changes in the *Abkari* administration in Orissa. His proposals were confirmed by the Government and the new scheme of administration on experimental basis was brought for implementation in the year 1847 but it was delayed as A.J. Mill left India on health ground. His successor F. Gouldsbury promised the Government to take personal drive in executing the new

23. *Ibid*, No. 4, January 30, 1840, Commissioner, Cuttack to Secretary, BCSO, January 8, 1840.
24. *Ibid.*
25. PBCSO, No. 46, April 4, 1844, Secretary, BCSO to Commissioner of Cuttack, April 3, 1844.

system. Finally the new system was introduced on August 1, 1847.[26]

According to the new system 2 *Abkari* Superintendents were appointed. They remained under the control of the Commissioner. One *Abkari* Superintendent remained solely in charge of Balasore district and one remained in charge of both Cuttack and Puri districts. Cuttack district was divided into 5 divisions, Balasore into 4 and Puri into 3. In the headquarters of the Sadar Division a Sadar Darogah was appointed and other Divisions remained under the charge of Moharirs. The Sadar Darogah and Moharirs were assisted by peons. Thus an elaborate administrative set-up was affected at a sanctioned establishment cost of Rs. 1,307 per month.

The new Commissioner F. Gouldsbury became very much concerned over the ganja plantation. In Cuttack and Puri districts the production rate of ganja was very high. It was a regular practice with the Collectors to destroy such illicit ganja plantation whenever it was brought to the notice of the Collectors. Over this question the Commissioner was not happy as the destruction was not permissible by the Regulation 7 of 1824. He sought the advice of the Board in this matter. The Board informed the Commissioner that there was no law to prevent the cultivation of ganja plant for private use. Hence the old practice of destruction was ordered to be abandoned forthwith. The old practice of obtaining pass from *Abkari* Department at Calcutta continued even after the introduction of the new system. One N.C. Das, *Abkari* Superintendent of Cuttack district detected cases of such nature that virtually allowed the illicit importation.[27] On getting such information the Commissioner moved the Board to discontinue the practice and finally this was discontinued. The Commissioner submitted his report to the Board of Revenue in 1851. He

26. *Ibid*, No. 31, April 29, 1847, Commissioner, Cuttack to Secretary, BCSO, April 7, 1847.
27. PBR, No. 126, March 13, 1851, N.C. Das, Abkari Superintendent, to Commissioner, February 21, 1851.

expressed his dissatisfaction on the performance of the *Abkari* Superintendents who worked diligently for the increase of the *Abkari* revenue in the province. The Commissioner again argued that the rate of increase of *Abkari* revenue in the first 5 years from 1847-52 was satisfactory. The average revenue was Rs. 51,722-7-8½ pies against the average of Rs. 49,523-1-8½ pies during the last years (1842-47).[28] He concluded that the new system was definitely better than the old system. For further enquiry the Member Board of Revenue, Henry Ricket arrived at Cuttack and submitted his report to the Government. In his exhaustive statement he pointed out that the illicit importation of ganja from Garhjats still continued in Cuttack. As regards Puri he found no significant increase of revenue out of ganja.

(*ii*) *Abkari Revenue*—The statistics submitted to the Board of Revenue revealed that the *Abkari* revenue collection in the year 1852-53 was Rs. 60,944 which increased in the subsequent years. In the year 1854-55 the *Abkari* revenue stood at Rs. 62,725 which increased to Rs. 77,663 in the year 1855-56 and Rs. 83,742 in the year 1856-57. It further increased to Rs. 93,667 in 1857-58. One hundred and sixty six persons were detained for violating the *Abkari* Law in 1855-56 out of which 81 persons were convicted.[29] In the year 1857-58, 64 persons were held for violation of *Abkari* Regulation and out of them only 31 persons were convicted.[30] Thus the illicit sale of excisable or *Abkari* articles was reduced to a considerable degree for which Government could fetch an encouraging *Abkari* revenue from Orissa.

The administration of Excise Department continued to be in that state of nature. Government did not like to

28. PBR, No. 56, July 23, 1852, Commissionar, Cuttack to Secretary, Board of Revenue, July 7, 1852.
29. RAB, 1855-56, Board of Revenue to Government of Bengal, No. 49, January 27, 1857.
30. *Ibid*, 1858-59, Board of Revenue to Government of Bengal, No. 41, January 24, 1859.

make any changes into the existing practice due to the appearance of Orisa Famine except in the matter of the illicit importation of Garhjat ganja into the regulated districts of Orissa. The old system of administration continued till the promulgation of a new Excise Act in 1878.

3. Excise Act, 1878

In 1875-76 the Bengal Government directed the Commissioner of Orissa to introduce auction system for country distilleries. This system was introduced to fetch more *Abkari* revenue. However, the Sadar Distilleries continued to manufacture. The auction system resulted with the decrease of revenue derivable from country spirit. In the year 1876-77 the Government realised a total amount of Rs. 3,10,469 as *Abkari* revenue.[31] Out of which Rs. 1,40,525 from Cuttack, Rs. 53,533 from Puri and Rs. 1,16,411 from Balasore were collected. In this revenue the note-worthy feature was the higher collection of duties from opium and ganja. In the year 1878-79 the *Abkari* revenue increased with an addition of Rs. 68,123 to the collection of 1876-77. The average *Abkari* reveuue during the last 5 years from 1873-74 to 1877-78 was Rs. 3,04,236 (Rs. 1,40,435 from Cuttack, Rs. 50,578 from Puri and Rs. 1,13,223 from Balasore) whereas the revenue of 1878-79 stood at Rs. 3,78,592 (Cuttack Rs. 1,67,639, Puri Rs. 59,068 and Balasore Rs. 1,51,885).[32] The main feature of the year was the large decrease in the consumption of country spirit and ganja and a large increase of sale in opium. The increase of the sale of opium was mainly due to the increase of retail shops since 1871-72. In that year the Government issued as much as 657 licenses in Orissa that practically increased the *Abkari* revenue.[33]

Bengal Act VII of 1878 was promulgated and extended to Orissa.[34] According to the provisions the administration

31. GAROD, 1876-77, pp. 18-19.
32. GAROD, 1878-79, p. 31.
33. RAB, 1871-72, p. 354.
34. BLCP, Vol. XXX, 1898, February 26, 1898.

of Excise Department was reorganised. A Commissioner was appointed to look into the administration separately. He was to act under the supervision of the Commissioner of Cuttack. The Act, provided for the establishment of a Sadar Distillery in each district. Government of Bengal directed the Commissioner of Cuttack for the establishment of a Sadar Distillery at Puri as the district did have a distillery before. The estimated cost of Rs. 124-10 annas payable from the Provincial Fund of D.P.W.D. was sanctioned and spent for the establishment of a Sadar Distillery at Puri.[35]

The new Act also provided certain preventive measures to check the illicit importation of Garhjat ganja. The Tributary States of Orissa for many years past constituted the principal problem of the Government in regard to the illicit importation of ganja into Orissa.[36] The safety of excise revenue in Orissa was at a stake. The Commissioner of Excise was directed by the Act to be extremely vigilant about the problem. Darogahs were appointed in frontier lines of Tributary Mahals to check smuggling. They were asked to issue pass to Garhjat Ganja for importation into Orissa. These preventive measures were resulted with the steady increase of *Abkari* revenue in the succeeding years.

(*i*) *Abkari Revenue*—In the year 1880-81 the total *Abkari* revenue collected from Orissa went upto Rs. 4,0?,690 against Rs. 3,78,592 in 1878-79. It further increased to Rs. 4,59,826 in the year 1881-82. The increase was chiefly on country spirit of Rs. 12,186, ganja of Rs. 10,785 and on opium of Rs. 27,708.[37] There had been a remarkable and steady increase of revenue on this head every year. The total amount realised from *Abkari* articles in Orissa in the year 1887-88 stood at Rs. 5,30,250 making an increase of Rs. 80,424 during last 7 years from 1880-81 to 1887-88. The total expenditure for the collection of revenue in 1887-88 was Rs. 18,243 only

35. File No. 93, 1878, T.E. Ravenshaw to Secretary, Board of Revenue, No 1716, March 27, 1878 (OSA).
36. RIHC, p. 353.
37. GAROD, 1881-82, p. 6.

after which the net gain was Rs. 5,12,007. There was a decrease of revenue in 1888-89 as the collection was only Rs. 5,22,438.[38] A further decrease occurred under the heads of country spirit and ganja. The consumption of these articles was affected to a certain extent by high prices and partly by the increase in smuggling from the Tributary States.

(*ii*) *Smuggling of Garhjat ganja*—To put an end to the vital issue of smuggling of Garhjat ganja the Government considered over the matter. Four proposals were placed before the Government. In the first place it was suggested to prohibit the cultivation of hemp plants (ganja plants) in the Tributary States. It was further proposed to prohibit the cultivation of the plant within 3 miles of British territory, to prohibit the importation of the drug into British territory and to raise the duty on imported Garhjat ganja to Rs. 4 a seer equalising its price with the duty of Rajsahi ganja. Out of these 4 proposals the proposal of prohibiting the cultivation within 3 miles of British territory and raising the price to Rs. 4 were accepted by the Government in the year 1892. The duty on all kinds of ganja was raised by Re. 1 per seer with effect from April 1, 1893.[39] Under the system of 1892 licensed wholesale and retail vendors were permitted to import Garhjat ganja under a pass from the Collector. To obtain such pass they were required to pay a fee of Rs. 2 per seer to the Government in advance. The maximum quantity of such importation was fixed at 1 maund at a time. The maximum possession of Garhjat ganja with the consumers was also limited. No consumer was allowed to be in possession of such ganja more than 5 tolas only. The previous limitation was 20 tolas per head.[40] This permission was given by the Government because the people of Orissa were using ganja as medicine sometimes. Some people were in habit of using the coarse and lower leaves of the ganja plant known as bhang daily as an intoxication and as a medicine also.[41] In view of this Government was not able to restrict

38. *Ibid*, 1888-89, p. 33.
39. BLCP, April 1, 1893.
40. RIHC, p. 354.
41. File No 91, 1891, G. Toynbee, Commissioner of Orissa to Board of Revenue, No. 6E, April 13, 1891 (OSA).

the complete abolition of the cultivation of the ganja plant. By introducing these new systems Government anticipated the steady increase of the *Abkari* revenue and the decrease of illicit importation of Garhjat ganja. Government believed that when the price of Garhjat ganja was increased the consumers were definitely to opt for Rajsahi ganja. But no remarkable change was noted. Illicit deal in Garhjat ganja continued. However these restrictions imposed in the year 1892 became beneficial to the Government.

Consequent upon these restrictions the *Abkari* revenue started increasing year by year. An amount of Rs. 6,10,535 was collected as *Abkari* revenue in 1893-94 against Rs. 5,60,977 in 1892-93.[42] But in 1895-96 the excise revenue was Rs. 5,71,526 which gave a deficit of Rs. 39,009 to the collection of 1893-94. This decrease was due to the decrease of sale in country spirit, ganja, bhang and opium. The decrease of sale was caused owing to the poor harvest in the year 1894-95 that had reduced the purchasing capacity of the people in general. The rate of total excise revenue from all sources per head of population was 2 annas 4 pies in 1894-95 against 2 annas 6 pies in 1892-93. This was not a healthy state of finance to the Government as reported by the Commissioner.[43] Keeping this in view the Government raised the rate of duty on all kinds of ganja except flat ganja with effect from January 1, 1894.[44] The excise revenue collection increased in 1897-98 to Rs. 6,62,775 which was further increased to Rs. 7,27,438 in the year 1898-99.[45]

4. Excise Act, 1896

The Government became interested in affecting some changes to the existing Excise Act. The new Act was enforced in the year 1898 with the title of Excise Act, 1896.[46] In the

42. GAROD, 1894-95, 1895-96, p. 44.
43. *Ibid.*
44. BLCP, March 31, 1894.
45. GAROD, 1898-99, p. 2.
46. BLCP, February 26, 1898.

new Act it was decided to introduce the Madras Excise system in Bengal. The Act adopted the system of levying duty on tax by taxing the trees tapped for sale as an intoxicant, by imposing a excise duty on ganja at the time of importation from Garhjats. The Government accepted also the recommendation of the Indian Hemp and Drug Commission and directed the Government to improve the provincial excise system in regard to the hemp and drug plants.[47]

In the year 1899-1900 some changes were affected in accordance to the provisions of the Act. The treasury price of opium was also raised from Rs. 32 to Rs. 33. The duty on flat ganja small and large twigs was levied at Rs. 6 and Rs. 5 per seer respectively. The system of taking the palm trees used for the preparation of tari was partially introduced. The outstill system which was abandoned from Cuttack district since 1890-91 was re-introduced. The restriction to issue opium to Garhjat States from Cuttack treasury since 1893-94 was declared to be valid. The legality of opening of new *golas* in Mayurbhanj and Nilgiri to store Rajsahi ganja was confirmed. These *golas* were opened from 1896-97. No ganja was allowed to be issued to these Tributary States from Balasore treasury. The cultivation of ganja plants in the Garhjat States was checked to a great extent. The services of the special staff in the Excise Department, entertained in the year 1896-97 for the suppression of smuggling of Garhjat ganja, were dispensed with. The nominal rate of tax on the distillery building at Balasore was imposed and realised from the sale of spirit at Balasore. In Cuttack all the excise buildings in charge of the Excise Department before the introduction of the Act were transferred to the Public Works Department for better maintenance. These changes in the excise administration resulted in the steady increase of *Abkari* revenue by the end of 1899-1900.[48]

The total number of shops of all kinds in the year 1899-1900 was 943 against 894 in 1895-96. The number of

47. *Ibid.*
48. GAROD, 1899-1900, Pr. 105, p. 27.

shops settled during 2 years 1895-96 and 1896-97 was nearly the same being 891 in 1896-97 but there was small but steady increase in the number since 1897-98.[49] The opening of more shops in Orissa to retail the excisable articles was felt. Vendors were generally inclined for opening of shops due to the restrictions imposed by the Government in illicit importation of Garhjat ganja during the eighties of 19th century.

The number of cases detected for violation of excise law gradually decreased from 306 in 1897-98 to 249 in 1898-99.[50] The total *Abkari* revenue from all sources increased to Rs. 7,34,098 in the year 1899-1900.[51] The increase of revenue was very high. The Commissioner attributed the cause of this increase to be influx of people for railway work in Bengal Nagpur Railway.

5. Rules for Tributary Mahals

As regards the excise administration in Tributary States the Government issued an order vide letter No. 1035, February 8, 1899 empowering the ruling Chiefs or Rajas to control the excise administration in their own kingdoms subject to the control of the Government.[52] The Government directed them not to allow any vendors to open shops within 3 miles of the frontier of the British territory. As per the directions all the shops meant for the sale of excisable articles were closed. As regards to the group of Sambalpur States transferred to the Orissa Division this 3 miles restriction was reduced to 2 miles vide letter No. 3051/148, May 29, 1888.[53] Thus the continuous headache of the Government in relation to the illicit cultivation of ganja and the illicit importation of ganja to the British regulated districts could be controlled by the application of

49. GAROD, 1899-1900, Pr. 102, p. 27.

50. *Ibid*, Pr. 9, p. 2.

51. *Ibid*, p. 27.

52. Selection Records (Feudatory States), p. 33, Secretary, Government of Bengal to Board of Revenue, No. 1035, February 8, 1899 (OSA).

53. *Ibid*.

the new regulation of the Government. The question of smuggling of Garhjat ganja into Orissa occupied the attention of the Indian Hemp and Drug Commission. In the interest of the excise revenue in Orissa the system of Cooh Behar was introduced in 1895 on an experiment basis in relation to the Tributary States. In 1901 on the recommendation of the Board of Revenue the system was adopted as a permanent arrangement in the Tributary Mahals of Orissa vide Government order No. 5669SR, December 6, 1901.[54] Cultivation of ganja was completely restricted and Government decided to supply it to Tributary States procuring from Rajsahi ganja *gola* under the same conditions observed in the regulated districts of Orissa.[55] In the Tributary States of Orissa the outstills were regularly put into auction. However the excise administration of the Tributary States was managed by the Rajas themselves throughout the 19th century under the guidance of the Superintendent of Tributary States as per the rules provided by the Acts in different times. The *Abkari* revenue collected from the State was fully enjoyed by the Rajas. Hence the new measures enacted and enforced by the Government was mainly to check smuggling of Garhjat ganja that was affecting the *Abkari* revenue of the Government. The new Act virtually afforded plenty of scope for the steady growth of the excise revenue of the Government.

In the changing circumstances of the excise administration the interest of the British Government could be materialised to a great extent. The unnoticeable and negligible excise revenue at the time of British conquest could be increased to the extent of Rs. 7,34,098 by the close of the century.

The Government not only legalised the process of manufacture of all excisable articles but also imposed new duties on various excisable articles affecting new administrative and legislative measures to fetch a significant excise revenue out of Orissa. Thus the commercial activities of the people

54. *Ibid.*
55. *Ibid.*

of Orissa were given a new lease of life by the establishment of a new regulated market. By the beginning of the present century the Government virtually monopolised the trade on all excisable articles. The Government withdrew the administrative powers of the Rajas of the Tributary Mahals. The aim of the Britishers at the time of conquest to Orissa could be successfully materialised through the monopolisation of the intoxicating, medicinal and excisable articles. The new zeal to monopolise the production of excisable articles and to collect more revenue as a perennial source of Government revenue by selling these articles through licensed agents or vendors could be materialised. The increase of consumption of these articles and the implementation of new excise rules in different times enabled the Government to yield more revenue. This new deal however did not bring any substantial change on the economic life of the people of Orissa rather it was a negation to the economic prosperity of the people.

B. CUSTOMS

*The same principle to collect more revenue for the Government from the Customs Department was affected since the British conquest. The British Government was only interested for more revenue from customs duties but in return, they did not invest much for the development of the ports and administration of the Customs Department, At times investments were made only when they thought of increasing the customs revenue by neglecting the interest of the people. People of Orissa in general were never allowed to opt for portal trade and to visit such custom houses or *chowkeys* due to high rate of customs duties. They were rather denied any sort of benefit or any hope of future gain. The unplanned way of implementing new customs rates and customs rules allowed the Britishers only for more profit through portal trade evading the customs duties, with no gain for the Orissan traders. As a result of which the people of Orissa refrained from their venture. Due to lack of interest and co-operation of the people, Customs

*Ports will be discussed in a subsequent Chapter.

Department could not operate well. The customs revenue gradually declined which had a tremendous impact on the economic condition of the Government and the people, which ultimately brought discredit for the Government.

Like excise duty the Government was collecting duties through custom houses. Duties realised from the articles of import, export and internal transit, formed the Customs Department of the Government. In the year 1804 just after the British conquest to Orissa the Governor General passed certain rules for the maintenance of its Customs Department in Orissa. From then Customs Department was established in Orissa to regulate the administration of ports on the coastal belt. By virtue of the rules passed in 1804, it was decided to impose or levy a single duty on the articles imported from any foreign countries either by sea or by land. It was further decided that the merchant should be allowed to carry his good to any part of the province the moment he paid the customs duty once on any custom house. They were not subject to any kind of oppression by the Government officers.[56] This system was in operation till 1858 when a new Act was promulgated for the smooth conduct of the Customs Department in Orissa.

Articles of every description except a few were subject to duty at the rate of 2½ per cent at the valuation specified therein in the *rawana*. This was applicable on the articles being imported by sea from Bengal or any other part of the British possession in India. The articles which were not subject to any customs duty were wheat, rice and grain of every description, horses, bullocks and quadrupeds of every kind, gold and silver bullion whether coined or uncoined, timber and wood usually used for ship and boat building, household or other purposes, pearls and diamonds or other precious metals, opium purchased at the Company's sale *gola* at Fort William, hackeries and carriages of every description, images intended for religious purposes of every kind and instruments of agriculture such as manufacture of ploughs and tools of every

56. BJP(C), No. 26, September 5, 1895.

description.[57] Any article not accompanied with a *rawana* was subject to the levy of duty at a higher rate specified in the Book of Rates. Export of salt petre from the province by sea or land was strictly prohibited. Similarly export of salt except on Government account or not being accompanied with a *rawana* for small quantities even for the use of crews of the ships or boats as the case might be, was strictly restricted. The export or import of gun-powder and arms and weapons into the province or from the province by land or by sea was prohibited.[58]

Government was very keen to check smuggling. For this it was provided in the rules that any article of any description and quantity when detected was to be confiscated by the custom houses. One-fourth value of the article so confiscated was to be paid to the man who informed about the smuggling, 1/4 of the cost was to be paid to the darogah of the *chowkey* where it was detected and the rest was to be credited to the Government account. Government officers appointed in the custom houses if were found negligent in their duties or if they were detected at the time of taking bribes either in kind or in cash from the merchants were liable for punishment. As punishment he was required to pay a fine four times to the amount so received by the officers besides being dismissed from his office. Thus the rule required the officers to be extremely vigilant in their duties.[59]

Under the provisions of the rules of 1804 collections of customs duty began. Government made arrangements to that effect. A Judge-cum-Magistrate was appointed as Customs Officer to collect customs. He was required to work under the supervision of the Commissioner, Cuttack. Towards the end of 1805 the Government ordered the Salt Agent to take charge of the Customs Department in addition to his duties. The Salt Agent, Cuttack expressed his inability to shoulder the responsibility of the Customs Department as he was 'busy in

57. BJP(C), No. 26, September 5, 1805.
58. *Ibid.*
59. *Ibid.*

maintaining his own Salt Department all the time.[60] Thus Customs Department remained in that state of affairs till 1810 when a new regulation was enforced for the Customs Department in Orissa. However with that arrangement the Customs Department had collected an average amount of Rs. 2,434 per month at the cost of only Rs. 49 for the collection work.[61]

By the Regulation 12 of 1805, all kinds of sayar duties (duties other than land revenue) were abolished. The duty was collected on goods of any descriptions separately at each of the custom houses. By which one article was subject to duties more than once in different *chowkeys* through which it passed through. This policy was regulated from England. In 1810 this system of customs collection was abolished. A new regulation was passed in April, 1810 superseding all the existing rules in Orissa with modified set of rules for collection.[62] In accordance with the rules a custom house was established at Balasore for the whole of Orissa. A Collector of Government Customs was appointed to be solely in charge of the custom house. He was kept under the control of the Board of Revenue at the Presidency Headquarters. The regulation also provided the rules for duty collection on different articles. This also enlisted the number of articles to be exempted from duty. It further envisaged that the articles once paid the duty, was not liable to pay the duty for the second time for a period of 1 year as the *rawana* accompanied with the goods remained valid for 1 year.[63]

1. Chowkeys

Under the custom house at Balasore the Government established 8 *chowkeys* at Baliapal, Rajghat, Remuna, Balaramghari, Bangreah, Fulwar, Churamáni and Dhamara. Out of

60. PBT (Customs), Vol. 23, p. 220, Collector of Customs to Board of Trade, September 22, 1806.
61. BJP (C), No. 27, September 5, 1805.
62. *Ibid*, No. 7, April 13, 1810.
63. *Ibid.*

these *chowkeys* Dhamara was situated at a distance of 48 miles. The nearest *chowkeys* were Fulwar and Bangreah.[64] These *chowkeys* were spread between rivers Dhamara and Subarnarekha. The establishment of the Central Custom House at Balasore was mainly due to the fact that Government wanted to regulate the administration of Balasore port which happened to be the main port of trade in the whole of Orissa. Even though there existed many smaller ports stretching from Dhamara to Chilka lake, the Government established *chowkeys* in Balasore district only with the hope of getting a good revenue from customs.

The management of the *chowkeys* was also regulated properly. In every *chowkey* a darogah or a *Muharir* was appointed. The salary of darogahs varied from Rs. 12 to Rs. 20 according to the importance of the *chowkey* where they were appointed. Similarly the *Muharirs* were getting their salary at the rate of Rs. 8 to Rs. 12 in the same manner as in the case of darogahs. To assist the darogahs or *Muharirs* of the *chowkeys* peons were appointed at a salary of Rs. 4 each. In the Sadar Customs Office at Balasore a *Sirastadar* and an English writer were appointed at a monthly salary of Rs. 40 each. To speed up the work of the Sadar Office alongwith the *Sirastadar* and English writer few *Muharirs* were appointed. Peons also were appointed to help the *Sirastadar* and English writer. The total establishment cost of the Head Office and *chowkeys* amounted to Rs. 366-3 annas per month in the year 1828.[65]

The Collector of Customs at Balasore was made vigilant over the proper functioning of the *chowkeys* and the *chowkey* officers. As per the code of conduct the Customs Officer was doing his duty. In case of any complaints received by him against any subordinates about illegal exaction of customs or receipt of any bribes, the Customs Officer was taking prompt

64. PBT (Customs), August 1829, Collector of Government Customs to Secretary, BCSO, August 13, 1829.
65. BCHR, Acc. No. 586, Collector of Government Customs to Civil Auditor, May 21, 1828 (OSA).

action on these matters. He conducted enquiries on the allegation by raiyats against Baliapal *chowkey* and recommended to the Board for punishment.[66]

2. Rules of 1820

Government wanted to regulate the Customs Department of Orissa smoothly. In view of this, Government made some new rules for the Collector of Customs to observe. Accordingly the Collector of Customs was directed to maintain a Free-Sea Register for the goods imported and to keep it in the custom house. As regards to the export of articles by the Government the Collector of Customs was required to receive an application in the same Form used by the Indian merchants. On receipt of such application mentioning the quantity and value of the articles the Collector of Customs was to depute an officer to the port at the time of loading the ship and to see whether the entry in the application was correct or not. On his endorsement the Collector of Customs was required to make an entry of the goods of export in a separate register, known as Free Export Register.[67]

Further this rule categorically declared that articles belonging to Military, Medical and Government Departments should be exempted from the duty of import, export and internal transit.

In the year 1821 an amendment of the existing rules was made by the Governor General in Council. This change was a tremendous help to the common people. Further, it was said that persons passing beyond the range of the *chowkey* and not entering the town of Balasore where the custom house was stationed, were allowed to carry any good not exceeding the value of Rs. 10 without paying customs duty.[68]

66. BdRP (Customs), No. 15, November 16, 1813.
67. PBCSO, July 1820, Secretary, Government of Bengal to Commissioner, Cuttack, No. 541, July 7, 1820.
68. BCHR, Vol. 22, Collector of Government Customs to Commissioner, Cuttack, July 20, 1824 (OSA).

In 1829 the Office of the Commissioner of Revenue and Circuit was created. It provided that the Customs Officer should make all correspondence in relation to customs with the Commissioner of Revenue and Circuit. It was again emphasised that the decisions of the Commissioner should be final in respect of all detentions, seizures, confiscation, remission of fines and other penalties. Again, the new provisions of 1829 empowered the Commissioner to appoint and dismiss all uncovenanted officers of the Customs Department. The Commissioner was to be guided by the rules and regulations in vogue or which might be implemented thereafter. The Board of Customs, Salt and Opium was maintained to supervise and control the Commissioner.

In accordance with the provisions laid down in the rules of 1829 the Customs Department functioned. Duties were collected. The rate of collection decreased. As per the statistics an amount of Rs. 60,670-5 annas were collected by the year ending 1828-29 from 1825-26 at a cost of total expenditure of Rs. 25,301-3 annas. The net revenue received from the customs thus became Rs. 35,369-2 annas on an average of Rs. 8,842-4 annas per year.[69] The annual income from customs in the year 1817-18 was Rs. 23,249-7 annas.[70] This decrease was due to the decline in the trade of cotton manufactured at Cuttack, which passed through Balasore Custom House.

The main portion of duties was collected from inland transit of goods. Out of the total collection of Rs. 60,670 5 annas from 1825-26 to 1828-29 an amount of Rs. 4,937-8 annas was collected in the sea-port and the balance was realised from the inland transit duties. In view of the small income of the Balasore Custom House, the Collector of Customs at Balasore suggested in his report to the Commissioner to abolish the Custom House at Balasore. He had

69. BCHR, Collector of Government Customs to Secretary, BCSO, August 13, 1829 (OSA).

70. RBR (Customs), Vol. 25, Accountant to Commissioner, Cuttack, October 23, 1818.

pointed out that the function of collecting that small amount of customs could easily be managed by the Calcutta Custom House. Henry Ricket, the Commissioner of Cuttack approved the proposal and wrote to the Board in 1836, as the Custom House only yielded a profit of Rs. 8,000 per annum the logic of its abolition could hardly be questioned.[71] But the Government was not prepared to abolish the Custom House immediately.

Arguments cropped in against and for the abolition of the custom house. Henry Ricket pointed out that transit duties were levied on the articles brought into the town or brought through the *chowkeys*. But articles were exempted from such duties which were not brought into the territory of the custom house, according to the Law passed in 1829. The collection of such duties formed the customs of Orissa. The export was only confined to rice which was an article of exemption. Thus the income from the customs decreased. In the year 1832-33 the duties both from import and export stood at Rs. 254-2 annas and it decreased to Rs. 69-6 annas in the year 1834-35. Thus the drastic fall in the collection of duties of customs supported the cause of minimisation in regards to the establishment of Customs Office. Ricket however did not suggest the abolition of port duty with the conviction that such abolition would be definitely injurious to Government revenue, derivable from the customs. After much of controversy the Board finally decided in April 1836 to reduce the establishment of Custom House at Balasore with the consideration that the maintenance of the Custom House at Balasore would not allow the merchants to defraud the customs payable at Balasore when the ports would be declared as free ports.[72]

3. Customs Rules of 1836

A set of new rules were prepared and were brought into

71. PBCSO, No. 79, March, 4, 1836, Henry Ricket to Secretary, BCSO, February 18, 1836.
72. PBCSO, No. 92, March 31, 1836.

force from 1836. This new system reduced the cost of establishment to Rs. 182 only. In the Sadar Office one English writer with a monthly salary of Rs. [illegible]0, one *Muharir* with a monthly salary of Rs. 10 and 2 peons with monthly salary of Rs. 8 each were maintained. Besides the Balasore Customs Office only 3 *chowkeys* at Baliapal, Churamani and Dhamara were retained and the rest were abolished. In each of these *chowkeys*, 1 *Muharir* with a monthly salary of Rs. 10 and 2 peons with the salarly of Rs. 4 each were kept to look after the administration of *chowkeys*. There was also an assistant to the Collector, Cuttack to help the Customs Officer in its Sadar Office. He was remunerated with a monthly allowance of Rs. 80 till 1848 when this post was abolished.[73]

The transit duty was abolished by this new system introduced in 1836. Consequently on this abolition the Balasore Custom House ceased to be a big source of profit of the Government.[74]

The detailed statistics on page 205 throws a flood of light about the position of income and expenditure following the abolition of transit duty at Balasore Custom House.[75]

In view of this extra disbursement according to the system of 1836 the Government again decided to reduce the establishment cost of Balasore Custom Office and *chowkeys*. Customs Office at Balasore was tagged to the Sadar Office in 1856 alongwith all *chowkeys*. From May 1856 the cost of establishment was reduced to Rs. 93 per month only, out of which in Sadar Office Rs. 53, in Dhamara *chowkey* Rs. 18, in Churamani *chowkey* Rs. 18 and in Baliapal *chowkey* Rs. 4 were spent.[76]

During the period from 1836-37 to 1856-57 the main articles of export were rice and paddy. The volume of export

73. BCHR, Acc. No. 648, Secretary, BCSO to Collector, Government Customs, Balasore, May 11, 1848.
74. PBCSO, No. 79, March 4, 1836.
75. *Ibid*, No. 36, January 17, 1839.
76. BCHR, Acc. No. 720.

Receipts	*1836-37* Rs. a. p.	*1837-38* Rs. a. p.
1. Duties realised on import	762-13-11	1,184-13-4
2. Duties realised on export	71-15-5	213-11-10
3. Sale of confiscated goods	—	—
4. Fines	—	122-13-5
5. Miscellaneous	605-6-8½	353-15-5
Total	1,440-4-½	1,885-5-0
Disbursement and charges		
1. Establishment cost	2,036-15-5½	2,184-0-0
2. Contingent charges	48-15-10½	65-14-9
Total	2,085-15-4	2,252-14-9
Excess of Deficit	645-11-3½	367-9-9

decreased to a considerable degree due to the fact that the export of rice and paddy was completely depending on the crops produced and ships not being available for export. All the ships were engaged in the Government salt monopoly and as such the availability of ships depended on the volume of salt trade conducted by the Government and the ships were made available only when the salt trade was completed. Thus the export trade in port under Balasore Custom House decreased.

According to the procedure followed by the Custom House, the Commissioner detected some discrepancy in respect of the quantity of loading and unloading. He said that the quantity of goods entered in the clearance certificate issued to the ships did not tally when the goods reached its destination. The Collector of Customs replied that when[4] the vessels were bound for Indian ports it was the usual practice to issue clearances to the vessels without being verified about the actual quantity of load. The quantity entered in the application for clearances were never taken into account. Sometimes the vessels were taking cargoes on the way. Very often the ship owners applied for clearances in advance before the loading operation was made in order to save time. In those cases clearances were issued for the quantity of cargoes of a particular description so applied for by the owner. But when the specified quantity of cargoes of a single description were not ready for loading the owners used to load cargoes of other descriptions. In that case it became quite natural to get discrepancies in the port clearances granted to the vessels and the actual quantity of cargoes reached in the ports of other descriptions. Hence the Collector was in argument that for this, the merchants were solely responsible and they were to be punished by the Government.[77]

4. Buoyage Duty

From 1846 Government imposed a new type of duty known as Buoyage Duty. This duty was to be levied on all vessels laden with cargoes other than salt visiting to all ports of Balasore. This Buoyage Duty was not applicable to salt as the salt trade was owned by the Government in those days. This new duty was called as Buoyage Duty because buoys were placed as signals by the Government on the mouths of the rivers to facilitate the Captains for easy entrance into ports. The rates of Buoyage Duty was fixed at Rs. 8 each on a vessel carrying less than 2,000 maunds of load, Rs. 10 each on a vessel with a load of 2,000 maunds and above and Rs. 15 each on a vessel with the cargoes above 5,000 maunds.[78] By the introduction of Buoyage Duty the income of the Government increased slightly. The total income during the period of 5 years from 1848-49 to 1852-53 stood at Rs. 12,287-11-5 pies against the establishment cost of Rs. 6,183-15-0 pies. The Government received a revenue of Rs. 6,103-12-5 pies.

77. PBCSO, August 1851, Collector of Customs to Commissioner of Cuttack, No. 17, August 8, 1851.

78. Collector, Government Customs to Henry Ricket, Member Board of Revenue, No. 14, November 25, 1853 (OSA).

Henry Ricket, the Member Board of Revenue in his report of inspection regarding Custom House of Balasore, said that the Balasore Custom House was established merely to check the evasion of the payment of port dues by the merchants at Calcutta.[79]

A small Marine Department was also maintained at Balasore. A master attendant remained in charge of the regulation of vessels, of buoys at the river mouths of Burabalanga and Dhamara and their Buoyage Duties thereof. Further he was required to assist distressed vessels and to take charge of wrecked property and to make annual supplies of opium, stationery etc. to Cuttack, Puri and Balasore.[80]

5. Customs Act, 1855

Buoyage Duty was imposed on every port but Government afforded no facilities in the river mouths except that of Burabalanga and Dhamara. A new Act was passed in the year 1855 by the Government of India. It was aimed at regulating the ports and port dues. According to this new Act port dues were to be collected from all the 8 ports of Balasore. The size of the ports and the volume of trade conducted in the ports were never taken into consideration by the Government of India at the time of its enactment. The Commissioner raised his voice against this Act. He said that this Act should not be applicable to the smaller ports even Dhamara. According to his view it should only be applicable to Balasore port, as Balasore port was dealing with a large volume of trade. To strengthen the argument of the Commissioner the master attendant Mr. White supplied the following statistics about the number of vessels visting to different ports from 1852-56.[81]

79. Selection from Records, Government of Bengal, No. XXX, 1853.
80. *Ibid.*
81. BRP (Customs), June 1857, W. White to Collector, Balasore, No. 95, June 18, 1857.

	1852	1853	1854	1855	1856
Subarnarekha	02	14	10	14	15
Sartha	22	42	46	35	37
Balasore	64	73	72	69	107
Lochanpur or Lychanpore	20	24	12	16	21
Chudamani or Churamani	14	04	06	19	39
Dhamara	38	34	56	31	08
Chhanoa	—	—	—	—	—

Mr. White further stated that no facilities were extended to smaller ports by the Government. Buoys were never placed in all the ports except Dhamara and Balasore. Thus the exaction of Buoyage Duty was nothing but a tax for only loading and unloading of cargoes in those smaller ports.[82]

Taking all the factors into consideration the Commissioner, Cuttack, suggested to limit the new Act of 1855 only to the Balasore port. These suggestions were never taken into consideration by the Government of India. In 1858 the Government of India prepared a scheme of regulations for the ports of Orissa. This new Act of 1858 declared all the ports, Balasore, Churamani, Lychanpore, Chhanoa, Sartha, Subarnarekha and Dhamara as one single port, that was Balasore port. The port dues were to be collected at the rate of 6 annas for every 100 maunds of cargoes of any descriptions. Amount of port dues received, as per this new rate, was required to be credited to a common fund named as Balasore Port Fund. All expenses for the maintenance of these ports were to be out of this Fund.[83] Thus this new Act brought a radical change in the administration of the main Custom House at Balasore.

82. BRP (Customs), August 1857, W. White to Collector, Balasore, No. 109, July 29, 1857.

83. ALC, India, Vol. III, Pr. 547 and 548,

The great Orissa Famine brought a change in the administration of the Customs Department. Many small ports vanished due to extra burden of tax imposed on them. False Point port was gaining popularity at the cost of the decline of smaller ports except Balasore. Government wanted to levy all types of port dues on False Point. But Sec. 33 of the Act of 1855 did not include False Point in the list of ports in Orissa.[84] Government introduced a special rule in 1861 for False Point.[85] As a result of which False Point was accepted as a port of importance. A custom house was established prior to it in the year 1860 which was specially meant for False Point.[86] According to the new rules the rate of customs duty at False Point was raised from Rs. 2 to Rs. 4 per ton of cargoes.[87] Initially a part time writer was appointed on an allowance. The writer was entitled to get his allowance so long as the vessels were present in the port and as long as he was engaged in the work of the custom house. Besides the writer, the Superintendent of the Light House and his assistants were also paid extra allowance for their services to the Customs Department when the vessels were present in the custom house.[88] The Custom House at False Point was maintained on a temporary arrangement basis till permanent staff were appointed. The administration of this custom house was regulated by the Collector of Cuttack. A Preventive Officer was appointed in the port at False Point in 1862 who was to take charge of portal communication and collection of customs dues. His salary was fixed at Rs. 30 per month. He thus functioned both, as a Preventive Officer and a Customs Officer.[89]

84. BRP (Customs), April 1871, Macferson, Collector of Customs to Commissioner, Cuttack, No. 2A, April 4, 1871.

85. *Ibid.*

86. PBCSO, May 1868, Armstrong, Collector of Cuttack to Commissioner, Cuttack, No. 7, May 2, 1866.

87. BdRP, January 1862, H. Bell, Jr. Secretary, Government of Bengal to Board of Revenue, Fort William, January 22, 1862.

88. PBCSO, May 1868, Armstrong, Collector of Cuttack to Commissioner, Cuttack, No. 7, May 2, 1868.

89. Resolutions, Finance Department, Fort William, April 9, 1862.

6. Customs Rules for False Point

The new rules for False Point Custom House were passed bearing in mind the environment and the difficulties encountered in loading and unloading of cargoes. As per the rules shipping bills were granted after due settlement of duties for goods. Boat notes were signed by the officer in charge of Customs and after that, boat notes were issued alongwith each despatch. The shipping bills were granted by the Collector, Cuttack after the payment of duties by the shippers. It was found that some difficulties arose out of the shipping bills. The figures entered in the shipping bill differed to the figure of the commodities arrived after careful examination by the custom house. This continued. Macferson, the Collector of Customs, pointed out that no other practice in realising the exact customs duty was ever possible under the existing rules of 1861.[90] Keeping this in view he suggested a change of rules, but no change was affected.

The Board of Revenue directed the Commissioner, Cuttack to implement the rules effectively in their letter No. 13C of January 23, 1871. But it was not possible to act according to the direction. As regards the import cargoes from foreign ports, the cargoes were taken to custom house where there was no officer to receive such goods. The only person who granted the pass to the unportionate consigner for delivery of goods, was a temporary staff. Thus strict vigilance could not be affected to yield customs dues out of the foreign goods. Under these circumstances it was suggested by Macferson to close the port till permanent arrangements were made and till False Point was declared as a regulated port of Orissa like other ports.[91] However the system continued without any alteration.

90. BRP (Customs), April 1871, Macferson, Collector of Customs to Commissioner, Cuttack, No. 2A, April 4, 1871.

91. *Ibid.*

Under the changing circumstances caused by the great famine, Government explored the possibility of making False Point as an important port to speed up the food supply into the province. Dhamara gradually ceased to operate any trade due to the silting of river Dhamara. Chandbali was not an established port, until it came into existence in 1872. Thus False Point attracted the concentration of the Government. Strict regulations were not enforced in this Custom House. The port was visited by 15 vessels in the year 1868-69 which was an increase in comparison to previous years. These 15 vessels included 7 steamers with 5,795 tons of load, 6 squir rigged with 918 tons of load and 2 native crafts having 74 tons of cargoes. These vessels brought both private and merchandise goods.[92] Out of these vessels no customs duties were realised. Only trade in paddy and grain was made by the year ending 1869 amounting 12,500 maunds of Rs. 19,209 value. These goods were exempted from customs duties. The trade in paddy and grain did not fetch any Government revenue from the Custom House at False Point. Not a single vessel from any foreign country visited any ports of Orissa in the year 1869.[93] During the whole year only Rs. 1,975 was received as import duty on the cargoes of the vessel Juhu Chism.[94] Except this amount, Government received no customs duties since 1866 upto 1869.[95] On the other hand the establishment cost increased. Due to the negligence of the Government to make permanent arrangement in the Custom House at False Point and to construct warehouses for the portal trade through the False Point, the revenue decreased. Hence the customs dues out of the portal trade remained stagnant with the figure of 1868.[96] This state of affairs continued to exist for some years.

92. BRP (Customs), August 1869, Macferson, Collector of Customs to Commissioner, Cuttack, No. 20, August 14, 1869.

93. *Ibid.*

94. *Ibid.*

95. *Ibid.*

96. BdRP, September 1868, Armstrong, Collector, Cuttack to Board of Revenue, No. 42, September 4, 1868.

The number of vessels visited the port at False Point increased by 34 in the year 1870-71. The total number of 105 vessels visited the port out of which there were 50 steamers, 4 British squir rigged, 28 British Indian squir rigged and 23 native squir rigged. The aggregate trade of the district of Cuttack at False Point amounted to Rs. 17,01,784 of which nearly Rs. 5,400 belonged to foreign trade.[97]

The vessel Bett started plying regularly between the ports of Calcutta, Balasore, Dhamara and False Point with passenger traffic and goods. Subsequently regular steamer service was started between Calcutta and the ports of Orissa. That indicated a progress in the portal trade of Orissa.[98]

The value of the foreign trade also increased at False Point in the year 1870-71. The total cost of foreign trade amounted to Rs. 53,705 against Rs. 30,852 in the year 1869-70.[99] The articles of export were grain and oil-seeds. They were exported to Ceylon and other European ports.[100] Out of this trade an amount of Rs. 4,326 was realised as duty but subsequently Rs. 1,125 were refunded as this amount was collected from a vessel carrying grains. An amount of Rs. 3,201 was realised as customs duty from exports in the year 1870-71.[101]

The value of import and export trade increased in 1873-74 in comparison to the year 1872-73 resulting in the increase of customs duty in the ports of Orissa. The trade statistics gives a clear picture about the increase of customs duty[102] as in Appendix 'F'.

The import and export in all the ports of Orissa increased further in 1878-79. Consequently with the increase of the

97. BRP (Customs), April 1871, Macferson, Collector of Customs to Commissioner, Cuttack, No. 13, April 5, 1871.
98. *Ibid.*
99. *Ibid.*
100. *Ibid.*
101. *Ibid.*
102. GAROD, 1873-74, p. 34.

portal trade, the Government customs duty also increased. The tonnage of cargoes correspondingly fluctuated. During the year 1878-79 Government collected customs duties to a considerable amount. An amount of Rs. 55,394 was collected as customs revenue from False Point in 1878-79, that being the highest turnover from that port till its decline. A clear picture about the total volume of import and export and the customs duty derived out of the trade can be drawn from the table as shown in Appendix 'C'.[103]

A total amount of Rs. 80,718 was realised as customs revenue in the year 1878-79 from the ports of Orissa against the collection of Rs. 72,067 in 1874-75 and Rs. 36,344 1877-78.

As regards False Point the Indian Ports Act was not extended to the port till 1375.[104] The Government of Bengal moved the Government of India to extend the Act to False Point but no action was taken. As the port was not regulated by law earlier the expectation of making it an important port and the collection of customs dues could not be materialised through the custom house. False Point partially was brought under the Customs Department. A Sub-Deputy Collector was appointed at the CustomHouse, False Point, after which the collection of customs dues gradually increased.

In the year 1882-83 from Subarnarekha the freight charges or transit duty of articles exported to Calcutta were collected to the extent of Rs. 15 on 100 maunds of rice, Rs. 14 on 100 maunds of paddy and Rs. 8 on firewood.[105] In the same year a fine of Rs. 10 each was collected by the Customs Officer, Subarnarekha from 2 merchants, Jagannath Kamila and Madan Behera having violated the customs rules of the port.[106] This gives a clear evidence that even though the port

103. *Ibid*, 1878-79, p. 18.

104. Malley, S.S.O., *Bihar and Orissa Cazetteer, Cuttack*, p. 168.

105. BRP (Customs), March 1882, Customs Officer to Collector of Sea Customs, Balasore, No. 52, March 7, 1882.

106. *Ibid*, February, 1882, Customs Officer to Deputy Collector in charge of Balasore, No. 69, February 20, 1882.

Subarnarekha was in a declining condition the Government received customs duty from the port.

Customs Regulation was extended to False Point. A Customs Officer was appointed in the Custom House at False Point to work independently. The Government worked out this new system after the year 1875 with the hope of getting more customs revenue from the port at False Point. No extra facilities like anchorage and storage were provided to this port. Even though lands were acquired at Jamboo for a better customs establishment with no expenditure from Government treasury, the scheme submitted before the Government was not accepted. As a result of which False Point which served the Government as well as the people during the period of Famine could not prosper.

7. Rules of 1893

The Lt. Governor of Bengal in exercise of the power conferred on him by Sec. 33 and 34 of Indian Ports Act, 1889 and with the sanction of the Governor General in Council passed some new rules for the Custom Houses in Orissan ports. These new rules came into force from May 1, 1893. According to the provisions it was directed that the Customs Officer should collect port dues or customs dues at the rate of 4 annas per ton upon every sea going vessels carrying 10 tons and above. It was again said in the provision that this rate of customs dues should not be levied on the mail steamer and the coasting vessels more than once in 60 days.[107]

In accordance with the rules laid down in the Indian Ports Act the custom house established at Chandbali port remained under the control of a Sub-Deputy Collector. In the year 1895 the administration of the Chandbali Custom House received a change. The posts of Port Officer and Customs Officer were amalgamated into one. This came into

107. File No. 35, 1893, Resolution of Government of Bengal, Marine Department, No. 9 (OSA).

effect from November 1, 1895. The salary of the new officer was fixed at Rs. 300 per month. The total amount of Rs. 3,600 as the salary of this Officer for the whole year was decided to be divided between Customs Fund and Ports Fund equally.[108]

8. Decline of Customs Duties and Consequences

With the new arrangements declared by the Government, high customs revenue was expected. Government was also very keen to regulate the Customs Offices in Orissa with a minimum cost of establishment. Orissa was denied the economic benefit out of the portal trade. The Government also received negative results out of the new customs rules. Nature worked on its own way. The silting of rivers did never allow the important ports to exist. With the facilities available the local merchants were not able to compete with the foreign merchants with whatever resources available with them. The greater volume of export of foodgrains had its impact. The import trade declined. When such was the state of affairs the Government went on imposing new types of port dues on the articles of import and export to yield a better customs revenue. These vital problems denied the Orissan merchants for better portal trade to earn economic prosperity for the whole of Orissa. Simultaneously the Government lost the customs revenue which could not reach upto their estimation.

The decline of portal trade and the duties derivable from it, mainly was caused, as a volume of trade in the ports of Orissa were diverted towards the Coast Canal after it was being ready in 1887 for traffic. The trade in Coast Canal increased having its corresponding decline in the portal trade. With the development of inland communication there started brisk inland trade in Orissa. Merchants preferred inland trade as the cost of the portal trade was much higher due to the heavy pressure of customs duty. The extension of railway to Orissa contributed further in the decline of portal trade.[109]

108. BLCP, March 28, 1896.
109. BLCP, March 1898, Oollin, Secretary, Board of Revenue to Government of Bengal, No. 240A, March 10, 1898.

The rise of price in foodgrains resulted in the price rise of other articles by which portal trade had a severe fall. As a whole the people of Orissa from the economic point of view were not benefited either out of the ports or from the portal trade.

As trade was concerned, the latter part of the 19th century following the years of Famine, was marked by an impressive increase of portal trade by the Government but on the other hand there was no increase of wealth and comfort in Orissa. It was because of the fact that the whole export trade was confined to foodgrains and other raw products of nature and the import trade was confined to finished goods of Europe. However the improvement of regular trade definitely gave this country an advantage of security against a second great Orissa Famine with the intensity of the first one by facilitating the mobilisation of labour and importation of foodgrains at call.

The expectation of T.E. Ravenshaw, Commissioner, Orissa Division was that the development of ports and sea borne traffic would affect a complete economic revolution for the Government through the collection of customs revenue changing a backward, isolated and unimportant country into a busy and prosperous centre of trade, which did not prove true.[110] Thus the expected customs revenue could not be collected by the Government rather the system of customs depreciated in the economy of the whole of Orissa. Government's zeal to realise more customs revenue proved fatal making the sea-shores of Orissa desert by the end of 19th century.

110. GAROD, 1876-77, p. 11.

5

Indigenous Industries and Impact of British Policy

Agriculture was the prime occupation of the people of Orissa but by no means the only occupation for their subsistence. Considerably a large portion of the population depended on industry. Industry and commence always played an important role in the economic prosperity of the people of Orissa. A large portion of the Orissan population was engaged in various types of industries down to the British conquest. Weaving was an important industry of the people. Large number of women in Orissa collected the family income by their earning from spinning, dyeing, tanning and by working in metals and from other Cottage Industries.

Pre-British Industrial Prosperity

The manufacturers of Orissa especially in cotton and silk textile had a wide range of demad in the Asiatic markets from the remote past. The Indian merchants with trade centres at Balasore, Pipili, Hariharpur and Hoogli carried on huge and extensive trade with Malaya, Indonesian Archipelago even before the arrival of the British merchants in these ports. In the 15th century the supply of Orissan textile to Malacca was made from the ports of Orissa. The merchants went to Bantam, Pegu, Tenaserim, Achim and even to the red sea ports of Aden and Jeddah in the Middle East.[1] The initiative and drive of the Dutch and English in the early part of 17th century opened new markets for Orissa cotton and silk textile manufacturers. The Japanese markets were opened for such silk manufacture of Orissa. The export of Orissan commodities like sugar, textile manufacture, earthen pots and other handicrafts was a net addition to the economy of this country. It reflected the industrial prosperity of Orissa before British conquest.[2] The textile commodities and sugar which were exported from Balasore had wide markets in Persia and Ceylon also.[3] These industrial products were sold in foreign markets in exchange of finished goods of European countries. The English merchant resorted to barter system for the textile products of Orissa especially. For better trade links gradually the Dutch and the English Companies assisted Indian merchants dealing with Orissan textile product with loans, vessels and other equipments for trade and industrial establishments.[4] The only consideration of controlling a vast hinterland for textile industry at Balasore prompted the English Company to exhaust heavy investment in Orissa. The English Company also decided to move from Hoogli to Pipili. The period of British advent ultimately forced the Dutch Company to quit Balasore.

Balasore was a cotton growing place. Cotton and Tasar manufacturers of this hinterland used to sell their products at Balasore. Most prominent places around Balasore for these manufacturers were Soro, Hariharpur, Mohanpur and Kashiyari. These places were specialising in the manufacture of Sannoes.[5] The articians of Soro had also their manufacturing centres in the outskirts of Balasore. Naturally for this the

1. Moreland, *A Study on the Indian Economic History* (India Edition), 1972, pp. 39-49
2. DWH, Vol. II, London, 1681-87, p. 239.
3. Arasratnam, *Dutch Power in Ceylon*, 1658-89, pp. 147 151.
4. Foster, W., *The English Factories in India*, 1661-64, p. 211.
5. Sirkar, J.N., *Studies in Mughal India*, pp. 228-29.

English merchants had the desire for heavy investments in and around Balasore. The textile industry flourished with the foreign patronisation in Balasore and other parts of Orissa but with the dawn of 18th century the Orissan foreign trade in sugar and textile faced problems in course of time. In 18th century uncertainties in the industrial economy crept into the minds of the merchants. The village level industries of Orissa could not sustain the heavy foreign competition and the financial exortions of the Muslim *fauzadars* and private traders for duty free trade. In the circumstances the foreign merchants looked for the help of native merchants. They were identified as *Dadani* merchants. The *Dadani* merchants worked as associates to the English merchants. During the first half of 19th century the East India Company had to fight with the challenges of these *Dadani* merchants and the rival parties to safeguard their investment and interest on textile industries in Orissa.[6] In 1751 the situation was completely changed. Bhonsle rulers of Nagpur assumed the power as rulers of Orissa. So also they obtained the control of tax collection. The British merchants feared to invest more on cotton textile industry with risk of getting frequent attacks by the Maratha *Bargis*. Consequent upon this the textile industry declined. In the second half of 18th century the Dutch and English factories could not withstand the blows of the Maratha misrule. Heavy demand of Bhonsle's regime made the cotton cultivation unremunerative. As a result of which the cotton weavers migrated to the outskirts of Balasore for protection particularly to Medinapur, Sunamukhi and Chandrakonas.[7] Thus by the time of British interference textile industry was in a state of decline.

The *Gossain* merchants had an important role to play with the growth of industry in the pre-British period. They had gradually monopolised the industrial system of Orissa. Their terms of contract with the cultivators and artisans were rigorous. Their money lending process was fixed at an

6. DSM, Vol. II, pp. 887-888
7. Dutta, K.K., *Studies in the History of Bengal Subah*, 1740-70, Vol. I, pp. 420-27, 435-36.

exorbitant rate of interest. This trend of the *Gossain* merchants kept the purchase money at a low rate. The artisans could not sustain such terrible loss. The entrepreneurs attached to the textile, sugar (Gur) and mustard oil industries were harassed by the *Gossain* merchants. All of the manufacturers and intermediaries felt the severe pinch of this financial instability.[8]

Thus the withdrawal of the investment of the foreign companies from the village based manufacturers, the tendencies of the *Gossain* merchants to exact more profit for their investment, the ruling anarchy on the trade routes, the migration of the weaving class and the harassment of the artisans in the hands of the money lenders together inflicted a death blow on the village based industry by the time the British conquest was affected in 1803 after the fall of Bhonsle's regime.

A. BRITISH INDUSTRIAL POLICY

The British officers after the conquest made no delay in analysing the conditions of the industries in Orissa. In 1805 they issued a detailed proclamation to regulate the commercial and industrial activities of Orissa and imposed excise duties on all types of manufactures.[9] The Company Government immediately thought of mobilising their investment on textile production in the coastal production centres of Balasore, Bhadrak and Jajpur.[10] They sent Mr. Brown from the Board of Trade to explore the possibility of mobilising more investment in varieties of textile products like *Mulmuls*, Terimdams and other thin muslins which were so long exported to Nagpur and other foreign countries. The Company decided to supply cotton thread to poor weavers of Bhadark, Jajpur and the neighbouring villages. The Company further proposed to engage these weaver families who in early 18th century

8. *Ibid*, pp. 463-64.
9. BJP(C), January 1805, C. Goram to Commissioner, Cuttack, January 26, 1805.
10. *Ibid*, No. 27, September 5, 1805, Commissioner, Cuttack to Chief Secretary, Government of Bengal, September 2, 1805.

migrated from Medinapur to settle in Orissa under the protection of East India Company. These weavers were habituated in making small and narrow cloths for the local use. The Company decided to engage these weavers to prepare long cloths and *Baptas* with the Company's investment.[11] In the first year the investment did not exceed Rs. 2,000 which negated the hope of raising it to Rs. 5,000. This was due to the refusal of weavers to enter into contract with the Company's textile investment.[12] No revolutionary change was affected in textile industry during the 1st decade of 19th century. The quantity of manufacture declined in 1825 compared with the previous year's for the dispute between the cloth merchants and their agents in Calcutta and for the competition the Orissan textile industry faced with Bengal goods and the goods of Lancashire. As such a sizeable quantity of textile products could find its way to Tributary Mahals. Hence the village based textile industry continued to depend on the consumption inside the country when the exportation was sealed.

With the renewal of the Company's charter the free trade policy was admitted in India. That was made applicable to Orissa also. The industries that afforded employment to the people of Orissa like stone cutting, capentry, boat building, manufacturing of brass utensils, gold and silver filigree work, dyeing and tanning and the village based weaving industry of Orissa did not interest the Company much but on other profiteering industry including heavy textile industry they desired to go with heavy investment.

The Company Government wanted to push their machine made textile goods into the markets of Orissa following the years of the continental blockade of Napolean Bonaparte. British machine made cloths comparatively cheaper in value easily captured the markets in Orissa. As a result of which the

11. *Ibid*, No. 30, April 1805, J.T. Brown to Thornhill, Secretary, Board of Trade, February 12, 1805.
12. BJP(C), No. 30, April 1805, Superintendent, Cloth Investment to Governor General in Council.

textile industries in Orissa declined. The weavers of reputation engaged in village textile industry were completely ruined who became the agricultural wage earners. For this one sided policy of the Company the weaving industry of this country did not exist by 1901-02.[13]

The most important indigenous Salt Industry of Orissa which afforded employment to many could not also thrive due to the fact that the Company Government wanted to monopolise salt trade and Salt Industry and the Company Government decided to impose the high rate of duties on salt. Further this Industry perished with the equalisation of duties with imported salt by which the salt prepared in Orissa could not challenge the competition with salt manufactured in Madras and smuggled through Khurda. The decline of this Industry was neither connected with the *Bargir hangama* nor connected with the collapse of law and order situation. But the expensive construction of embankments, unhealthy climate, lack of fuel lands near the *Aurangs* and the rise of wage caused by the rise of prices of commodities had pernicious effect on the rise of the cost of manufacture of salt. On the other hand the selling price of salt remained static. These factors made the production unremunerative and unattractive to the wage earners engaged in salt fields.

When most important industries like textile industries and Salt Industry having the British interest for which they were prepared to invest could not thrive after the withdrawal of the investment policy of the Company Government, it is impossible to think of the prosperity and continuity of other industries in Orissa which existed in Pre-British period. To add to this the monopolistic theory adopted by the Company and the restriction imposed by the Laissez-Faire policy to withdraw direct assistance by the East India Company Government virtually were responsible for the decline of industries in 19th century.

13. Mukherjee, P., *History of Orissa*, p. 480.

B. COTTAGE INDUSTRIES IN 19TH CENTURY

1. Weaving (Textile) Industry

Orissa had a wide reputation in textile industry in the past. The Oriya merchants had good business in many of the South-Eastern countries. The Europeans were fully acknowledging the calicoes of Balasore, Bhadrak and Harispur (Hariharpur). The products of these places received heavy appreciation in Europe.[14] Fine muslin of Gulnagar in Kendrapara Sub-Division in Cuttack district had once a good reputation inside and outside India.[15] Besides cotton cloths of coarse variety were made in many villages for local use only. Sometimes the products of this weaving industry were not merely sold in the localities but were also sent to *hats* for sale.

The village weavers used to manufacture their products through *Tantas* (hand made looms). The weavers were identified in the society as *tantis.* With the help of these primitive instruments it was not possible on the part of the weavers to get good outturns to compete with the mill made textiles in the markets of Orissa. Consequent upon this stiff competition many of the weavers' family tried to get their livelihood from agriculture. Weaving then was not carried on as an organised industry but it was confined in the homes of the weavers themselves who were frequently agriculturists. Most of the weavers were completely ruined. Only 4 weavers possessed valid license under the License Tax Act by 1880.[16] This village based industry thus could not thrive. Nevertheless it is interesting to note that the number of cotton weavers increased by 35 per cent since 1901 in Orissa.[17]

The main cause of decline of this weaving industry in Orissa was the floating of Lancashire textile products and the

14. BdRP (Customs), March 1818, C. Becger, Collector of Customs, Balasore to Commissioner, Cuttack, March 2, 1818.
15. GAROD, 1899-1900, Pr. 35, p. 9.
16. GAROD, 1880-81, p. 13.
17. Malley, S.S.O., *Bihar aud Orissa Gazetteer, Puri*, p. 203.

European machine made textiles which were superior than the product of Orissan weaving industry. The texture and the price naturally attracted the consumers in the markets. The sale of the products of the Bombay group of mills virtually made the final blow on the local cotton textile industry. Most of the weavers' family who had the reputation for their craft and efficiency were completely ruined and they were left to the mercy of other income groups As per the survey of 1901-02 there was no manufacture of weaving products of importance in Orissa.[18]

2. Tasar Weaving Industry

Weaving of Tasar silk on a small scale was carried on in the village of Gopalpur in Dharmasala thana in the Cuttack district.[19] The Silk Industry like the cultivation of betel leaf was introduced by a few Bengali families. Having migrated to Cuttack from Burdwan or Medinapur they were engaged in this Industry. There were about 600 persons engaged in this Tasar Weaving Industry. They used to do this for the last 7 generations.[20] Almost every family owned a loom and managed to earn 2 annas a day per person. They did not like to go for any other profession as they were always self-sufficient for family maintenance. They were following the simplest method of weaving through the help of looms. Tasar cloth was also manufactured in Puri district to a small extent.[21] This Industry provided employment to a good number of skilled weavers.

3. Metal Industry

There were a number of metal workers in Orissa during the Pre-British period. Dhenkanal, the Tributary State earned a good name in this Industry. Iron was being extracted from hills of Dhenkanal. Many people were engaged. The persons

18. Mukherjee, P., *History of Orissa*, p.480.
19. Malley, S.S.O., *Bihar and Orissa Gazetteer, Cuttack*, p. 152.
20. *Ibid.*
21. GAROD, 1890-91, p. 8.

engaged in this were remunerated at the rate of Rs. 3 per month.[22] Many ironsmiths were earning their livelihood being engaged in the Iron Ore Foundry in Sambalpur and Phuljhar etc.[23] A little iron smelting was also carried on in the hilly estate of Sukinda in Cuttack district that afforded employment to many.[24] Iron used in the temples of Orissa built many centuries ago gives a clear evidence that Iron Industry existed earlier in Orissa much before the extension of the British administration to this country.

4. Brass and Bell Metal Industry

The utensils of daily use for eating purposes formed a universal need of Orissa. These utensils were manufactured in village industries. These industries were not common. Utensils made of brass and bell metal were in common use of the people of Orissa. Brass utensils were made out of an alloy of copper and zinc. Bell metal was the composition of high tin, bronze containing upto 30 per cent tin and some zinc and lead. This mixture of metals called *Kansa* was in extensive use in manufacturing household utensils. Copper and bronze utensils or vessels were generally used in temples of Orissa. Bell metal and brass ornaments were also in extensive use amongst the women in Orissa.[25]

A good number of brass and bell metal workers lived in different parts of Orissa. These workers were called *Thataris*. *Thataris* continued to manufacture their articles during the whole of British period. Ghantimunda in Cuttack district at a distance of about 16 K.M. from Cuttack town occupied an unique place in making *Kansa* and brass utensils.[26] Kantilo in Cuttack district at a distance of 35 K.M, from Banki town manufactured utensils of brass and bell metals.[27] Balakati in

22. Toynbee, G., *A Sketch of the History of Orissa*, pp. 180-182.
23. GAROD, 1872-73, p. 9.
24. *Ibid*, Pr. 35, p. 9.
25. *Ibid*, 1899-1900, p. 9.
26. GAROD, 1890-91, p. 8.
27. *Ibid*, 1889-90, Pr. 57, p. 9.

Puri district was also famous for this Industry.[28] Bhuban in the present Dhenkanal district was also famous for this. The existence of *Thatari* families in large number speaks about their monopoly in this Industry at Bhuban. The products of Brass and Bell Metal Industry were sold in the Tributary States and to a limited extent in the neighbouring districts.[29] This Industry for the obvious reasons of its common necessity by the people could not decline. Furthermore this Industry did not face any competition in the market with the finished English goods. As a result of which the Brass and Bell Metal Industry continued to exist without any trouble providing ample employment opportunity to many Oriya artisans.

5. Filigree Industry

The goldsmiths and silversmiths of villages earned their livelihood regularly out of filigree works. The making of ornaments in gold and silver was their professional business. Cuttack earned a worldwide reputation for filigree work. The workers used to prepare fine delicate knotted specimens of gold and silver ornaments. The articles prepared by them could be small and big but were used on special occasions. Mirror holders, rose water sprinklers, small boxes, temples of miniature forms, animals and birds etc. were skilfully prepared by filigree workers of Cuttack town. This unorganised cottage industry afforded employment to about 400 families in Cuttack town and more than 2,000 families in the interior.[30] To make it an organised cottage industry, Utkal Gaurab Madhusudan Das, the pioneer of modern industry established the Orissa Art Wares at Cuttack that afforded employment to these artisans in a organised manner. Specimens of filigree works of Cuttack were sent to European exhibition which received European appreciation.[31]

28. *Ibid*, 1890-91, p. 8; Malley, S.S.O., *Bihar and Orissa Gazetteer, Puri*, p. 211.
29. GAROD, 1899-1900, Pr. 35, p. 9.
30. Malley, S.S.O., *Bihar and Orissa Gazetteer, Cuttack*, p. 150.
31. Mukherjee, P., *History of Orissa*, p. 179.

Gold was found in Tirka river near Angul and in Brahmani and Subarnarekha river beds.[32] Goldsmiths of Orissa made use of this gold in making ornaments as required by the customers. Though the income was not very high a number of families were able to survive on this gold trade and industry.[33]

6. Hide Industry

Another important article of export from Orissa was hide. The dense forests of Orissa afforded plenty of opportunity for this trade. The spread of Leather Industry in Northern India demanded plenty of hides from different parts of India. The business community rushed to Orissa to take advantage of the availability of hides in large quantity. Cuttack district alone exported 13,979 pieces of hides at a cost of Rs. 23,053 during the year 1869-70.[34] During the year 1876-77 Balasore port exported 1,39,863 pieces, Cuttack exported 74,234 pieces and Puri exported 2,14,106 pieces of hides to different places.[35] The value of export of hides from Orissa reached at Rs. 5,00,000 in the year 1898-99. This figure revealed a remarkable achievement in this Hide Industry and trade.

The communities which collected animal skins preferably big animals belonged to rural areas. They belonged to the lowest caste of the Society. Leather manufacture had many phases from the beginning of skin collection to the last of delivery of finished leather goods. These phases were monopolised by the skilled class. The tanners, leather dyers and shoe makers were all experts in their own profession. All skilled

32. File No. 126, Misc. Collection IV, Application of H. Miller Co. for grant of concession for monopoly of washing of gold of Brahmani (OSA); BRP, Nos. 38-46, May 1890.

33. Jena, K.C., *Socio-Economic Conditions of Orissa (19th century)*, p. 127.

34. BCHR, Macferson, Collector of Customs to Grey, Assistant Collector of Customs, False Point, No. 21, July 9, 1870 (OSA).

35. GAROD, 1876-77 and 1877-78.

workers other than the shoe makers were called *chamars*, shoe makers known as *mochis* were not as common as the *chamars*. *Mochis* were found generally in small and big towns. These families were getting their bread from this Hide Industry in Orissa.

The businessmen of Northern India exploited the situation and engaged their agents for the collection of hides from interior junglee villages of Orissa. The *mochis* who were manufacturers of leather goods could not withstand the competition when the North India businessmen were ready to give high prices for the hides. Many leather workers were thrown into unemployment though the middle men belonging to Orissa engaged for the procurement of hides were benefited. Consequent upon the export of hides in large quantity from Orissa the leather cottage industry declined which was again reflected on the economy of this group of families. This change in the trend of hide business crippled the local Leather Industry.[36] The Utkal Tannery, the first organised Leather Industry also received the same injury for its decline. One or two small tanneries managed to exist in Cuttack to manufacture ladies' shoes, ordinary leather suitcase etc.[37]

7. Pottery Industry

The potters were important members of the village community all over Orissa. Earthen pots were used by every family for cooking, carrying water from the ponds to the house and fields, for the purpose of storage and religious functions.[38] In any case every house required earthen pots always. The supply of pots to every house became the universal need. This kept the potter of a village always busy in his profession with his wheel as instrument. The potters were neither poor nor very rich. The services of the potters were always acknowledged and nowhere it was challenged in Orissa.

36. Dutta, R.C., *Economic History of India*, Vol. II, p. 253.
37. Mallev, S.S.O., *Bihar and Orissa Gazetteer, Cuttack*, p. 153.
38. GAROD, 1899-1900, Pr. 38, p. 9.

The *handis, kalasis* and *surehis* of various size were the products of the pottery. Pottery thus provided the means of livelihood to the potters' family throughout Orissa.

8. Stone Carving

In the statement of E.B. Havell in the monograph "Stone carving in Bengal" published in 1906 it was said that within the area in Bengal as a stone building country Orissa excelled other places.[39] Under the patronage of native dynasties of early time a great style of stone architecture and stone carving was developed. In the ornamentation of temples and other works of stone which were built in different times in the district of Cuttack and Puri in Orissa, carvers acquired the most extraordinary technical skill. There were stone carvers found in many places in Orissa. In spite of the discouraging condition around them they were in no way inferior than others in artistic perception and technical skill. The Director General, Archaeological Survey in 1902-03 said that the work of the modern stone mason a native of Bhubaneswar and of surrounding places did not lag behind the old working style.[40] The stone carvers of Orissa one day had excelled others in producing bold effects of light and shade that made a statue more lively. Thus the stone carvers, the wage earner group were superior to the stone artisans of European countries.

A small colony of stone carvers settled at Naltigiri (Lalitgiri) about 50 K.M. from Cuttack town used to make images of Gods of continental design. This Industry was introduced for the first time there by the Marathas but it could not make any progress. Manufacture of stone vessels of soft stone was confined to Puri district.[41] Families of stone carvers were also manufacturing stone vessels of different size in many Tributary Mahals like Nilgiri and Dhenkanal. Stone Carving Industry had its origin from very ancient days in Orissa which was originally patronised by the native kings and

39. Malley, S S.O., *Bihar and Orissa Gazetteer, Puri* (Quoted), p. 208.
40. *Ibid.*
41. GAROD, 1890-91, p. 8.

gradually it had its decline due to the localisation of the products inside Orissa only. However during old days a good number of stone carvers were getting their subsistence out of this cottage industry.

9. Paper Industry

Paper used to be manufactured largely at Padmapur a place about 9 K.M. from Cuttack town on the Cuttack Kendrapara main road. In old times the Paper Industry of Padmapur was supplying paper as per the demand of the Orissa Division.[42] Paper was manufactured in this Industry out of bamboos and the colour of this paper was brown. This Industry declined owing to the competition with the imported cheap paper of better quality. The manufacture of this paper continued however upto 1896 and this was used in Cuttack Collectorate as Fly-Leaf because of its durability.[43]

10. Rope Industry

Rope and twine making afforded a livelihood for nearly 4,300 persons in Orissa.[44] Ropes were manufactured from cocoanut fibre. This Industry was very much present in almost all the villages in Puri district as cocoanut plants were plentily cultivated in this district. There was a small quantity of export trade in rope after meeting the general demand of rope all over Orissa.[45]

11. Sugar Industry (Gur)

Sugar was not manufactured in Orissa though sugarcane was cultivated. Sugarcane was mainly used for the preparation of molasses (Gur) for local consumption. This molasses manufacture was only made for a small period of 1 or 2 months a year. Many people were engaged in this by which

42. *Ibid*, 1894-95-96, p. 13.
43. *Ibid.*
44. Malley, S.S.O., *Bihar and Orissa Gazetteer, Puri*, p. 211.
45. *Ibid*, GAROD, 1894-95, p. 13.

they could collect the required quantity of molasses for home use and the rest were exported to other neighbouring places.

12. Bamboo and Cane Industry

Different kinds of articles manufactured from bamboo and cane were required by the people of Orissa for daily use. Bamboo workers were busy round the year in preparing articles of daily use such as baskets, bamoo mats, bamboo umbrellas, chairs and screens. Bamboo weaving was a simple craft which was monopolised by certain lower castes who were identified in the society as *Damas*. They were professional hereditary class engaged in the home industry and no other class ever tried to harm them for earning their livelihood. Such bamboo articles were extremely durable. During the absence of electricity bamboo fans were used in the Government Offices and in the houses of the rich men of Orissa. This Bamboo and Cane Industry existed extensively in almost all the villages of Orissa. A good number of people were engaged in this Industry and they were earning their livelihood out of this.

13. Carpentry Industry

The village carpenter was another useful member of the society. Even family required his help both for household furniturs and wooden tools. The cultivators in the field require implements for cultivation, the oilman required the instrument called *ghani* for the preparation of oil from the oilseeds, the weaver required looms for weaving and the potters required the wheel. Doors and windows were required for the construction of houses. For the grandeur of the Court, the monarch required aristocratic furniture. A carpenter was called upon to satisfy every section of the society who was in habit of making these articles at his own home and at home of other persons who called on him. As an useful[4] member of the society in every village of Orissa carpenter families lived. Artistic and decorative toy making was known to the carpenters of Orissa. The artistic engraving on the wooden plates fitted in many ancient temples testified the artistic quality of toy making of the carpenters of Orissa. The economic condition of the toy makers was definitely better than the ordinary carpenters all over India.[46] This was also true in the case of Orissan carpenters. General carpenters were getting their subsistence very comfortably in Orissa. The blacksmiths were also useful men in every village who belonged to the class of carpenters' family in Orissa.

14. Oil Pressing Industry (Ghani)

Oil was a main need for every household in Orissa. Oil was used for cooking and burning lamps before the use of Kerosene oil. Mustard oil was used for cooking, cocoanut oil was used for body masssage and castor oil was used to light lamps. The oil of every variety was manufactured by a class called oilman or *Teli.* He was using the *ghani* to get oil from oilseeds in a simplest method by the help of oxen. *Teli* or oilman was found in each and every village of Orissa. The oilman of Orissa used oilseeds cultivated in every part of Orissa as a major crop, as his raw materials. The *Teli* community remained engaged in their hereditary profession round the year in Orissa. This Oil Pressing Industry or *ghani* usually established by the *Telis* at their homes afforded employment to this community throughout Orissa.

15. Fishing Industry

Fishing was the occupation of an important section of the people of Puri. This district was the only one in the old Bengal Province with an open coast from which deep sea fishing could be carried on. The deep sea fishing was conducted not by local Oriyas but by Telgu settlers from Ganjam. They were called as *Nulivas*, who were found to have settled in Puri town, Nuagaon, Arkhakuda, Khirisai, Ramalenka, Sahadi and Manikpatna.[47] They used both Oriya and Telugu Language and gradually they became the permanent

46. Chopra, Puri and Das, *Social, Cultural and Economic History of India*, Vol. III, p. 159.
47. Malley, S S.O., *Bihar and Orissa Gazetteer, Puri*, pp. 204-205.

settlers of Puri district. Owing to the absence of any large markets in the neighbourhood most of the fish they collected were dried in the sun. They used to sell these dried fish throughout the year. Large varieties of fish were salted and exported to Calcutta and Tributary States. Some of these big varieties of salted dried fish was also exported to Calcutta by rail after Orissa was linked with Calcutta.[48] Fishing Industry was found on the coast of Chilka lake. The *Nulivas* living near Balugaon followed the same process and exported their products to Madras by rail when the East Coast Railway line was opened for traffic in 1897.[49] Thus Fishing Industry provided employment to a good number of poor people of Orissa. This also procured timber, wheat and oilseeds for consumption in Orissa from Tributary States in exchange of dried fish.[50]

16. Handicraft Industry

There were other minor Handicraft Industries in Orissa. The high standard Handicraft Industry was found in Puri district that manufactured *chandua*, very attractive for its decorative value made of small pieces of coloured cloths. This Industry existed at Pipili about 30 K.M. from Puri town.[51] These *chanduas* and *samianas* were used during festivals. Pipili also manufactured decorative umbrellas for temple use. Other art industries which included ivory carving and carpentry, horn toy making etc. were found in Cuttack district.[52] Palm Leaf Industry was carried on at Bahugram 15 K.M. from Cuttack town. It prepared delicate palm leaf baskets of different size and other palm allied articlesr[53] Shell ornaments were made to a limited extent in the Killa Kanika.[54] The shell articles were also manufactured by the skilled workers of

48. *Ibid.*
49. GAROD, 1899-1900, p. 31.
50. *Ibid*, 1882-83, p. 17.
51. Malley, S.S.O., *Bihar and Orissa Gazetteer, Puri*, p. 213.
52. GAROD, 1890-91, p. 8.
53. Malley, S.S.O., *Bihar and Orissa Gazetteer Cuttack*, pp. 153-54.
54. Settlement of Kanika, p. 15.

Puri town, which were collected from the seashore. Handicraft Industry in this way afforded employment to workers.

17. Murdanga Industry

Religious functions were very common in Orissa. The spread of Vaisnavism and the spread of Chaitanya cult in Orissa inspired many for sankirtan. Sankirtan parties required *Murdangas* as an musical instrument. These *Murdangas* were manufactured in Dharmasala in Killa Darpana in Cuttack district.[55] These *Murdangas* were widely in use throughout Orissa for its superior tone and better finish. A number of families engaged in this Industry were getting employment. This Industry as was solely dependent on the local patronage it could not thrive as an important Industry to share with the economy of this country. Moreover it could not compete with the *Murdangas* manufactured at Nadia in Bengal. As a result of which this Industry declined.

18. Stone Quarry Industry

There were no mines of importance in Orissa. Laterite, sandstone and limestone were quarried from the hills and were used for road metalling and building purposes. Following the years of famine the Government changed the economic policy and resolved to allot more funds for the construction of good all weather roads. Completion of Bengal Nagpur Railway lines was decided by the Government. Construction work was expedited. Stones mainly from Choudwar quarry and from quarrys around Dharmasala were collected and used in the construction of railway bridges.[56] The owners of these mines had done handsome business with the authorities of the Bengal Nagpur Railway Company. The following statistics gives a clear idea about the amount of business transaction of different years in stone.[57]

55. Settlement of Darpana, p. 6.
56. GAROD, 1899-1900, p. 10.
57. *Ibid.*

1896	Rs. 15,703
1897	Rs. 94,852
1898	Rs. 6,10,149
1899	Rs. 3,35,231

Besides this laterite stones and sandstones were used for construction of good roads. Out of these figures it can be firmly said that Stone Quarry Industries continued to provide employment to a large number of workers in Orissa. This Industry was in a better perspective but this could not thrive as the owners were not able to invest after the completion of the railway work.

C. CAUSES OF DECLINE OF THE INDIGENOUS INDUSTRIES

All the indigenous industries of Orissa managed to continue on the local patronage. The life of the industries generally depended on the internal and external trade, the availability of raw materials at a low cost on the markets where the articles would be sold, on the communication facilities, on the present currency system and finally on the competition with the finished goods available in the markets. All these factors had tremendous impact on the prosperity and continuity of cottage industries in Orissa.

The industries of Orissa were mainly meant for local demands. The weavers, the potters, the *chamars,* the *mochis,* the carpenters, the goldsmiths, the *damas* and other professional hereditary skilled workers, were always busy in manufacturing their articles to meet the local demands. They were allowed in many cases to enjoy service tenure lands even by the settlements made by the Britishers. They always wanted to satisfy their masters being the villagers. They did never think to produce qualitative goods to face competition with machine made finished goods. Even though the products of such industries deeply attracted the Englishmen, yet due to lack of proper guidance the artisans were not able to keep up the standard of their manufactured articles. Before the advent of the British administration the Orissan industries were getting the support of the kings or rulers but the British administration gave no attention to the prosperity of these industries. The ruler and the traders being the same British people the interests of the industries naturally hampered. So long the local people went on patronising the local products these industries could thrive. Pottery, carpentry and other local cottage industries were never taken into consideration by the Britishers. Weaving, Hide and Paper Industries were facing lot of competition with the finished goods of cheap rates imported by the English administration. Thus the trade interest of the British trading community were fixed on these Industries. As a result of which big industries like Weaving, Paper, Hides and Metal gradually declined when the local patronage was withdrawn due to heavy pressure from the administration.

It is also important to note that marketing was not developed in Orissa. There were no good markets for the sale of articles. The products were sent by the manufacturers to nearby *hats* for sale twice a week. Robert Ker was the first British Officer who felt the necessity of an open market. His initiative resulted with the opening of a public market in Cuttack town. Lease were temporarily granted and the shops were exempted from tax.[58] This was the only open market of its kind in Orissa. The manufacturers were to depend on the local *hats* to sell the articles where there was no competition and where the articles were purchased by the traders or intermediaries at a lower price and sent them to urban markets to sell at higher price thus squeezing the economic gain of the manufacturers.[59] The absence of free and open markets inside and outside Orissa thus allowed the economy of the manufacturers to dwindle to further loss. Consequent upon this the decline of the indigenous village industries, became very clear.

58. R. Ker, Magistrate to Board of Revenue, September 1, 1806 (OSA).
59. Mishra, S., *Economic Survey of Orissa*, Vol. I, p. 379.

The British administration gave a deaf ear to the improvement of communication facilities for Orissa. Orissa was virtually an isolated tract till 1897 when East Coast Railway line was ready for traffic.[60] When easy and cheaper communication facilities were not available the manufacturers neither were able to procure raw materials from distant places at cheap rate nor could sell the articles in urban markets at higher rates. Under these conditions the artisans of Orissa were forced to remain at the mercy of the local traders and were forced to accept a low price below the production cost. Following the year 1866 though communication facilities were provided yet by then the delicate financial condition of the industries did never allow the owners to opt for a new trade technique.

The great famine desperately dislocated the economic condition of the people of Orissa. The manufacturers were no exception to starvation during the famine years. The manufacturers being pauper owed to the pressure of the English traders. The English administration volunteered to supply capital to the skilled artisans to produce their goods and naturally imposed new regulations on them. The contract obviously helped the English traders but not the manufacturers of Orissa. The artisans however tried their utmost to revive their industries but the appearance of famines continuously at short intervals ruined them. As a result of which they became unable to pay back the loans and as such they were asked by the English administration to give their finished goods as per the price determined by them. The method of collection became oppressive and arbitrary. Under these peculiar conditions the industries vanished from Orissa.

After the famine the price index gradually went up. The rise in price of foodgrains had tremendous impact on the industries. The artisans used to earn less and were required to pay more for foodgrains and other articles. During the period from 1814 to 1890 there was 50 per cent rise in money wages for a ordinary worker and there was 125 per cent rise

60. GAROD, 1899-1900, p. 31.

in price of the cost of living.[61] The purchasing capacity for an individual diminished to a great extent. This was reflected on the village based industries. The monopolistic view of the English traders aggravated the delicate economic situation of the industries. The low price finished goods were flooded into the markets of Orissa. The manufacturers were not able to withstand the competition and thus sold the articles in low price forgetting the marginal profit what they were getting previously. The artisans thus became the worst sufferers due to abnormal price rise of foodgrains and the change of price of other articles of common llfe. This forced the manufacturers to abandon the idea of the reorientation of their industries. The Weaving, Hide and Metal Industries etc. became the prey to this cause of the decline. Under this situation the production capacity went down gradually and the industries declined.

The prosperity of industry and the growth of trade and commerce was directly connected with the currency system. *Kauris* were the medium of exchange during the Maratha Government and in earlier times.[62] The assessment of the country was always calculated and collected in *Kauris*. *Kauri* maintained the Government rate of exchange of 4 *kahanas* and 2 *panas* to the rupee in the market until 1808 and then fell as low as 7 *kahanas* per rupee in the markets of Cuttack district in 1812.[63] During the first phase of the British rule the scarcity of *Kauris* was felt as the army people were paid heavy through *Kauris*. At this critical moment the pilgrims visiting Orissa were pressing hard for *Kauri* currency.[64] This was evident from the letter of Harcourt to Mr. Shaw, Private Secretary to the Governor General "we are very much distressed for want of small coins or *Kauris*."[65] The landlords were given option to

61. Toynbee, G., *A Sketch of the History of Orissa*, p. 193.
62. Wilson, C.R., *Early Annals of English in Bengal*, Vol. II, Part I, No. 1014.
63. BRC, No. 42, October 24, 1817, Sherer, Accountant General to Government of Bengal, July 28, 1817.
64. Roy, B.C., *Foundation of British Orissa*, pp. 189-190.
65. Harcourt to Mr. Shaw, Private Secretary to Governor General, August 9, 1804, MSS No. 1361, p. 33, Quoted by B.C. Roy, *Foundation of British Orissa*, p. 190.

give the land revenue by *Kauris*. On the other hand the landlords were reluctant to pay the land revenues through *Kauris* as the exchange price of *Kauris* remained the same and as they felt it unwise to carry *Kauris* from their estate to the Government treasury. The question cf currency system did not receive proper attention of the Government and as such in many cases at the time of business transaction there were troubles. The foreign traders wanted to follow the Government rate of exchange whereas the local traders wanted to collect higher rates of 7 *kahanas* instead of 4 *kahanas* as fixed by the Government. The village artisans were not willing also to sell their products on rupee. As a result of which the products of village industries of Orissa could not be displayed in the markets of any other province and as such were meant for local use only. Orissa was exporting rice in large quantity every year. From seventies of 19th century there was steady rise in export and import trade of Orissa. For import of various kinds of finished goods Orissa was to pay heavy cost through rice only. As a result of which the price of rice increased that affected the cultivators to a great extent. On this situation the manufacturers of interior villages expressed their inability to sell their manufactured goods with the exchange of rupee. The period of stagnancy came in. The local industries for this also started declining.

The administration invited rich Bengalis to Orissa as landlords. They had money but they had no interest to invest capital on industry. Rather they were busy in diverting their capital to Bengal market. They drained the raw materials to Calcutta and earned their fortune. On the other hand the Government did not care for this nor was interested to patronise the local industries. When the administration was callous and failed to formulate any industrial policy and major capital investment and the self-centred landlords of Bengal having no interest to patronise local industries and the manufacturers being penniless following the onslaught of famines, it could be sheer foolishness to set up better industries in Orissa.

The people of Orissa did not receive proper attention of the British administration. Most of the officers were unable to understand the economic problems of Orissa. Most of the regions of Orissa remained in inaccessible forests. When the British officers could not reach the villages they had to depend solely on the opinion of the subordinate officers who were again ignorant about the economic system of the people and the country. This was one of the vital reasons why many of the economic problems concerning industry, trade and commerce could not be examined by competent authorities. Therefore, Orissa had to suffer from the maladjustment of the industrial economy whereas the other provinces marched ahead on the path of economic prosperity and industrial growth.

The monopolistic theory of the British administration worked very effectively in Orissa in relation to industry. The Company came as a trading community when entered into Orissa. They initially were not interested in trade either with Orissa or to establish industries. Rather they became busy in exporting raw materials to England and importing English finished goods to Orissa. The Weaving Industry faced a stiff competition with machine made English cloths in the market. As a result of which the products of that Industry which had a long heritage for its design, beauty and durability in Orissa gradually declined. This happened also in the case of many other industries. When the local industries became helpless and they faced heavy competition it was impossible to think of the prosperity of the Orissan industry. Under this rule Salt Industry of Orissa vanished. Hide Industry was monopolised by North Indian business community. Metal Industry was compelled to be closed as all the raw materials were drained for their use. The manufacturers could not withstand the competitive markets. As a result of which the industries in Orissa declined towards the end of the eighteen nineties.

The decline of ports of Orissa was injurious to the trade and industry of this country. Some of the ports of Orissa specialised in rice export only. The ports of Puri and Balasore were specialised for rice export throughout 19th century. The

English administration exported rice from Orissa to a dangerous level for which they attempted to make all the ports busy round the year. They had exported nearly 30,00,000 of maunds of rice by the end of the century.[66] For this it was impossible on the part of the traders to import some raw materials for the use in industries. That hampered the outturn of some of the big industries existed in Orissa like Weaving and Metal Industries etc. The manufactured goods could not be cleared up through the ports and were accumulated. The manufacturers on this situation could not dare invest further on their industries. Thus limiting the ports mainly for rice export and import of English finished goods never facilitated the small entrepreneurs to sick their fortune through industrial growth. Thus the decline of ports had relation with the decline of indigenous industries of Orissa.

The decline of these village based industries was ultimately resulted with the growth of the poverty of the people. When the industries were closed the artisans engaged in those industries were thrown out of employment. These artisans tried to be accommodated in the only alternative that was agriculture. The number of wage earners gradually increased. Agriculture could not absorb these categories of new wage earners. As a result of this poverty of the artisans knew no bounds. When majority of the individual artisans suffered, this had a serious impact on the economic growth of Orissa. In this economic state of life in Orissa towards the end of the century a modest attempt was made for industrial regeneration by Utkal Gaurab Madhusudan Das.

D. ATTEMPTS FOR INDUSTRIAL AWAKENING

People of Orissa were not allowed to have any mechanised industry of any kind and size till the beginning of the 20th century. Neither the British administration nor any British Company intended to use the resources of raw materials

66. Maddox Report, Vol. I, pp. 128-29.

available in Orissa by opening new mechanised industries. Lack of communication facilities throughout the century for a commercial prospect was felt by the Britishers and as such the administration became keenly interested to realise heavy excise duty only from village based industrial products.[67] The policy of the British administration under the East India Company and the Crown was completely a negation to the encouragement of the industries in Orissa. They desired to cripple small industries that existed in Orissa and to monopolise the markets through the English finished goods. Under these circumstances no money lender dared invest their money for the venture of establishing new industries. Moreover the people of Orissa were not so advanced to accommodate new ideas to establish new mechanised industries in this period.

On the opening of railway lines in Orissa towards the close of 19th century some people were inspired to introduce a new industrial life for the people of Orissa. They could feel the benefit of the communication facilities through which raw materials could be procured easily for industries and the finished goods manufactured by the industries could be sent to different markets to fetch more profits. The confinement of the manufacturers to the local *hats* could easily be avoided. This being the basic need of industrial growth Orissa witnessed a new ray of hope of economic upliftment in the beginning of 20th century.

Utkal Gaurab Madhusudan Das made a laudable venture to improve the economic condition of the people and the local manufacturers as well towards the end of 19th century. Under his patronage a factory was started, provided with scientific appliances to afford employment to many.

Orissa Art Wares was his first creation in 1899-1900 that

67. BJP(C), January 1805, C. Goram to Secretary to Commissioner, January 26, 1805.

could provide employment to 100 men initially.[68] This establishment was first started in his residential campus.[69] Many were engaged in the delicate craft of gold and silver filigree works for which Cuttack was famous from time immemorial but which due to absence of local support could not continue for a long time. The products of this Warehouse received deep appreciation from different countries of Europe.[70] He had spent the major share of his own purse for the running of this Industry that afforded employment to many families and that could revive the lost glories of Oriya artisans. It became the first organised factory in Orissa started by private enterprise. According to Mahatma Gandhi, Mr. Das was himself interested in teaching the youth of this country the dignity of labour and he gave practical proof of his teaching by establishing at great sacrifice a tannery at Cuttack and the Warehouse in his own residential campus.[71]

This factory Utkal Tannery was established in the year 1905 on about 40 acres of land near Cuttack station on which he had invested a considerable amount of his own. In the words of Sir Ganesh Dutta Singh, Minister, Local Self Government of Bihar and Orissa. "He was generally generous and charitable. He was very keen on the industrial development of the country which he considered essential for providing labour to the poor and with this idea he started Utkal Tannery which unfortunately was the cause of his financial ruin. He was keen for its development and he made considerable sacrifice for it. In order to teach shoe making he himself became a shoe maker."[72]

The products of Utakal Tannery excelled the quality those of other countries abroad. The quality and durability of the products of this factory commanded the use of the boots

68. GAROD, 1899-1900, p. 9.
69. Mohanty, S., *Madhusudan Das*, p. 136.
70. *Ibid*; National Register of Private Records, Webster's remark on Orissa Art Ware, February 17,1900 (NAI).
71. Das, Miss. S., Edt. *Madhusudan Das as seen by many Eyes*, p. 1.
72. *Ibid*, p. 38.

by even the soldiers during the first World War.[73] This complement was made by Bodharam Dube. He was thus called as the pioneer of a national industry. As ill luck would have it this great Industry met with a failure. But Madhusudan Das did a pioneering job by giving impetus to the people of Orissa for the development of such ideal industry to make this underdeveloped country developed one economically, providing employment opportunity to thousand.

Madhusudan Das accused the British administration mainly for the decline of Orissa economy caused by the decline of industries, which existed through many hardships. He said in a paper statement in the daily "The Oriya" that it was the divide and rule policy of the administration that had disunited the zeal of the Orissan artisans for the development of industries in Orissa.[74]

The venture of Utkal Gaurab Madhusudan Das to give a new lease of life to the people of Orissa through industrialisation could not prosper due to lack of financial support from any quarter as stated by Dr. Rajendra Prasad, the Ex-President of India.* The zeal of establishing industries in Orissa vanished when Madhusudan died in February 1934. Orissa thus remained in darkness in respect of advanced scientific industries even after his death.

The view of the British administration throughout the 19th century thus did not encourage the people for the rapid growth of industries in Orissa. The administration continued to remain as a disinterested onlooker towards the growth of industries. It was thought by them that Orissa should remain as an agricultural region so that exploitation could be possible. This belief was resulted with the decay of the industries in

73. *Ibid*, p. 41.

74. Mohanty, S., Madhusudan Das, p. 159.

*Mourning and appreciation of Dr. Rajendra Prasad on the day of Funeral Ceremony of Madhusudan Das. Edited by Miss. Sailabala Das.

Orissa. When industries declined the professional workers opted for agriculture and as a result of which they gradually became unskilled labourers forgetting their own profession. Unemployment problem became acute. Orissa remained as an exporting land rich with raw materials not being explored in the map of British empire.

6

Trade and Commerce

A. TRADE

Pre-British System

Orissa had trade relations with foreign countries from earlier times. The ancient sailors of Orissa regularly made trade relations without any fear. Kali Das described the king of Orissa as "Lord of the Sea" in his Raghubansa. That testified the truth of Kalingan trade through sea and ports. The floating of coloured paper boats on the day of Kartika Purnima by every Oriya family every year reminds us about the hundreds of merchants who used to set sail on the ocean to sick wealth by commercial relations with foreign countries. It is presumed that Orissa had also trade relations with Africa from the representation of a giraffe sculptured in Konark. From different sources it is confirmed that Orissa had extensive maritime trade relation with foreign countries from very ancient time. However this maritime trade could not continue to exist due to the recession of sea water from the old ports, lack of protection from the monarchs against the heavy competition that the Orissan merchants faced and lack of resources for trade of the primary producers, the tendency of shifting of the capital from trade towards landed property closed the glorious sea-trade prosperity of Orissa towards the close of 17th century.

The ports of Orissa along the coast lines played an important role in the growth of sea-borne trade. In the first half of 17th century different European communities made their appearance in the sea coast of Orissa. The wealth, the opulence of the province, plentiful of raw materials, various types of manfactured goods deeply attracted the foreigners to establish their settlements on the coast of Orissa.

1. Arrival of European Traders

The Portuguese sailors, who were disliked by the people of the Coromandal coast were in search of new places to establish their settlements. They came to the coast of Balasore and finally settled at Pipili much before 1599.[1] Pipili became the first port of Orissa to welcome the foreigners. The Dutch followed them. They arrived in the Pipili port in the year 1625 as the second rival foreign business community in Orissa.[2] Due to rivalry with the Portuguese the Dutch shifted their concentration to Balasore port in the year 1633.

The English true to their national character as traders came to Orissa much earlier than they came as ruler in 1803. The English came to Orissa in 1633 and established their factories at Hariharpur and Balasore.[3] In the following year they established a factory at Pipili.[4] The French also joined in this commerial competition and established their factory at Balasore. Hariharpur and Balasore came next to Pipili. Hariharpur for this became the second port in Orissa to be visited by the foreigners. Among these Balasore became the most important trading centre and port in Orissa. European

1. *History of Portuguese in Bengal*, pp. 97-98.
2. *Ibid*, p. 97.
3. *Bengal District Gazetteer*, Balasore, p. 37.
4. *Ibid*, p. 33.

communities had their factories as well as settlements in Balasore town.

2. Orissan Ports (19th Century)

Balasore port could not continue to remain as an important port for a longer period. Thomas Motte who was sent as an emissary to Sambalpur Diamond Mines by Clive in the year 1766 enrouted through Balasore.[5] His statement threw sufficient light on the commercial activities of English, French, Dutch and Portuguese merchants in Balasore. G.F. Lackie who was on deputation to Nagpur through Balasore observed that Balasore was a flourishing maritime trade centre but due to the decline of the quality of the cloths, manufactured in Balasore, the factories were in wretched condition.[6] The commercial activities of the people of Orissa by that time were in a declining state. Soon after the British conquest the Government became very keen to promulgate new regulations for the sea-borne commercial activities in Orissa.

Before the initiation of the British regulation, maritime trade continued to attract a quite good number of nations to establish their factories on the mouth of rivers of Balasore and Puri. Thus before the British conquest many ports existed in Orissa.

(*i*) *Pipili*—Pipili was situated at a distance of 30 miles north of Balasore on Subarnarekha river. In the past Pipili occupied a unique position among the ports of Orissa. Pipili welcomed the Portuguese sailors by the middle of 16th century A.D.[7] Since then it became an important seat of the Portuguese. Portuguese sailors were expelled from Hoogli in 1631 and from Hijli in 1636. After this they concentrated their business activities in this port. Gradually the Dutch and English appeared as rival trading communities near Pipili at

5. *Early European Travellers in Nagpur Territories*, p. 1.
6. *Ibid*, p. 52.
7. Maddox Report; p. 38.

Balasore and Hariharpur. But Pipili was retained as an important port for Portuguese. Bruton described in 1663 Pipili as a port town of Portuguese where the Portuguese were the residents.[8] The Portuguese with collaboration of Arkanese had turned this port as a slave market. This became the vital cause of the downfall of the Portuguese power in the coast of Orissa and finally they were expelled from Pipili by Sahajahan the Mughal emperor. Following this downfall the Dutch established a factory at Pipili. The Dutch continuously exported salt from this port to different places. The English followed the Dutch and established a factory at Pipili in 1635.[9] Pipili flourished as an important commercial centre of foreigners. Nature played her own role in the decline of this commercial port. Rapid silting of Subarnarekha and the formation of sand bars around the river mouth affected the usefulness of this port. High floods of river Subarnarekha gave a death-blow to this port when the remnants of the port were washed away by the flood water in 1642.[10] The prosperous commercial port of Pipili turned to be an insignificant and ignoble village where poverty reigned over the inhabitants.[11] Before the British conquest this port did not get a place in the list of ports of Orissa to draw the attention of the British Government for its development.

(*ii*) *Hariharpur*—In May 1633 the English sailors reached Hariharpur (Modern Jagatsinghpur) port in the hope of a settlement there. Due to the regular feature of silting deposit in the river the port of Hariharpur was found to be unsuitable for any commercial activities by the English. The English merchants decided to confine their sea-borne trade in Balasore only. Thus the port Hariharpur vanished from the map of sea coast by the end of 17th century.[12]

8. *The History of Portuguese in Bengal*, pp. 97-98.
9. Maddox Report, p. 38.
10. *Ibid*, p. 43.
11. *Bengal District Gazetteer*, Balasore, pp. 37-38.
12. *Ibid*, p. 39.

(*iii*) *Balasore*—Balasore was discovered by the English in the year 1633. Balasore was situated on the river Boorabalanga (Budhabalanga), at a distance of 16 miles from the coast. Consequent upon the abandonment of Pipili Dr. Broughton secured the permission for erecting a factory at Balasore. The ruins of the little colony at Pipili was removed to Balasore. A new village for foreigners came to light. The Barabati village was established on the right bank of the river Boorabalanga, a mile below the site of the modern town Balasore. A factory of English sprang into existence by the year 1640.[13] This factory was on one side by a river and the other 3 by a deep moat and a native village, sprang up rapidly. The village was inhabited by the artisans and weavers engaged by the Company for its manufacture. The main articles of trade in those days were *satran* a type of coarse long cloth and muslin. Orissa was very famous for the muslin cloths manufactured mainly at Balasore. In the year 1641 the condition of the factory at Balasore port became very unsatisfactory and its abolition was ordered.[14] Francis Day visited the Balasore and Hariharpur port in 1642 and recommended for the improvement of both the factories. Under this unhealthy situation Balasore port was retained till 1651.[15] Hopkins was appointed as the British Agent at Balasore.[16] Trade in calicos, silk and saltpetre increased. A change came over the situation when Aurangzeb ascended the throne in 1658. The permission granted by Sahajahan was immediately cancelled and he demanded annual customs duty to the extent of Rs. 3,000. The Mughal Governor at Balasore also demanded the anchorage charges on the English. Balasore thus remained as mere port upto 1663.[17] Captain Health was deputed by the Court to find out a suitable place in the coast of Bay of Bengal for sea-borne trade. Captain Health reached Balasore on November 16, 1688.[18] In that year the hostilities between the Mughals and

13. Maddox Report, p. 38.
14. *Early Annals of English in Bengal*, pp. 19-20.
15. *Ibid*, pp. 21-22.
16. *Ibid*, p. 32.
17. *Ibid*, pp. 47-49.
18. Maddox Report, p. 38.

English reached a height when the Company's servants came in a body from Hoogly to Balasore. Two English factories were seized and the inmates were made captives. Consequent upon this Captain Health burned and plundered Balasore town.[19] Nature also worked to hasten the closure of the port. Boorabalanga deposited silt on the mouth making the Balasore port inconvenient for the trade by the year 1700. From 1751 the decline of the port became quite visible. This important port of Orissa was ultimately abandoned before 1786.[20] G F. Lackie, a member of a party deputed by Lord Cornwallis to Nagpur passed through Balasore on March 22,1790. According to his observation Balasore was formerly a flourishing port.[21] This flourishing port was discovered by the Britishers when they entered into the city in 1803 and found the port in a delapidated condition. A house at Barabati was identified as the factory building of the English. However this port was declared as a port of Orissa in 1858. Following the years of famine the Government decided to improve the ports of Orissa. For better convenience the Chandbali port and False Point received due consideration of the Government. The Collector, Balasore in 1873 said that "all Orissa is being sacrificed to False Point chimera."[22] Balasore port thus could not grow further as an important port in Orissa.

(*iv*) *Dhamara*—Dhamara was formed as a guard to the estuary on the mouths of rivers Brahmani and Baitarani. This condition attracted the English settlers to use it as a port of importance. This port was also declared as an important port of Orissa in 1858. Dhamara was an useful port even at the time of British conquest in 1803 where from rice and salt were exported to Bengal.[23] Dhamara port even existed in a very wretched condition by the end of the year 1894. There

19. *Ibid.*
20. *Ibid.*
21. *Early European Travellers in Nagpur Territories*, pp. 52-53.
22. GAROD, 1872-73, T.E. Ravenshaw to Secretary, Government of Bengal, No. 271, July 23, 1873.
23. Toynbee, G., *A Sketch of the History of Orissa*, p. 88.

one Custom House and one Pilot House to give shelter to pilots of the vessels coming to the port.[24] Thus Dhamara continued to serve as a port of Orissa upto 1894.

(v) *Subarnarekha*—Subarnarekha was situated in the mouth of river Subarnarekha. It was not far from Pipili port. After the decline of Pipili port the Europeans shifted their centre of activities to this port with a view to reach a vast interior area of Orissa. No permanent improvement of this port was undertaken as it involved a great engineering skill and a heavy cost. Dense forest on the bank of the river Subarnarekha provided ample facilities for smuggling. This smuggling was found to be a difficult task on the part of the Government to stop. This port gradually declined. However Subarnarekha port was declared to be a port of Orissa in the year 1858 in accordance with the Act II of 1858. Subarnarekha was found to be not very useful during the period of famine as it afforded no facility for food supply to Orissa. In the year 1882-83 an amount of Rs.20 was spent towards the cost of repairing of this port.[25] This is a clear evidence that Subarnarekha existed as a port of Orissa in 1882-83. Owing to the silting of the river mouth and the construction of Coast Canal and the abandonment of salt manufacture in Orissa, Subarnarekha port ceased to operate any sea-borne trade. This port is represented by Batanga and Madhata on the Coast Canal and Barabati on the Gochhida river.[26]

(vi) *Sartha*—Sartha was situated at the junction of 2 rivers Panchapara and Sartha which flowed into the Bay of Bengal a few miles below Subarnarekha. Due to the silting of rivers this port became unsuitable for accommodating vessels. Hence the Government paid no attention to improve this port but this was declared as a port of Orissa in the year 1858.[27]

24. File No. 159/1894, Board of Revenue, Commissioner of Customs to Board of Revenue, No. 948, September 24, 1894 (OSA).
25. PBCSO, March 1882, Customs Officer, Subarnarekha to Collector of Customs, Balasore, No. 131, March 7, 1882.
26. Maddox Report, p. 43.
27. *Ibid.*

Panchapara has taken the place of Sartha port in the course of time.

(*vii*) *Churamani*—Churamani was an open road-stead on the mouth of the river Gummere a branch of Kansbas. Before the British conquest to this country this port was chosen as a centre of business activities of the Britishers. In the year 1803 considerable quantities of rice and salt were exported from this port. This port was included in the list of the ports according to the provisions of Act II of 1858. Mathormohan Padhi, a merchant of repute wanted to improve the condition of the port by removing the silt before 1874. Partially he was successful but the port fell into disuse by the deposits of silt and mud.[28]

(*viii*) *Lychanpore*—Lychanpore was not far away on a small creek of the river Lychanpore. It also played an important role in the growth of sea-borne trade in Balasore district as well as in Orissa. This port was also included in the Act. It could not afford any help to the Government during the period of famine. Gradually it ceased to exist in Orissa as Government did not like to spend further on this port.

(*ix*) *Chhanoa*—Before the British conquest this port also occupied a place among the ports of Orissa. It was situated on the mouth of Chhanoa river. This port vanished by the time the Act II of 1858 was introduced in Orissa for better port administration.

(*x*) *Chandbali*—Consequent upon the outbreak of the famine the Government wanted to expedite the supply of foodgrains for the people of Orissa. By that time all important ports were felt to be useless for the purpose of supply. This new port of Chandbali was opened in the year 1872.[29] It was an inland port on the river Baitarani running through Cuttack and Balasore. It was situated 15 miles lower down the river

28. BRP, November 1875.
29. GAROD, 1873-74, p. 10.

Dhamara at the confluence of the Matai river.[30] It was on the Balasore side of the river Baitarani 25 miles from the coast. The port was accessible by tidal creeks 25 miles to the north and 70 miles to the south.[31] This port became the centre of trade in Orissa in the second half of 19th century. It absorbed the trade of the old port Dhamara. During the whole period of famine this port had helped the Government in respect of the import of foodgrains to Balasore and Cuttack districts. The importance of Chandbali gradually increased when the importance of other ports of Balasore district declined. Due to the landing problem in the port at False Point all big vessels were directed to Chandbali. When this port was growing rapidly in the whole of the coast a storm passed over the port on September 22, 1885 devastating the port.[32] This port was also called as Ravensport after the name of T.E. Ravenshaw.

Before the opening of the Chandbali port the sea-borne trade virtually was in a collapsing stage. According to the statement of Beams, Collector, Balasore it was observed that, "A stranger coming by sea to Balasore on seeing our harbours would think he had arrived at the dominions of some independent native Chiefs who did not know what were the requirements of the civilised countries in respect of portal accommodation. He would be extremely surprised to find himself in the territories subject to the greatest maritime power, the world has ever seen."[33] When Orissa was isolated from the rest of the world Chandbali helped the people as well as the Government to keep up the standard of the sea-borne trade in Orissa. Light steamers ran almost daily to and from

30. Maddox Report, p. 43.

31. BRP, November 1868, H.L. Dampier, Secretary, Government of Bengal to Government of India, No. 3345, October 22, 1868.

32. Buckland, C.E., *Bengal under Lt. Governor*, Vol. II, p. 822.

33. GAROD, 1872-74, T.E. Ravenshaw to Government of Bengal, No. 271, July 23, 1873.

Calcutta and this Chandbali port became an important place for coastal trade.[34]

(*xi*) *Ports of Puri*—The ports of Puri district were opened for navigation in 1860. The ports of Puri were Puri, Devee, Sahandu, Mettacooah, Futtypore and Nundla.[35] These ports were in better position during 19th century but due to lack of proper maintenance and supervision these ports were turned simply to be road-stead. These ports did not allow the vessels during North-West monsoon.[36] Puri remained behind other districts in respect of ports. Its only port Puri was an open road-stead and owing to the surf, loading and unloading difficulties, and lack of storage facilities it could not compete with other ports of Orissa in allowing vessels to and from it.[37] However Puri port continued to function till the dawn of 20th century.

(*xii*) *False Point*—False Point was the most important port in the district of Cuttack. It was situated at the mouth of river Mahanadi at a distance of 70 miles from Cuttack town. This port was used in the past as an important port but in course of time it had its decline. The port was opened in the year 1860 for open sea-borne trade with places other than Orissa proper. It was by far the best harbour on the coast of India between Hoogly and Bombay.[38] False Point had never a fair chance prior to famine. There were no means of communication except in the rainy season. Between 1860 and 1862 an Agency was established there only to export rice from Cuttack. Messrs Robet Charriol commenced rice trade

34. GAROD, 1873-74, p. 10.
35. BRP, November 1868, H.L. Dampier, Secretary, Government of Bengal to Government of India, No. 3345, October 22, 1868.
36. BRP, July 1877, J. Beams, Commissioner, Cuttack to Government of Bengal, No. 600, July 18, 1877.
37. GAROD, 1876-77, p. 12.
38. RCF, Vol. I, Part II, Pr. 30.

there.[39] But there was no means of disembarking the cargo and passengers at the place of anchorage. The Agency, established there, was abandoned during the period of famine as there was no prospect of any further rice deal. The coasting steamers to and from Calcutta usually passed it twice a month east way without any notice.[40] The horrors of famine forced the Government to take notice of this port which was in a ruined condition. During the years of famine Government was exploring every means of throwing supply into the province. False Point harbour formed the main source of entrance by which food was brought into the province. In complying to the demand of the Famine Commissioner which declared it as a best harbour in the whole of India the Government decided to make this harbour a good and all weather navigable port for Orissa. The investigation about the possibility of making it as a great port was conducted. After this the harbour was properly surveyed and deepened and the channels were clearly buoyed off and it was connected with Cuttack through Kendrapara Canal. After the commencement of these preliminary works this port remained open throughout the year.[41] It was expected by the Government confidently that False Point would grow into an important harbour in Orissa that would afford facilities for import and export of articles.

A large volume pf rice was exported to different foreign places. To regulate the export trade the Government felt the necessity of appointing a preventive officer at False Point. The Governor General in Council approved the proposal of the appointment of a preventive officer at a monthly salary of Rs. 30.[42] The appointment was made with effect from 1862 in the Customs Office at False Point. Even though the Customs

39. BRP (Customs), Decemher 1879, Macferson, Collector of Customs, to Commissioner, Cuttack, No. 56, December 17, 1879.

40. *Ibid.*

41. *Ibid*, November 1868, Dampier, Secretary, Government of Bengal to Government of India, No. 3345, October 22, 1868.

42. Fort William Indian House Correspondence, Resolution, Finance Department, Fort William, April 9, 1862 (NAI).

Office was established in 1860, it could not levy customs duties on the articles of import and export. The Collector, Cuttack submitted a proposal for the appointment of a writer in the Custom House to maintain accounts when he found a large quantity of rice was exported from the port. On the proposal, the Board of Revenue agreed and informed the Collector, Cuttack in their letter No. 1360, November 20, 1860 to appoint a writer.[43] Gauri Sankar Ray was appointed as a part-time writer in addition to his excise work on the basis of an extra allowance.[44] Thus False Point became a prominent port in Cuttack district that had attracted the Government for its better administration. False Point was not recognised by the Act II of 1858 and as such duties were not levied on the import and export articles to and from this port. A set of special rules were passed by the Board to regulate the trade at False Point from 1861.[45] According to the rules shipping bills were granted after the settlement of duty was made and Boat notes were signed by the proper Customs Officer.[46] False Point was maintained after this by the control of the Government.

A scheme was put forward in the year 1875 when Government felt the necessity of improving this port following the years of famine. An estimate of Rs. 2,33,000 was recommended to the Government for the development of the port.[47] Government decided to acquire a vast area for the construction of the port. Maharanee of Burdwan donated a vast area of land at Jamboo. For the purpose of demarketing the boundary of the land the Government sanctioned an

43. BdRP, November 1860, Secretary, Board of Revenue to Collector, Cuttack, No. 1360, November 20, 1860.
44. PBCSO, May 1868, Armstrong, Collector, Cuttack to Commissioner, Cuttack, No. 7, May 2, 1868.
45. BRP (Customs), April 1871, Macferson, Collector of Customs to Commissioner, Cuttack, No. 2A, April 4, 1871.
46. *Ibid.*
47. Malley, S.S.O., *Bihar and Orissa Gazetteer, Cuttack*, p. 168.

amount of Rs. 3,670 debitable to the Provincial Funds.[48] The aim of the Government became very clear and favourable. But the expectation of any financial gain was not felt by the Government as it was found impossible to prevent the silting up of the harbour and thus the idea of development of the port was abandoned.

False Point served as an important port of Orissa in the latter part of 19th century. The quantity of import and export increased year after year. A quantity of 400 bags of rice was exported in the year 1867-68 and it increased to 68,421 bags in 1869-70. Similarly 13,979 pieces of hides were exported in the year 1869-70 whereas not a single piece was exported from this port either to any other ports of India or to the ports of foreign countries in the year 1867-68.[49] Hence this port continued as a busy port of Orissa in the seventies of 19th century. The comparative statement gives a clear picture about the increase of import and export trade at False Point for a period of 18 years from 1860-61 to 1878-79[50] as shown in Appendix 'H'.

Thus the sea-borne trade in an increasing manner turned the port False Point as an important port in Orissa.

3. Portal Communication

The position of portal communication in Orissa changed. There was a remarkable improvement in the sea-borne trade through the ports of Orissa. In spite of all the handicaps ports like Chandbali and False Point received the attention of the Government to handle the sea-traffic from Calcutta. The

48. H.H. Risley, Under Secretary, Government of Bengal to Secretary, Board of Revenue, No. 116 (OSA).
49. BRP (Customs), July 1870, Macferson, Collector of Customs to T. Grey, Assistant Collector of Customs, False Point, No. 21, July 9, 1870.
50. GAROD, 1878-69, p. 20.

number of vessels visiting different ports increased rapidly. The statistics enumerated below gives a clear evidence of the increase of the portal communication in Balasore port.[51]

Vessels visiting ports of Balasore

1869-70	1870-71	1871-72	1872-73	1873-74	1874-75
232	277	275	345	405	387

Similarly the tonnage of vessels coming to Puri stood as 10,553 in 1874-75 against 1,356 in 1868-69. Towards the latter part of 19th century foreign trade became more active. The British Indian Steam Co. made False Point as a place of their business activities. French ships from Mauritius were visiting Orissan ports to import rice and oil-seeds to their country. In the year 1868-69 the total transaction of foreign trade was Rs. 6,39,031 which rose to its highest point in the year 1877-78. During the years from 1881-82 to 1888-89 the ports of Orissa were busy in dealing with foreign trade. A variety of new factors prevailed over the sea-borne trade. These new problems had terrible impact on the economic prosperity of the people of Orissa. The value of import of foreign goods in 1881-82 was Rs. 66,99,026 and the value of export was Rs. 68,42,784. These figures increased to Rs. 91,15,021 on import trade and Rs. 96,53,531 on export trade in the year 1884-85. The value of import and export further increased in 1894-95. The total value of import and export in the ports of Orissa was Rs. 1,19,73,792 in the year 1884-95 against the last year's figure of Rs. 1,14,59,770.[52] Towards the end of the century in 1899-1900 the value of total communication (export and import) remained as Rs. 1,20,75,438.[53] It gave an increase to the cost of 1894-95.

51. BRP, November 1875, RAC, 1874-75.
52. GAROD, 1894-95-96, Pr. 103.
53. QAR.

The amount of import always exceeded the amount of export. The main articles of export were foodgrain, agricultural and forest products and the imported articles in all the ports of Orissa were metal, gunny bags, kerosene oil, sugar, tobacco, lead, copper, zinc, glassware, liquors, spices, gold, silver and other machine made fancy goods including cloth. The heavy burden caused by the imported articles was to be entirely shouldered by the only important item of export of rice. Due to the increase of export of rice the increase of price of rice was affected. Consequent upon the increase of price of rice, the main food of the people of Orissa, the people lost their purchasing capacity. When they lost their capacity to purchase foreign goods the volume of trade in foreign articles naturally decreased. Thus the quantity of export resulted in the decrease of import. The heavy drain of the foodgrains put the people of Orissa into hardship. The imported cloths replaced the hand-made cloths in the market. As a result of which the indigenous industries perished. The rise of price of rice was felt as a great hardship to the population of shopkeepers and the Government employees as well in Cuttack town.[54] Thus the system of import and export through the ports of Orissa had terribly affected the economy of Orissa throughout 19th century.

The extension of railway to Orissa contributed much to the decline of portal trade in Orissa. The deteriorating condition of ports of Orissa, the callousness of the Government to improve the condition of the ports, the heavy rate of duty an the articles of import and export and the abandonment of salt manufacture accelerated the process of decline of the sea trade in Orissa towards the end of 19th century. As a result of which the economic conditions of the province naturally declined.

54. GAROD, 1877-78, J. Beams, Commissioner, Cuttack to Government of Bengal, No. 600, July 18, 1877.

B. COMMERCE

Regulated markets, internal communications, investment capacity of the people, media of transaction and duties imposed by the Government on articles, play dominant roles in the growth of commercial activities of a community so also of a province. Lack of well organised markets in Orissa afforded no facilities to the people to grow as a commercial race in the whole of 19th century. Internal communication facilities received no Government care. The manufactured goods could not reach the markets to fetch better profits to the manufacturers. Agricultural products, forest products and products of the indigenous industries were forced to be confined to the local markets (hats) for its sale. The Orissan merchants did not find any prospect to develop the commercial zeal inside the country. The financial conditions of the merchants were not well. They had no investment capacity that added injury to the commercial prosperity of the people. As a result of which the merchants of other regions inclined to invest their money to pursue their commercial activities in Orissa exploiting the backwardness of the people following the years of British conquest. To add to this the British Government brought new regulation to levy excise duty on certain articles locally manufactured and sold. By this the free commercial policy that prevailed throughout the Maratha period was changed. The good state of commercial activities in the beginning of 19th century received a drastic change by the new regulation in 1805.[55] Like salt monopoly the British Government decided to control the management of excisable articles immediately after their conquest.

Markets serve the purpose of sale and purchase of goods. The manufacturers and the merchants dealing with different descriptions go to the markets to sell their goods and purchasers go to the markets to get their required quantity of goods in exchange of cash or kind. Before the British conquest

55. RBR, Acc. No. 3, Vol. 351, C. Goram to Secretary to Commissioner, January 26, 1805 (OSA).

to Orissa the people followed the barter system to get their goods. The medium of exchange was mainly foodgrains when silver coins (sicca) replaced the *Kauri* in Orissa. The old practice naturally discontinued.

Pre-British System

There existed no regular markets in Orissa at the time of British conquest. Every village was a self-dependent unit. Whatever a particular village community could not produce according to their need they usually depended on the neighbouring village for that. The villagers in that case were not required to go to distant places for getting their articles of necessity. But if the needs could not be satisfied within the immediate vicinity the villagers had to run to the weekly markets or *hats* of a number of neighbouring villages at regular intervals. The weekly markets served the purpose of irregular commercial centres of the villages. Sometimes the villagers due to distance did not go to the weekly markets and remained contented with the goods available in the immediate neighbouring village. But to get some indispensable goods they had to depend upon the distant weekly markets even if they faced difficulties. Beyond these there prevailed the system of annual fairs or *melas* to which the villagers of number of villages eagerly looked forward to buy commodities of specialised nature which came from distant places of production. The needs of village community were satisfied in this manner in Orissa before 1803. By the help of such irregular markets proper display of local products could not be made to attract a number of customers. As such the manufacturers had to wait for the day of such weekly markets to sell their goods. Sometimes the manufacturers had to return with their goods from such *hats* due to absence of intending purchasers or to sell the goods at cheaper rates below the cost of production.[4] In that case manufacturers of such articles were demoralised and in the long run the goods vanished from such markets. Such temporary markets did not provide proper incentive to manufacturers to produce more goods when such manufacturers were deprived of their dividends from the business. Merchants also received such type of problems in irregular markets. When a merchant collecting goods of different descriptions visited a weekly market and found no customers on that particular day in the market he never inclined to visit such unpredictable market in the subsequent days and sought his fortune elsewhere. In that case the people of sorrounding villages ultimately suffered, when they could not get their requirements from the *hats*. Such handicaps naturally did not afford any facility to the growth of commercial activities of Orissa.

1. Market System

(*i*) *Cuttack*—Robert Ker, Magistrate, Cuttack was not satisfied with such irregular marketing system in Orissa. He became the first English Officer to think of this. He suggested to the Bengal Government for opening of regular markets as the basic support of the commercial prosperity of this country. In his letter to the Board of Revenue he submitted proposals for opening of new regular markets in Cuttack town and in some important business centres. On getting recommendations Government granted lease of lands to intending merchants of Cuttack town to open shops in the town. These shops were exempted from rent and tax of any kind.[56] Shops were opened in the central places of Cuttack town. Cuttack town sprang up as an important regular commercial centre during 19th century. Agricultural products of permanently settled estate like Kanika, Kujang, Darpan, Aul etc. were brought to this centre for sale to the merchants coming from Madras, Bombay, Ceylon, Laccadive, Maldive islands and other European countries.[57] In the course of time Cuttack occupied an important place from commercial point of view in the whole of Cuttack district. It dealt with goods of various descriptions. Forest products

56. RBR, R. Ker, Magistrate, Cuttack to Board of Revenue, November 1, 1806 (OSA).

57. Settlememnt of Kanika, p. 15; Settlement of Darpan, pp 1-6.

like hide coming from mainly Tributary Mahals to this market were sold to merchants coming from Kanpur in North India. They regularly visited this market and made it as their base of commercial operation. In the year 1869-70 Cuttack market made hide business to the extent of Rs. 23,053 with the Kanpur merchants. It only exported 74,243 pieces of hides through False Point in 1876-77.[58] Cuttack town earned a worldwide reputation in filigree works. European merchants mainly depended on Cuttack market to get best variety of filigree works that afforded commercial benefit to a large number of skilled workers. Specimen of this filigree work were displayed in the European exhibition mainly exported from Cuttack market.[59] This is a clear evidence about the importance of Cuttack town as a commercial centre in the Orissa Division.

False Point was recognised as an important port of Orissa in 1860-61. During the years of famine Cuttack was made a main business centre in rice trade. It was linked by canal with False Point. Brisk rice trade was conducted in Cuttack town. Beside the articles of export the main articles of import like cotton, kerosene oil, various types of metals, gunny bags, etc. were brought to Cuttack town from False Point. Merchants of different interior villages came to collect these articles from Cuttack market for onward trade in villages. Thus during 19th century Cuttack market remained busy as an important commercial centre. This new regular marketing system accelerated the growth of commercial activities of the people of Orissa.

Besides Cuttack town proper there were other towns in Cuttack district such as Jajpur, Jagatsinghpur and Kendrapara town. Markets flourished in these places. Irregular and regular markets continued to function. The importance of Kendrapara increased because it was nearer to False Point and

58. BRP (Customs), 1870, Macferson, Collector of Customs to T. Grey, Assistant Collector of Customs, No. 21, July 9, 1870.

59. Mukherjee, P., *History of Orissa*, p. 179.

the market was connected with False Point through Taladanda and Kendrapara Canal.[60] Agricultural products could be brought from neighbouring villages for exportation through False Point and through Chandbali via Pattamundai. Subsequently after the emergence of Chandbali port in 1872 Pattamundai market served as a feeder market of Chandbali.[61] Jajpur market could supply plenty of foodgrains to Dhamara port and subsequently to Chandbali port. Thus by the end of 19th century a number of new markets sprang up to facilitate the commercial activities of Cuttack district.

(*ii*) *Balasore*—Balasore on the bank of river Boorabalanga was selected as an important market by the European communities. After the decline of Pipili and Hariharpur, Balasore port turned to be the business centre of Europeans even in the latter part of 18th century. English settlers constructed buildings in the town of Balasore. The ruins of Barabati is the clear evidence of the old Balasore town.[62] The importance of the market disappeared by 1786.[63] When English entered into the town they were simply charmed with the geographical phenomenon of the town and decided to develop the marketing system of the town which would afford commercial benefit to them as well as to the local artisans. Balasore became a regular market in the district. Articles of import could be easily brought to this town and were distributed to the merchants for local sale in the interior villages.

Bhadrak emerged as an important market in Balasore district consequent upon the formation of Chandbali port. Bhadrak was connected with the port either via Ruknadeipur or Basudevpur road. This town was also directly connected with a road. The surplus produce of the South East of the district of Balasore could be brought to the market which were

60. GAROD, 1873-74, p. 10.
61. *Ibid.*
62. *Early Annals of English in Bengal*, pp. 19-20.
63. Maddox Report, p. 38.

sent mainly for exportation. It became a feeder market that functioned regularly.

Remuna was another important business centre in the district. It was a centre of brass metal merchants.[64]

Jamjhari market, 29 miles below Balasore used to derive its supply of salt manufactured in *Aurangs* of South East of the district.[65] This centre served as a salt market and thus attracted the attention of the Britishers during 19th century.

Beside these commercial centres there were number of important markets in Balasore district such as Baliapal, Basta, Kamarda, Jaleswar, Nangaleswar and Singla which were famous for rice and salt business. These business centres helped to a great extent to the growth of commercial activities of the district. There existed a number of irregular centres or *hats* which were treated as feeder markets to the main markets. With the existence of such business centres Balasore flourished materially in 19th century.

(*iii*) *Puri*—Marketing system was not modern in Puri during the time of British conquest. Rivers of the districts were useless for internal trade. In rainy season there were heavy floods and in other seasons the river beds were dry. Due to the work of nature the whole district remained backward in commercial activities. People were contented with what they got out of their lands. Puri town could only give commercial facility because the pilgrims visited Lord Jagannath. Puri town turned to be a regular market getting goods from neighbouring villages particularly agricultural products for the consumption of pilgrims. Puri port was brought under the Port Act of 1858. Consequent upon this Government decided to use this port for rice exportation to different places. Warehouses were constructed in haphazard manner. Towards the close of 19th century ports of Puri were abandoned and salt

64. *Ibid*, p. 29.
65. *Ibid*.

manufacture was stopped at Chilka for which Government did not pay much attention for the development of markets. However this town was used as an important commercial centre even after the decline of ports which rested mainly on pilgrims.

Khurda the seat of Hindu Rajas sprang up as an important commercial centre. Agricultural and forest products from different *killas* could easily be brought to this centrally located place.[66] From these goods were sent to Puri and Cuttack town. Khurda remained as an important business centre till the opening of the East Coast Railway line when the centre was shifted to the Railway Station at Jatni.[67]

Beside Puri and Khurda there were other business centres like Pipili, Gope, Balakati, Balugan and Astarang. Pipili began to grow for the pilgrims who used to take shelter there on their way to Puri. Balakati was a centre of bell metal and brass metal utensils. Merchants of Tributary Mahals used to visit this market regularly to get utensils.[68] These important places thus afforded facilities for the growth of commercial activities of the people and the merchants of Puri district. As feeder markets there existed a number of *hats* in every administrative division of the district.

Markets and marketing system continued to play their roles in the commercial prosperity of the people of Orissa. The growth of markets was linked with the communication facilities like roads and railways through which goods produced or manufactured in the interior village areas could be easily brought without heavy cost. Without good roads neither raw materials could reach the doors of the manufacturers nor the finished goods could reach the consumers. As a result Orissan economy remained stagnant as a whole.

66. Settlement of Khurda, pp. 1-3.

67. GAROD, 1899-1900, p. 31.

68. *Ibid*, 1890-91, p. 8.

2. Communication System

(*i*) *Roads*—There was no want of communication along roads for the purpose of commercial traffic during 18th century in Orissa. The country was intersected by a number of roads. Cuttack being situated in a strategic point served the purpose of a connecting link between Bengal, Madras and Nagpur. It was the only town between Bengal and Northern Sarkars. The familiar road that connected Bengal with Cuttack ran through Medinapur, Jaleswar, Basta, Ramachandrapur, Balasore, Soro, Bhadrak, Dhamnagar, Arakpur and Padmapur.[69] This was the only route generally used by the pilgrims of Northern India when they came to visit Puri. The same route was used by Motte in his march to Sambalpur in 1766. Lackie also used this road when he was deputed by Lord Cornwallis to Nagpur Court in 1790 alongwith George Forster.[70]

There was a regular road from Cuttack to Nagpur which ran through Banki, Baideswar, Padmavati, Kantilo, Barmul, Boud, Sonepur, Ratanpur, Lanji and Tharse to Nagpur.[71] There were 2 other roads from Cuttack to Nagpur which were not frequently used by the people or by the Government as these roads passed through dense forests.

Bengal-Cuttack road passed to Madras through Puri and Ganjam. Travellers coming from Northern India on Badsahi road and from Central India through Barmul pass crossed the Kathajoori river to go to Puri through Balianta and Pipili. The road from Cuttack to Puri was the continuation of Bengal-Cuttack road that passed through Balianta, Balakati and Pipili.[72]

Khurda, the seat of the Hindu Raja of Orissa was not connected with Cuttack and Ganjam directly during the period

69. Runnel, J., Memoir of a Map of the Mughal Empire, p. CXXX.
70. *Early European Travellers in Nagpur Territories*, p. 52.
71. *Ibid.*
72. Sirkar, J., *History of Bengal* (Edt.), Vol. II, pp. 208-09.

of Maratha administration. Dense forest regions between Khurda and Ganjam did not permit the Maratha ruler to construct direct roads between Khurda and Ganjam. Khurda had a regular land connection to Puri. The road that connected Khurda with Puri passed through Sahajpur and Kalupada crossing Daya river and joined with the main Cuttack-Puri road at Pipili.

By the time the Britishers came to Orissa these important roads were used by the people for mercantile traffics. Britishers became interested in the development of these roads for the purpose of commercial prosperity of the Company. Many new roads were added to the existing roads. Roads were constructed and maintained by different agencies. Provincial roads paid for out of the Provincial Funds and were kept under the charge of the Public Works Department of the Provincial Government. The second category of roads were paid for out of the District Road Fund and were under the immediate charge of the District Engineer. Local Board roads were maintained by the Local Boards purely for local utility. The cost of maintenance of such roads were paid out of the Local Board Funds.[73] The District Boards maintained the District Board roads within the boundary of the district, roads passing through the *killas* of permanently settled estates were also maintained by the District Board. But the Rajas or Zamindars were required to pay the cost of the maintenance of such roads to the District Board under which the *killa* came.

The first among the Provincial roads was Grand Trunk Road which ran from Medinapur in Bengal Presidency to Ganjam in Madras Presidency. It entered the Cuttack district at Akhayapada, 46 miles from Cuttack town. It was raised and metalled and crossed the rivers Baitarani, Kharsuan, Brahmani and Mahanadi by ferries. Passing through western hills it reached Cuttack town where it was divided into two, the Cuttack to Puri road and Cuttack to Ganjam road.

73. Maddox Report, p. 7.

Cuttack to Puri road was generally known as Jagannath Road which was constructed between 1811 and 1812 in place of the old pilgrim road.[74] There were 2 other Provincial roads, the first from Cuttack to Sonepur, mostly unmetalled and the second from Cuttack to Sambalpur through Athagarah.[75]

The principal District Board Roads of Cuttack district leading to Cuttack town the main commercial centre were constructed in the latter part of 19th century. These roads were of better use.

Cuttack to Taladanda, 44 miles length out of which 13½ miles were metalled. It was an all weather road.

Cuttack to Machhgaon, 32 miies leaving Taladanda Road at 11th mile was metalled upto 14th mile from Cuttack.

Cuttack to Chandbali Road passed through Pattamundai having a length of 63 miles.

Phulnakhara-Madhab Road joined the Cuttack-Puri Road at 16th mile from Cuttack.

Tangi to Haripur Road connected the Garhjats with Grand Trunk Road at 10th mile from Cuttack.

Jajpur to Kuakhia was a bad road with a length of 25 miles. It was not bridged at Kharsua and Brahmani.

Jajpur-Kendrapara Road connected these 2 important towns for commercial benefits with a length of 25 miles.

Beruan to Kalamatia was unaccessible during rains, the length being 16 miles.

Jajpur was connected with the Pachhikote estate by a road. This road was 19 miles long and was a good road partly bridged.

Salipur to Chhatia Road crossed 2 rivers having the length of 18 miles. It was not an all weather road as the road was unbridged.

74. *Ibid.*
75. *Ibid.*

Besides these important roads there were small roads in good condition in the district of Cuttack such as Pattamundai to Sudipur, 11 miles long; Jagatsinghpur to Jajpur with a length of 8 miles, Jagatsinghpur to Tirtol, 9 miles long; Beruan to Balichandrapur, 14 miles long and Jajpur to Kyanti having a length of 17 miles.[76]

Local Board Roads were many but all these roads were only fair-weather roads in Cuttack district.

Puri District possessed many roads maintained by Provincial Government, District Boards and Local Boards. These roads were

Pipili to Khurda, 15 miles long joined Ganjam and Jagannath Road at Mukundaprasad near Khurda.

The Khurda to Kalapathar through zilla Kuspala and Manikgora, 17 miles long joined the Provincial Road, Cuttack-Sonepur Road near Kantilo.

A district branch road left the Khurda-Sambalpur Road at Baghamari was extended upto Itamati, a commercial centre of Nayagarh Raja.

Sunakhala, a village on the district road between Baghamari and Bolegarh was connected with a road made by the Raja of Ranpur that further was linked with Ganjam Road near Tanghy.

A district road was stretched from Balugaon on Chilka lake to Banapur.

A good road was made by the Estate Improvement Fund from Chandka to Khandagiri and Bhubaneswar, 11 miles long again being connected with Sardeipur and Balianta Road.

A road was maintained by the District Board stretching from Khurda to Patnaikia on the Jagannath Road having a length of 22 miles.

76. Maddox Report, p. 8.

A district road was constructed between Sunakhala and Aitpur with a length of 34 miles.[77]

Grand Trunk Road ran for a length of 95 miles from and to the end of Balasore district. It afforded communication facilities with Medinapur and Calcutta in the North and Cuttack and Ganjam on the South. It was built by Capt. Sackville between 1812-20 the portion in Balasore district being opened in 1821.[78]

The Balasore District Board maintained 38 roads with a total length of 309 miles in the district only. These roads were unmetalled and many of them were fair-weather roads which were impassable for cart traffic even during the rains. In the North of the district especially these roads were subject to high flood of Subarnarekha. In June 1898 the Kamarda-Baliapal, Baliapal-Basta, Kamarda-Jaleswar and Singla-Nangaleswar Roads were breached in many places due to high flood. Bridges over these roads were washed away by the heavy flood. As a result these roads turned to be unsafe for cart traffic. There was another important road that connected Balasore and Mitrapur and Remuna. This was named as Panchapara-Haladipada Road. Gopinathpur to Soro and Anantapur to Soro Roads were opened for cart traffic by the District Board. A road from Jamjhari market was stretched to Basudevpur which met the old Salt Road. It was extended further upto Bhadrak. The most important road in the district was Bhadrak-Chandbali Road. Salt and other agricultural products of the district were enrouted to Chandbali port for exportation either via Ruknadeipur or via Basudevpur.[79]

In addition to these district roads there were maintained 67 village roads with a total length of 200 miles under the control of Balasore Sadar and Bhadrak Local Boards.[80]

77. Settlement of Khurda, p. 24.

78. Maddox Report, p. 27.

79. *Ibid*, p. 29.

80. *Ibid*.

Sambalpur-Medinapur service track opened in the year 1842 that passed through Keonjhar Tributary Mahal that allowed mercantile traffic straight from Calcutta to the Garhjat States of Orissa.[81]

Thus roads in the whole of the province afforded ample facilities to the growth of commercial prosperity of the people. These roads were very useful to carry mercantile traffic from interior villages to important markets where from goods of various descriptions were sent for exportation to nearby ports and gave an income to the Government in the form of road cess.

(*ii*) *Navigable Canals*—Following the years of famine the Canal Projects were initiated by the Government with a view to afford irrigation facilities as well as navigation benefits to the people. Taladanda Canal, Kendrapara Canal yielded revenue for the Government out of water communication in these canals. After the construction of Coast Canal direct water route could be possible from Cuttack to Bhadrak. The main aim of connecting Hoogli with Cuttack through the Coast Canal though was not materialised still it afforded facilities for commercial benefits to the merchants of Orissa. Easily the mercantile goods could be routed through Coast Canal that yielded profit to the merchants and revenue to the Government. The mercantile traffic through these canals were stopped after the opening of Bengal-Nagpur Railway in Orissa.

(*iii*) *Railways*—The people of Orissa from time to time claimed for the opening of Railways in Orissa. They could visualise the material benefit from the railways. The people of Orissa pressed the Government hard to construct railway lines in Orissa. Utkal Sabha went on demanding for this.[82] Committees were formed in Cuttack, Balasore and Puri with a view to pressurise the Government for railway lines in Orissa.

81. Settlement of Keonjhar, p. 24.

82. *Utkal Dipika*, No. 12, March 23, 1888.

Committees after careful consideration placed before the Government, proposals about the route for the construction of railway lines. These Committees suggested that the new railway lines should be stretched from Raniganj to Puri when the Government were thinking to stretch it from Sambalpur to Cuttack.[83] The prolonged silence of the Government was criticised by the people on mauy occasions.[84] The Government argued that the construction of railways were expensive because of the innumerable bridges to be constructed. Lt. Governor, Sir Asley Eden visited Orissa in 1878 to make an extensive enquiry about railways. He made it clear that canals would be more useful than railways for the province.[85] Government after the completion of the canal projects reconsidered the matter and it was decided finally that Howrah to Puri railway lines should be opened. The construction work was expedited and the railway line between Howrah to Puri was ready for traffic by April 1900.[86] Kuakhai Bridge was completed by March 31, 1900 which started from December 26, 1897 at a cost of Rs. 14,51,000. Mahanadi Bridge at the cost of Rs. 26,88,200 was completed within 2 years. The cost of Kathjoori Bridge was Rs. 13,55,000 and was completed within 3 years. Birupa Bridge at an estimated cost of Rs. 6,18,550 was complete within 2 years.[87] Before the inauguration of this line the East Coast Railway line linked Orissa with Madras in the year 1897.[88] The long awaited claim of the people of Orissa could be materialised by the Government. Orissa thus ceased to be considered as an isolated Province of India. The consequences of these railway lines were far reaching. Internal trade could increase tremendously no doubt but it became instrumental in the decline of many indigenous industries including Salt Industry. The immense benefit derivable from the railways could be easily felt by the people in general and

83. *Utkal Dipika*, No. 33, August 13, 1881.

84. *Ibid*, No. 9, February 28, 1880.

85. *Ibid*, No. 12, March 23, 1878.

86. *Ibid*, No. 18, May 5, 1900; GAROD, 1899-1900, p. 31.

87 *Ibid*, No. 18, May 5, 1900.

88. GAROD, 1896-97, 1897-98, p. 2.

by the merchants in particular, when they used the railways to speed up their commercial traffic to destinations at a very low rate of freight charges.

With the development of internal communication there was brisk internal trade throughout Orissa, causing harm to the sea-borne trade. Consequent upon this Government completely ignored the canal projects. Canals were still used by the merchants for the growth of their commercial activities as railway lines were not made available everywhere. As such the commercial growth could not reach upto expectation making the Orissan economy stagnant.

3. Impact of the Commercial Policy

Under these state of commercial rivalries the merchants of Orissa could not derive exclusive benefit as they were not rich to compete with the foreign merchants, as the price of the commodities were growing up, as there were insufficient water route and as they could not make use of the railways. To add injury to the backwardness of the people of Orissa the Government had imposed new taxes on articles in different times with the hope of getting more revenue. The Government was callous and was a silent observer to this economic backwardness of the people throughout the century. As a result of which commercial activities of the people of Orissa declined.

During the first half of 19th century the export and import trade was monopolised by the East India Company Government. The second half of 19th century was anticipated with a marked and impressive increase in both export and import trade due to the improvement of internal communication and improvement of the ports following the years of famine. The hope of having a complete revolution in the economy of the province by changing the backward isolated unimportant country into a busy and prosperous centre of trade[89] could not be realised. There was no sign of wealth and

89. BRP, July 1877, J. Beams, Commissioner, Cuttack to Government of Bengal, No. 600, July 1877.

comfort among the people. It happened due to the fact that the trade of the province was only confined in the export of foodgrains and other raw materials over which the Government was very much interested and the import of finished goods. The improvement of communication and the establishment of regular trade links with different places became a protection against future famine through labour mobilisation and importation of foodgrains of other places. The mobilisation of labour was further increased by the extension of railways. True to British policy it showed a familiar colonial pattern of administration. The improvement of communication facilities enabled the affected mass to take their shelter for food in urban areas and to find their employment elsewhere.[90] It also rendered ample provision for the transportation of grains to the affected areas immediately which was considered difficult previously. Though the facilities for trade and commercial activities of the people of Orissa were provided yet they were negligible to challenge the colonial attitude of the business community on Orissa to which Government was only a silent observer. But the material condition of the people was never improved as the benefit of the commercial policy was mainly enjoyed by the outsiders.

90. Moral and Material Progress Report, 1911-12, p. 379.

Conclusion

Nineteenth century was a period of transition in the history of Orissa. Within 13 years of the East India Company's administration there broke out the Paik Rebellion, a clear sign of discontentment of the people of Orissa against early British socio-economic policies. The British instituted a searching enquiry into the conduct of their own affairs in order to avoid similar revolt in future, but they had no occasion to think if Orissa required the same attention as the neighbouring territories of Bengal or Madras. Orissa seems to have been left singularly neglected and thereby denied of many advantages. The changes in the method of administration destroyed the infrastructure of the economic development of the province in consequence of which many skilled workers were thrown into unemployment.

The land revenue administration in India was of the deepest interest to the East India Company as it ultimately was connected with the material well-being of a predominantly agricultural nation. It was more true in case of Orissa. At the time of their occupation of this province the Company anticipated the financial benefit for which they wanted to help the landed class. As such they assured the landed class of best possible protection in future recognising their interest in agriculture.* As land revenue was a major part of the Company's total

*Secret and Political Consultations, March 1, 1804, Harcourt and Melville to Government of Bengal.

revenue in Orissa, the authorities were prompt in introducing settlements. But the temporary settlements from 1804 to 1837 brought untold misery and sufferings to the people including landlords. The concerned officers were interested to get more *Jama* for the advantage of the Company without caring for the results of such short-term settlements.

The first 30 years' settlement became effective in 1837. It could not provide adequate safeguards to poor tenants and cultivators from the oppreesion of the Zamindars. The land holders were also uncertain of their future, and actually before the expiry of the term of the settlement in 1867 many of them had allowed their cultivable lands to fall barren so that their *Jama* would not be enhanced. That was one of the contributing factors for the disastrous Famine of 1866. Both the land holders and tenants in that grave calamity and the Government had no option but to permit the old settlement to continue for a period of another 30 years. Such an extension of the term of the settlement helped the province to recover, to some extent, from the damages sustained in 1866-67. But the lots of the poor cultivators could not improve. The peasantry suffered in abject poverty as before.

The settlement of 1897 was introduced keeping in view the disastrous consequences of the Famine and the defects of the settlement of 1837. To help the Zamindars the portion of the assets taken as revenue was reduced. It was obvious from the consequent decrease of the sale of the estates for non-payment of the Government dues by the Zamindars. The agriculture community heaved a sigh of relief due to the removal of over-assessment in many cases. Further to improve the condition of the tenants the Bengal Tenancy Act of 1885 was extended to Orissa and it succeeded to restrict the exaction of illegal *abwabs* or cesses by the land holders. Thus by the end of the century only the peasantry in Orissa reaped some benefits from the enactment of the British authoritiee. However the British policy towards the Feudatory States of Orissa remained more or less unchanged in consequence of which the people in Garhjat States could not improve their lot in any way.

The Famine of 1866-67 marks a dividing line in the history of modern Orissa. After the searching enquiry into the cause of the mortality of about one million of people the British administators gave up their attitude of complacency. In the post-Famine period they gave some attention to such socio-economic problems like education, irrigation and communication etc. They no doubt initiated certain bold measures on matters of irrigation but the projects almost ended in failure because the Zamindars were apprehensive of increase of their *Jama* if their lands would be covered by the irrigation system and the poor cultivators were more fearful of the enhancement of their land tax. Thus the economic prosperity due to irrigation as in some parts of Madras Presidency remained far from realisation in Orissa.

Salt manufacture in the long coastal tract of Orissa was a traditional local industry in the province. It produced the finest salt in Eastern seaboard of India. The British administration controlled it through monopoly and after the abolition of monopoly in 1863, through excise system and finally they closed the whole sea-coast of Orissa from the manufacture of salt. The consequences of the British salt policy in Orissa was disastrous from many directions. First the price of salt increased which caused the hardship to the people, secondly with the abolition of the monopoly the manufacture of the article declined and many poor salt workers were thrown into unemplopment. In fact, in the Famine of 1866 many of them perished due to lack of any fruitful occupation. Hardly with the restriction of manufacture, the importation of large quantity of Liverpool salt took place which finally resulted in the final closure of this profitable Orissan industry. It increased the miseries of the people manifold, and caused economic hardship for the landless labourers of the coastal tract and they ran away from the coastal tract of Orissa to distant places for their livelihood. Hence it retarted the prosperity of the province.

The increase of the consumption of excisable articles even at high rates enabled the Government to use this elastic source of revenue as a major percentage of the total annual revenue, that altimately impaired the economic life of the people of Orissa.

Orissa had a long established reputation in many cottage industries from time immemorial especially Weaving and Filigree Industry had attracted the attention of Europeans from medieval time. But 19th century, as in other parts in India, cottage industry had declined due to British policy. It brought about disastrous consequences and immense economic hardship to the people in course of time. The famous Filigree Industry suffered due to lack of patronage either by the Government or by any private enterprises. Only in the last decade of the century Madhusudan Das* one of the makers of modern Orissa established Orissa Art Wares to help economic revival of the poor province. He also gets the credit of introducing the first power machines in his Orissa Tannery established in 1905. He produced finest shoes and even exported to foreign countries for the use of soldiers in the 1st World War. Thus the atmosphere of economic regeneration by indigenous organisation was ushered in the beginning of 20th century.

Orissa's glorious maritime trade and flourishing ports had considerably declined by the time of the British occupation of Orissa in 1803. The new administration could not do anything to check the decline and in fact the abolition of salt monopoly almost closed the ports of Orissa from outside communication. The British administrators bitterly realised their neglect of Orissan ports when they failed to import rice and paddy to coastal tract to save the people. Naturally after the Famine some attempts were made to improve the port of False Point and at the same time a new inland port at Chandbali was established. It was linked with Cuttack, the capital of the province through navigable canals. Attempts were made to link Chandbali with Calcutta through Çoast Canal

*Madhusudan Das was one of the makers of modern Orissa. He was the founder of Filigree and Leather Industries at his residential campus at Cuttack. He was a member of the Bengal Legislative Council.

Project. It helped to a great extent for the increase of the portal trade. Both import and export increased considerably through the inland water communication before the introduction of railways. It helped to some extent to ease economic hardship of the common people.

The Britith authorities tried to improve communication to Orissa by improving a number of roads and by extending waterways communication but Orissa was denied of the benefit of the extension of railways as in other parts of India. It was neglected till the end of the century and only in 1899 the first line was thrown open to the general public in the coastal tract of Orissa. However the most important factor, that contributed to the emergence of a new socio-political and economic consciousness in Orissa by a slow rise of middle class intelligentsia, was the establishment of a college and a number of schools after the Famine.

The extension of the railways by the end of 19th century finally ended the isolation of Orissa. It also helped to increase the commercial activities of the people and greater mobilisation of labour.

G. Toynbee, the Commissioner of Orissa observed in 1892, "In all direction and on all sides the immense strides made by the province generally in education, commerce, irrigation, communication and general wealth and prosperity are conspicuous to the most casual and superficial observer. And yet one looks below the surface, the great mass of the people live in the same lives and have the same limited hopes and aspirations that they had 30 years ago."* The statement thus acknowledges that Orissa remained virtually a backward province in comparison to other provinces of British India.

To consider the balance-sheet of the trend of the economic development of 19th century it is logical to say that the period before the famine left a legacy of stagnation, unpredict-

*GAROD, 1891-92, p. 29.

able economic deterioration which was accentuated by a process of stabilisation and a comparative prosperity following the years of Famine. The continuous drain upon the provincial economy with no equivalent return of any kind led to the accumulating poverty of the people that accounts for the economic backwardness of the province throughout 19th cnetury. In spite of the Government's manifold reformative measures, the conditions of the majority of the population remained unsatisfactory. Consequently, the economic prosperity of Orissa remained a distant object. However, the process of stabilisation contributed its share to the slow growth of middle class intelligentsia which led to the establishment of 'Utkal Samilani' in 1903. It was an organisation which spearheaded the movements for alround improvement of a people neglected for ages.

APPENDICES

APPENDIX 'A'

Statement showing the Settled Assets and Settled Revenue with percentage in the Settlement of 1897

District	*Exsisting Assets*	*Exiting Revenue*		*Settled Assets*	*Settled Revenue*	
		Percen-tage	*Amount Rs.*		*Percen-tage*	*Amount Rs.*
Cuttack	18,47,400	38	7,14,100	20,72,900	53	10,99,300
Balasore	9,88,800	38	3,77,290	11,51,400	59	6,29,073
Puri	5,37,700	51	2,92,800	6,43,300	58	3,76,700
	34,09,900	41	13,84,190	38,67,600	54	21,05,073

APPENDIX 'B'

Statement showing the Annual Rate of Tribute, Estimated Rent and the Area of Tributary Mahals

State	*Tribute* *Rs. a. p.*	*Area in sq. miles*	*Rent Rs.*
1. Athagarh			
Former	6,848-8-7	250	15,000
Present	4,445-0-0		
2. Athamallik	450-0-0	300	8,000
3. Boud	750-0-0	700	25,000
4. Baramba	1,310-9-10	150	12,000
5. Dhenkanal	4,780-5-15	10,000	50,000
6. Duspalla	620-2-9	500	20,000
7. Hindol	516-12-14	200	9,000
8. Keonjhar	2,790-11-3	22,000	30,000
9. Khandpara	3,948-5-2	300	20,000
10. Mayurbhanj	1,001-0-0	15,000	50,000
11. Nilgiri	5,617-6-9	400	16,000
12. Narsinghpur	1,364-8-15	250	12,000
13. Nayagarh	5,179-14t16	1,900	35,000
14. Pallahara	266-10-8	20	1,500
15. Ranpur (Runpur)	1,313-4-6	200	15,000
16. Talcher	974-10-16	250	12,000
17. Tigiria	826-13-9	150	8,000

APPENDIX 'C'

Statement showing the Detail Account of Relief Operation

District	*Quantity received in local stores and Relief Committees*	*Quantities issued for consumption*				*Total consumed*	*Without labour*	*Light labour*
		To Govt. Deptt.	*To public*	*For sale at cheap rate*	*Starving*			
Cuttack	1,48,767	3,282	49,754	31,520	52,565	1,37,121	12,381	7,177
Balasore	75,427	4,473	10,526	11,643	46,816	73,458	21,945	4,552
Puri	47,383	1,028	18,973	5,940	16,626	42,567	3,205	3,426
Total	2,71,577	8,783	79,253	49,103	1,16,007	2,53,146	37,531	15,155

APPENDIX 'D'

Col. Gulliver's Statistical Account of Canal Project in Orissa

Name of Canal	*Length of navigable canals (miles)*	*Length of irrigable canals (miles)*	*Area irrigable from the distributaries (acres)*	*Length of distributaries (miles)*	*Cost of distributaries per acre*	*Length of village canals (miles)*
Kendrapara	70½	70½	94,200	252½	Rs. 568	74¼
Pattamundai	—	48	—	—	—	—
Taladanda	27	27	15,636	65¼ nearly	Rs. 26	—
Machhgaon	—	19	38,275	123	Rs. 646	—
High Level Range I	33⅛	33⅛	58,060	108	Rs. 925	23½
Range II	12¾	12¾	—	—	—	—
Range III	17½	17½	—	—	—	—
Total	160⅞	227⅞	2 06,172	548½	—	101¾

APPENDIX 'E'

Detail Statistics of the Abkari Revenue

	1837-38		1838-39	
Name of the articles	*No. of shops*	*Amount realised Rs. a. p.*	*No. of shoys*	*Amount realised Rs. a. p.*
Cuttack				
Opium	1	8,428-1-2	1	7,438-0-0
Liquor	18	2,221-8-6	15	2,674-2-23
Tari	150	2,163-10-7	138	1,883-14-11
Ganja	1	3,102-8-0	1	2,737-8-0
Total		15,995-12-3		24,784-3-2
Balasore				
Opium	2	13,456-14-8	1	12,648-0-0
Liquor	6	556-6-5	6	595-0-5
Tari	4	841-14-6	4	771-13-2
Ganja	22	463-12-10	22	471-7-4
Total		15,319-0-5		14,486-4-11
Puri				
Opium	6	1,169-0-0	6	2,325-0-0
Liquor	31	1,382-7-5¼	21	1,968-13-2
Tari	50	1,017-15-3¼	50	1,017-15-3½
Ganja	7	1,043-10-0	—	—
Total		4,613-0-8½		5,311-12-5½

APPENDIX 'F'

Statistics of Trade and the Increase of Customs Duty (1872-73 and 1873-74)

Name of the Port	No. of Vessels				Trade value of Export and Import			
	Entered		Cleared		Export		Import	
	72-73	73-74	72-73	73-74	72-73	73-74	72-73	73-74
					Rs. a.p.	Rs. a p.	Rs. a.p.	Rs. a.p.
Cuttack	75	106	80	101	8,21,429-0-0	10,60,432-0-0	8,49,547-0-0	11,42,893-0-0
Puri	31	33	29	33	1,95,533-0-0	3,15,034-0-0	74,959-0-0	35,237-0-0
Balasore	345	405	351	479	3,99,208-0-0	16,31,708-14-0	2,50,488-0-0	17,13,158-8-5

Receipts								Expenditure	
1872-73				1873-74				1872-73	1873-74
Duty	*Port dues	Others	Total	Duty	Port dues	Others	Total		
Rs. a. p.	Rs. a. p.	Rs. a. p.	Rs. a. p.	Rs. a. p.	Rs. a p.	Rs. a. p.	Rs. a. p.	Rs. a. p.	Rs. a. p.
1,833-0-0	—	—	1,830-0-0	12,373-5-8	—	41-4-2	12,414-9-8	8,887-0-0	4,868-2-0
—	—	—	—	30,531-0-0	—	—	30,531-0-0	277.0-0	12,540-4-5
6,712-0-0	2,772-0-0	1,599-0-0	11,083-0-0	8,274-2-7	3,567-6-8	1,011-2-3	12,852-11-6	340-0-0	2,280-15-0

APPENDIX 'G'

Statistics showing the Total Volnme of Import and Export and the Customs Duty derived out of it

Districts	*Vessels entered*		*Vessels cleared*		*Value of Import*	*Value of Export*	*Customs Revenue*
	Vessels	*Tonnage*	*Vessels*	*Tonnage*	*Rs.*	*Rs.*	*Rs.*
Cuttack							
1874-75	110	1,18,375	108	1,20,041	9.11,659	17,00,471	43,000
1877-78	202	1,40,952	187	1,41,838	36,23,812	36,74,817	20,635
1878-79	179	1,38,676	173	1,38,498	19,28,230	28,28,183	55,394
Puri							
1874-75	32	10,553	31	11,618	54,361	5,32,259	25,534
1877-78	20	8,019	21	10,130	62,929	5,62,895	—
1878-79	42	9,724	39	8,782	1,30,302	3,95,484	2,213
Balasore							
1874-75	387	51,689	456	59,877	26,26,837	21,38,305	3,533
1877-78	535	73,635	513	68,495	53,68,743	58,63,579	15,709
1878-79	362	49,924	433	57,396	35,82,421	49,24,834	23,111

APPENDIX 'H'

Statement showing the Detail Increase of Import and Export Trade at False Point

Year	No. of Vessels	Tonnage	Value of Import Rs.	Value of Export Rs.	Total Rs.
1860-61	4	2,830	—	67,590	—
1861-62	10	7,756	—	2,46,570	—
1862-63	6	4,016	—	1,78,020	—
1863-54	16	8,681	3,30,930	1,88,280	5,19,210
1870-71	105	52,744	1,32,355	6,69,757	8,02,112
1871-72	86	72,525	9,00,133	4,75,700	13,75,838
1872-73	75	69,999	8,49,547	8,21,429	16,70,976
1873-74	106	86,597	11,42,893	10,60,432	22,03,325
1874-75	110	1,18,375	9,11,659	18,00,471	27,12,130
1875-76	133	1,57,468	13,80,653	12,71,575	26,52,328
1876-77	166	1,49,515	11,88,073	29,06,105	4,940,178
1877-78	202	1,40,952	36,04,023	36,73,016	72,77,039
1878-79	179	1,38,676	19,28,230	28,28,182	47,66,412

Glossary

Abkari	Excise (Opium, Ganja and Liquor).
Abra	a superior variety of kurkutch salt.
Abwab	miscellaneous cesses, charges levied by zamindars or public officers illegally in addition to the regular assessment on the land.
Amil	an officer of Government in the financial department especially a collector of revenue; also himself a farmer, or contractor for the revenue under the native system and vested with supreme authority, both civil and military in the district which he framed.
Amin	a native surveyor of land, an officer who measures the land in the settlement, also a native officer of Government employed either in the revenue department to take charge of an estate and collect the revenue on account of Government.
Amala	a native officer of judicial court or revenue office.
Aurang	a manufacturing division of salt agency.
Baboo	clerks engaged in revenue offices, especially Bengalis.
Bapta	a type of cloth of mixed tasar and cotton threads.

Bahal	a revenue plot.
Bakshi	commander-in-chief.
Bardaranjagir	a rent-free tenure enjoyed by the family members of the estate holders or zamindars.
Bargi	a band of cavalry forces of the Bhonsle of Nagpur.
Bazar	a market.
Bazefasal	crops of inferior quality.
Baziaftidar	a holder of resumed rent-free lands.
Bebarta	the adviser of the king or Dewan.
Bepari	a businessman, a dealer, a merchant.
Bheti	a present to the zamindars or revenue officers by the cultivators.
Bhowri	a house for boiling salt.
Bibhachina	a present by the cultivators to the zamindars at the time of marriage ceremony of the zamindars' family members.
Burkundza	a matchlock man but commonly applied to a native armed with a sword and shield who acts as a doorkeeper, watchman, guard or escort.
Chakla	a large division of a province comprehending a number of parganas.
Chamar	a low caste skilled leather worker other than shoe maker.
Chandina	home-stead land.
Chandinadar	a holder of home-stead lands.
Chandua	a decorative, attractive handicraft product used in functions over-head.
Chaprasi	a peon.
Charchitti	a delivery order.
Chattis	a name given to a collection of choolhas.
Chhatak	one-sixteenth part of a seer.

Choolha	a fire place for boiling brine.
Chooleas	superintendents of choolhas who contract.
Chowkey	a station of police or of customs, a post where a guard is placed.
Choukidar or Chowkidar	a village watchman, a police or customs peon.
Churrus	a narcotic and intoxicant, a portion of hemp plant.
Cutcherry	a court or an office or a place where any Governmental business is transacted.
Dadani	advance payment.
Dakhilkharaj	transfer of land with area and rent to the name of new owner and incorporation of the same in the record.
Dalai	a sub-ordinate officer in command of paiks.
Dalbehera	headman among paiks, an officer in command of paiks.
Damos	a class of skilled workers preparing bamboo baskets.
Darbar	a court, a royal court, an audience.
Darogah or Darogha	an officer-in-charge of the division of salt agency of a police station, a manager, a superintendent especially the chief native officer of police, customs or excise station.
Dastipadika	local measuring rod of land.
Debottar	rent-free lands belonging to temples.
Dewan	a minister, a revenue minister, a chief of state.
Dharmasala	a resthouse for pilgrims.
Diha	a revenue division in a permanently settled estate.

Dustak	a passport, a permit, a warrant. In Orissa it was applied especially to a process by which a revenue defaulter was compelled to pay any balance that might be due to him.
Ekrarnama	an engagement, an agreement, assent, ratification.
Faujdar or Fauzadar	the chief of a body of troops.
Ganda	one unit of native currency system.
Ganja	a kind of intoxicating drug prepared from the hemp plant, an intoxicant used by the people.
Garah	a fort.
Garahjat	tributary states of Orissa.
Garibapraja	poor tenants.
Ghani	an oil mill used by a class of local people called as teli to prepare oil from oil-seeds.
Gola	a warehouse, a place in which grain or salt is kept for a season; also a grain or salt market, a place where grain or salt is sold wholesale.
Gossain	a religious.
Goomasta or Gumasta	an agent or a manager, a confidential representative appointed by zamindars to collect their rents.
Handi	an earthen pot for cooking.
Hat	a market held on certain days in a week.
Hinayat jagir	jagir held by low caste people.
Jagir	a tenure common under the native Government in which the public revenues of a given tract of land were made over to a servant of the state, service land.
Jagirdar	a holder of jagir.

Jama	a total amount of rent or revenue payable by a cultivator or a zamindar including all cesses.
Jamadar	an officer of police, customs or excise second to the darogah.
Jheel	a narrow water course from hills to low lands.
Kahan	a measure of kauri currency.
Kalasi	an earthen pot for keeping water during religious functions.
Kamilbaziaftidar	a holder of resumed rent-free lands.
Kansa	a bell-metal utensil.
Kanungo	a revenue officer who under the native Governments recorded all circumstances within their sphere which concerned landed property and realisation of the land revenue etc.
Kauri	a small shell found in Indian ocean used as money.
Khandayiat	the head of paiks employed in rural police work holding their lands at a quit rent.
Kharcha	expense, disbursement.
Khas	as a revenue term it is applied to the management of estates and the collection of revenue by officers of the Government without any intermediate person between them and the cultivators.
Khasmahal	district held in the management of the Government.
Khasara	a field index to the map containing one entry for each field or separate plot belonging to one cultivator specifying the names of the owner and the occupier, its area, the crop borne in it and a description of the nature of the soil.

Khariddars	a purchaser of proprietary rights in small plots of land from the zamindars.
Khatian	a record containing a list of tenants of the village with details of the land held by each, the rent payable for them, and the class of tenancy to which holding belonged.
Khewat	a record which contained the names, tauzi numbers, areas and proprietors of each estate of which any lands were situated in the village.
Khond	a tribal people inhabitating the hill tracts of Orissa.
Khoraki	diet allowance.
Khorakposak niskar	a rent-free tenure towards the diet allowance and clothing allowance.
Khudkhast	permanent tenure holders on land; personal cultivation by land holders.
Killa	a state of khandayiat, a permanently settled estate, a tributary state, a fort.
Killazat	a killa which was resumed and given temporary settlement.
Kist	instalments of rents.
Kistbandi	settlement of the revenue by instalments
Koppali or Copalli	resinous exudation from a tropical tree grown in the garahjat states, a part of hemp tree, collected from the living tree which is used as an intoxicant.
Koomtees	a mercantile community from Madras Presidency.
Kothi	a store room.
Kurkutch or Karkatch	salt obtained by solar evaporation.
Lakhraj	revenue-free land.
Lakhrajbahal	land confirmed without revenue.

Machhadia	a fishery.
Magon	borrowing.
Mahajan	a money lender.
Mahal	a province or district, in the language of Bengal regulation a mahal is called an estate and is defined as any parcel or parcels of land which may be separately assessed with the public revenue; the state of tributary king.
Mahalla	a division of a town.
Mahalwari	system of land revenue assessment in which the unit of assessment is a mahal not an individual holding.
Mahaprasad	holy food of Lord Jagannath.
Mahanta	the head of a matha.
Mahula or Mowah	a small fruit of a tree out of which liquor is prepared locally.
Malangi	a manufacturer of salt.
Malikana	allowances paid to the proprietor of an estate on his becoming recusant.
Marfatdar	custodian.
Matha	a religious institution resembling a monastery.
Mauza	a village or a group of villages.
Mela	a seasonal fair.
Mochi	a shore maker.
Mufassil	the villages in general, the station in the villages as opposed to sadar or principal town or station.
Mughalbandi	a long strip of cultivated land lying between hill tracts and sea; revenue assessed lands of Cuttack, Balasore and Puri districts settled by the Mughals.
Muddut	collection of portions of hemp tree, narcotic, sometimes used as medicine.
Muharir	a clerk, a writer.

Mukaddam	the headman of the village, a class of proprietary tenure holders or sub-proprietors.
Munsi	a secretary, a writer, a term applied by Europeans usually to interpreters of Persian and Hindustani.
Mulmul	a fine variety of cotton cloth.
Murdang	a musical instrument commonly used in sankirtan party, elliptical shaped earthern pipe, one side narrow and one side broad, covered with hide, produces fine tone.
Nalas	a water course, a drain.
Nankar	an assignment of a portion of land or revenue of an estate made to the Zamindar as his subsistence allowance.
Nayabadi	rent fixation on new lands fit for cultivation.
Nisi-baziaftidar	a holder of resumed rent-free lands.
Nuliya	Telugu settler from Ganjam engaged in sea fishing as profession.
Nuzrana	a present to the superior, a present to the zamindar by the cultivator, forced contribution.
Padhan	a class of proprietary tenure holder.
Paik or Paika	the paiks constituted a local militia holding the lands of the military chiefs or Rajas by tenure or military services.
Pana	a sum of 80 kauri shells equal to 20 gandas, 16 panas make a kahan.
Panga	salt produced by boiling the brine.
Pahani	a water course to the fields from distant water reservoirs built by the cultivators.
Pahi	non-resident.
Parcha	an abbreviated khatian.
Pargana	a tract of the country comprising many villages; name of a fiscal division of the Mughals and Marathas.

Parwana	an order, a written command, a letter from a man in power to a dependant.
Patta	a document given by the collector to the zamindar specifying the conditions on which the lands are held and the rents payable, a deed of lease.
Patwari	a village accountant.
Peskash	a tribute or quit rent, a fine or present to the ruling power on receiving an appointment of revenue.
Pirottar	rent-free lands held by Muslim monastery.
Pitrali	lands enjoyed through ancestors.
Raiyat	a cultivator, a farmer, a peasant.
Raiyatwari	system of revenue settlement directly with the individual land holders the revenue demand being periodically re-assessed.
Raja or Rajah	the king.
Rajkumar jagir	rent-free tenures enjoyed by the prince permanently.
Rajwara	hill tracts of Orissa ruled by semi-independent kings.
Rawana	a pass, a certificate from a collector of customs authorising goods to pass without payment of further duty, a passport.
Ruidad	an agreement between the Government and the zamindars.
Sadar	usually means the chief seat of Government, principal town or city as opposed to muffasil.
Sadar Jama	the sum total of revenue payable to Government exclusive of charges of collection etc.
Sahukar	indigenous banker and money lender.
Salami	a complementary present to a superior upon being introduced to him.

Samanta	a near relative to the Raj family to work during social functions.
Sanand	a grant, a charter.
Sarbarakar	a minor revenue official, in Orissa the title was given to village accountant when he was the general director and manager of the revenue affairs being paid by a percentage on the collection of his village.
Sevaka	service tenure holder.
Sayer	taxes other than land revenue; transit duties.
Sicca	a stamped coin, especially the name of the silver currency of the Mughal kings adopted by the Indian Princes and eventually by the East India Company.
Sikim Zamindar	a purchaser or recipient of proprietary rights in small plots of land from the zamindar.
Sirastadar	a record keeper.
Sthaniya	local.
Subadar	the Governor of a province, a viceroy under the Mughal and Maratha Governments.
Sunia	day fixed by the zamindars for the clearance of the revenne by the cultivators.
Surehi	an earthen pot manufactured by the potter to keep water cool with a narrow long neck.
Tahasil	sub-division of district or estate.
Tahasildar	a native collector of revenue in charge of a tahasil.
Taluk	a portion of zamindari, an estate applied to a tract of proprietary land usually small, a division of a province.

Talukdar	the holder of a taluk, a collector of revenue from the cultivators of a taluk.
Taidad	a document of contract of salt manufacture.
Tandakar	monetary punishment.
Tanki	a quit rent.
Tankidar	a holder of small areas permanently assessed at a quit rent.
Tanta	handmade loom used by the weaver class.
Tanti	weaver class.
Taqavi or Tuccavee	a kind of loan given to the cultivators by the Government for productive purposes.
Tari	fermented juice of palm tree.
Tauzi	a field index register.
Thani	resident.
Thatari	manufacturer of brass and bell-metal utensils.
Teli	oilman, a man doing business in oil.
Telinga	he whose mother-tongue is Telugu.
Toila or Taila	temporary lands fit for temporary cultivation.
Vakil or Wakil	an agent, an attorney, a person invested with authority to act for another.
Zilla	a district, a division.
Zamindar	a landlord, a proprietor directly responsible to the Government for the revenue of the land he possesses.
Zamindari	the office and rights of the zamindar.

Bibliography

(Consulted at the National Archives of Indla, New Delhi; State Archives of Orissa, Bhubaneswar; State Archives, West Bengal, Calcutta; the Archives of the Board of Revenue, Orissa, Cuttack and National Library, Calcutta).

1. Original Source

A. Manuscript Sources—Official Records

Bengal Revenue Proceedings from 1815-1900

500 Volumes have been consulted containing

(i) Bengal Revenue Proceedinge—Land Revenue.

(ii) Bengal Revenue Proceedings—Miscellaneous.

(iii) Bengal Revenue Proceedings—Customs.

(iv) Bengal Revenue Proceedings—Salt.

(v) Bengal Revenue Proceedings—Finance, Separate Revenue, Salt.

(vi) Bengal Revenue Proceedings—Excise.

(vii) Bengal Revenue Proceedings—Irrigation.

(viii) Bengal Revenue Proceedings—Civil Judicial.

(ix) Bengal Revenue Proceedings—Criminal Judicial.

Bengal Revenue and Agriculture (Famine) Department Proceedings, 1879-1900, 20 Volumes.

Proceedings of Board of Customs, Salt and Opium, 1819-1890, 50 Volumes.

Proceedings of Bengal Legislative Council, 1850-1880, 30 Volumes.

Proceedings of the Board of Revenue, Miscellaneous, Customs and Excise, 1805-1890, 40 Volumes.

Proceedings of Bengal Public Works Department, 1862, 1863, 1868 and 1869, 4 Volumes.

Balasore Salt Records, 1803, 1875, 65 Volumes.

Balasore Custom House Records, 1805-1875, 25 Volumes.

Board's Revenue Collections, Vol. 582-587, 6 Volumes.

Bengal Revenue Consultations, 1822.

Cuttack Revenue Records, 1803-1820, 17 Volumes.

Cuttack Salt Records, 1803-1875, 70 Volumes.

Records of the Orissa Canal Projects, File No. 111, 1869, Relevant Papers.

Records of the Board of Revenue, Lower Province, File No. 125, File No. 66 of 1892.

Records of the Board of Revenue,

File No. 93 of 1878 (Excise),

File No. 91 of 1891 (Excise),

File No. 159 of 1894 (Customs),

File No. 35 of Collection of Government Customs.

Records of the Customs Department, 1820-1827, 5 Volumes.

Salt and Excise Records,

Letter No. 665S, 1901, Assistant Commissioner, 24 Pargana to Commissioner, Excise, Salt, Bengal.

Letter No. 46, 1901, Commissioner of Orissa to Commissioner, Excise, Bengal.

Letter No. 1586S, 1901, Commissioner, Excise, Salt, Bengal to Secretary, Government of India.

Letter No. 655TF, 1901, Secretary, Government of Bengal to Secretary, Government of India.

Copy of a letter, September 1, 1806, R. Ker, Magistrate, Cuttack to Board of Revenue.

Selection from Records of the Government of Bengal paper relating to Orissa Canals, 1869-1877 and 1881-1883, Calcutta.

Selection from Records of the Bengal Government, No. XXXV (Reports of the districts of Puri and Balasore, Henry Ricket, 1853), Calcutta, 1859.

Selection from Records of the Bengal Government, XXIV, No. 3, (Papers on the Settlement of Cuttack and on the State of Tributary Mahals), Calcutta, 1867.

Selection of Records on Feudatory States of Orissa Divisions and Rules applicable to them, Part I, Calcutta, 1907 (Confidential).

B. Printed (Records and Report)

Abstract of Regulation of Government, W. Blunt (Compiler), 1826-28, 4 Volumes.

Acts of Legislative Council of India, Fagan (Edt.), Vol. II, Calcutta, 1862.

Bihar and Orissa Gazetteer, Cuttack, Puri and Balasore, S.S O. Malley, Calcutta, 1929.

Bengal District Gazetteer, Calcutta, 1906.

Calendar of Persian Correspondences, 4 Volumes, Records Department, Calcutta, 1911-1949.

Collection of Treaties, Engagements and Sunands relating to India and neighbouring countries, C.U. Aitchison (Edt.), Vol. II & III, Calcutta, 1892.

Diary of Streynsham Master, T. Richard (Edt.), Vol. II, Lonnon, 1911.

Diary of William Hedges, Colonel Henry (Edt.), London, LXXXVIII.

Early European Travellers in Nagpur Territories, Nagpur, 1930.

East India Report of Famine Commission presented to both the Houses of the Parliament, London, 1881.

Final Report on the Survey and Settlement of the Province of Orissa, S.L. Maddox, 1890-1900, Vol. I & II, Calcutta, 1900.

Final Report on the Revision Settlement of Orissa, J.F.W. James, 1906-1912.

Final Report on the Survey and Settlement of Killa Aul, D. Bose, 1892-1901, Calcutta, 1901.

Final Report on the Survey and Settlement of Killa Darpan, H.K. Mohanty, 1901, Calcutta, 1901.

Final Report on the Survey and Settlement of Killa Kanika, S S. Hussain, 1889-1894, Calcutta, 1900.

Final Report on the Survey and Settlement of Killa Kujang, 1892-1899, Calcutta, 1900.

Final Report on the Survey and Settlement of Keonjhar State.

Final Report on the Survey and Settlement of Khurda Government Estate, Teylor & Maddox, 1897-1898, Calcutta, 1901.

Fifth Report of the Select Committee of the House of Commons on the affairs of East India Company, 1812.

Guide to Orissa Records, Orissa State Archives, Bhubaneswar, 1962-1963.

General Administration Report, Orissa Division (Annual), 1850-51 to 1898-99, 49 Volumes.

History of Portuguese in Bengal.

Imperial Gazeteer of India, Vol. II & III.

Memoirs of the Map of Mughal Empire, J. Runnel, PCXXX, London, 1793.

Memoirs of the Bengal Civilian, J. Beams, London, 1961.

Moral and Material Progress Report, 1911-1912.

Narrative of the Principal Events, Prinsep (Edt.), 1813-1814, London, 1820.

Narrative of the Principal Events connected with Flood Embankment in Orissa and the Origin and Development of Orissa Canals, 1840-1900, W.A. Inglis, Calcutta, 1900.

Orissa Project, Contract between the Secretary of State and the East India Irrigation Company, 1861.

Private Records (Orissa), Index Volume, National Archives, Delhi.

Quinquennial Administration Report, Orissa Division, 1900-1901 to 1904-1905.

Report on the Administration of Bengal (Bengal Presidency), 1830-1831 to 1880-1881, 50 Volumes.

Report on the Administration of Salt Department, 1830-1831 to 1885-1886, 55 Volumes.

Report on the Administration of Salt Revenue in Madras Presidency and Orissa, 1866, 1867, 2 Volumes.

Report on the Administration of Salt in the Madras Presidency, 1888-1889.

Report on the Abkari Revenue of Lower Province, 1845-1846, Calcutta, 1847.

Report on the Abkari Revenue of Lower Province, 1852-1853, Calcutta, 1854.

Report on the Abkari Revenue of Lower Province, 1857-1858, Calcutta, 1859.

Report on the Abkari Revenue of Lower Province, 1862-1863, Calcutta, 1864.

Report on the Abkari Revenue of Lower Province, 1880-1881, Calcutta, 1882.

Report on the Salt in British India, Bengal, Part II & III, Volume 25 & 26, George Plowden.

Report of the Commissioners appointed to enquire into the Famine of Bengal and Orissa, 1866, 2 Volumes.

Report of the Orissa Famine Commission, 1866 with Appendix.

Report of the Indian Famine Commission, 1880, Part I

Report of the Indian Famine Commission, 1898 with evidence Volume,

Report of the Indian Famine Commission, 1901 with evidence Volume.

Report of the Irrigation Commission, 1901-1903, Part II.

Report of the Commissioners appointed to enquire into certain matter in connection with the Orissa Canals, 1884-1885.

Report on the Mahanadi River, 1881, A. Cotton, Calcutta.

Report on the River Mahanadi and its distributaries, 1863, R. Temple.

Report on the District of Cuttack, Henry Ricket, Calcutta, 1858.

Report on the District of Balasore, Henry Ricket, Calcutta, 1858.

Report on the Bay of Bengal, False Point and Jumboo Port, Patna, 1923.

Report on the manufacture of Salt and the system of Administration of Salt Revenue of Balasore, Cuttack and Puri Districts forming the Orissa Division of Bengal Presidency, 1883, G. Rundall.

Report on the Village Watch on the Lower Province of Bengal, D J. Mcneil, Calcutta, 1866.

Report on the Administration of Feudatory States of Orissa, 1908-1909.

Report on the Indian Hemp and Drug Commission, 1893-1894.

Report of the Commissioners appointed by the Parliament to enquire into the sale and manufacture of Salt in British India, Vol. 26, 1856, George Plowden.

Report of the Inundation Committee of Orissa, 1866.

Report on the Maritime trade of Bihar and Orissa, 1935-36, Patna, 1937.

Report on the Embankment of Orissa, 1871.

2. Newspapers and Periodicials

English

The Hindu Patriot.

The Englishman.

The Friend of India.

Calcutta Review, 1850-1870.
Journal of the Asiastic Society of Bengal.
Orissa Historical Research Journal.

Oriya

Utkal Dipika, 1866-1903.
The Balasore Sambada Bahika, 1870, 1871, 1872.

3. Secondary Works

Abul Fazal, Ain-i-Akbari, translated by H.S. Jarrat, Calcutta, 1891.

Agarwal, S.C., Salt Industry in India, Simla, 1937.

Baden Powell, B.H., The Land System of British India, 3 Volumes, Oxford, 1892.

Beams, John, Notes on the History of Orissa under the Mahammadan, Maratha and English Rule (Edt.), N.K. Sahu, Calcutta, 1956.

Banerjee, R.D., History of Orissa (From Earliest Time to British Period), 2 Volumes, Calcutta, 1930.

Basu, B.D., Ruin of Indian Trade and Industries, Calcutta, 1935.

Bhatia, B.M., Famines in India, 1850-1945, Bombay, 1963.

Buckland, C.E., Bengal under the Lt. Governors, 2 Volumes, Calcutta, 1902.

Chopra, Puri & Das, Social, Cultural and Economic History of India, 3 Volumes, Delhi, 1974.

Cheng Hang Seng, Agrarian Regions of India and Pakistan, 1950.

Das, B.S., Studies in the Economic History of Orissa from Ancient Time to 1833, Calcutta, 1978.

Das, Suranarayan, Desaprana Madhusudan (Oriya), Cuttack, 1971.

Das, M.N., Economic and Social Development of Modern India, Calcutta, 1959.

Das, Miss. Sailabala (Edt.), Madhusudan Das as seen by Many Eyes (Oriya), Cuttack, 1935.

Dutta, R.C., Economic History of India, 2 Volumes, Government of India Publication, Delhi, 1963.

Dutta, K.K., Studies in the History of Bengal Subah, 1740-1770, Vol. I, Calcutta, 1963.

Fawcett, C., The English Factories in India, Vol. II (New series).

Habibulla, A.B.M., The Foundation of Muslim Rule in India.

Hunter, W.W., Land System in Bengal, Vol. I, London, 1894.

Hunter, W.W., History of Orissa, 2 Volumes, London, 1872.

Hunter, W.W., Indian Administration. London, 1882.

Jena, K.C., Socio-Economic Conditions of Orissa during 19th Century, Delhi, 1978.

Marx, Capital (Moscow Edition), 3 Volumes.

Mahatab, H.K., History of Orissa, Part II, Cuttack, 1969.

Mohanty, Surendra, Stabdira Surya, (Oriya), Cuttack, 1970.

Mohanty, Surendra, Madhusudan Das (Oriya), Cuttack, 1972.

Mukherjee, P., History of Orissa. Utkal University Publication, Vol. IV, Cuttack, 1964.

Mukherjee, P., Gajapati Kings of Orissa, Reprint, Cuttaek, 1981.

Memoria, C.B., Agricultural Problems of India, Allahabad, 1976.

Patra, K.M., Orissa under the East India Company, New Delhi, 1971.

Pattanaik, C.C., The Famine and some Aspects of the British Economic Policy in Orissa, 1866-1905, Cuttack, 1980.

Prinsep, H.T., Transactions in India, 1813-1823, London, 1825

Ray, B.C., Foundation of British Orissa, Cuttack, 1960.

Ray, B.C., Orissa under the Marathas, Allahabad, 1960.

Sirkar, J.N., Studies in Mughal India.

Senapati Fakirmohan, Autobiography (Oriya) Reprint, Cuttack, 1969.

Sinha, N.K., Economic History of Bengal, 2 Volumes, Calcutta, 1961-62.

Stirling, A., An Account (Geographical, Statistical and Historical) of Orissa Proper or Cuttack, Calcutta, 1904.

Sarkar, D.C., Studies in Indian Coins, Calcutta, 1968.

Srivastav, B., Trade and Commerce in Ancient India, Varanasi, 1968.

Taylor, Famines in India, their Remedy and Prevention, London, 1874.

Toynbee, G.A., Sketch of the History of Orissa, 1803-1828, Calcutta, 1873.

Travelyan, Charles,A Report on the Inland Customs and Town Duties on the Bengal Presidency, Calcutta, 1835.

Wilson, C.R., The Early Annals of the English in Bengal, 3 Volumes, London, 1895.

Wilson, C.R., English Chiefs at Balasore in the Bao of Bengal, Calcutta, 1895.

Index